The Executive Committee of the Southern Baptist Convention
1917-1984

Albert McClellan

The
EXECUTIVE COMMITTEE
of the
Southern Baptist Convention
1917-1984

BROADMAN PRESS
Nashville, Tennessee

Library of Congress Cataloging in Publication Data

McClellan, Albert A.
  The Executive Committee of the Southern Baptist
Convention, 1917-1984.
  Bibliography: p.
  Includes index.
    1. Southern Baptist Convention. Executive Committee—
History. 2. Southern Baptist Convention—History.
3. Baptists—United States—History. I. Title.
BX6462.M35 1985   262'.06132   84-29349
ISBN 0-8054-6576-6
ISBN 0-8054-6577-4 (pbk.)

Acknowledgments

This book about the Executive Committee had to have a point of beginning. Some suggested 1927, for that was the date of the restructuring, thought by many to have been also the date of origin. Austin Crouch, the first executive secretary, headed the 1928 report to the Southern Baptist Convention as "The First Annual Report . . . " and so on, for many years. Others said that 1917 was the true date and proved it by the records. The *SBC Annual* for that year plainly shows that the Convention established an Executive Committee with some of its duties almost identical to the duties assigned to the 1927 Executive Committee. As I puzzled over the beginning, I discovered that from 1845 the Southern Baptist Convention had been in a way its own executive committee, especially in those areas not assigned to the two mission boards. This prompted me to ask what had happened in ancient times that had led to the creation of the very special kind of Southern Baptist organization that was established in 1845, out of which the Executive Committee had emerged. My conclusion was that while the Executive Committee was indeed organized in 1917, its agenda really began with the early interdependent relationships of Baptists in England. The first two chapters of this book were written to describe the progress of some of the precedents in Baptist history that led finally to the idea of an executive committee or executive board in Baptist life.

The book also had to have an ending time. Of course, history never ends, but the book had to end. At first, it seemed to me that a proper time would have been with the retirement of Porter Routh. But that would not do, for as important as he was in the life and work of the denomination, the Executive Committee went inexorably past his retirement. History has a way of ignoring retirements and calendars. It stretches like the flooding of the early morning summer sunlight across rivers and mountains, leaving nothing untouched, unexposed, or unchanged. I had to bring my story to an end, yet I could write no more than I had the perspective from which to see and understand. So quite arbitrarily, I terminated my accounting with the spring of 1984.

Objectivity was another problem. At first, I imagined that I could be totally objective. That illusion lasted to about the fourth page of the first chapter. Although I refused until the last few paragraphs of the book to use the first person singular, I was nevertheless present, prominently by name a few times but subtly hidden in the judgments and interpretations many times. I would like to apologize for this, but it would be useless. I would be found out again and again.

There were other people who helped make this book. First, Mabel Helm McClellan, my wife. Without her, it would not have been finished. In those months when I was lost in a storm of books, microfilm, annuals, letters, reports, minutes, blank sheets of paper, jumbled computer screens, ruined diskettes, unheard groanings, and occasional utterances, I would cry out, "I cannot do it." She would simply say, "You can, you will, you must."

Then, Harold Clark Bennett, the executive secretary-treasurer of the Executive Committee. He envisioned the book and led the committee to commission it. I was inspired by his unhampering interest and his constant affirmation. But occasionally, I chaffed under the Damoclean Sword of his unrelenting reports to the Executive Committee in which he kept saying that I would finish the book on time, but now, I am grateful for his persistence.

Porter Routh, the immediate past executive secretary-treasurer, whose forty-year knowledge of the Executive Committee is quite well known, helped me understand many obscure points. Duke K. McCall, also a former executive secretary-treasurer, helped me see into some of the shadows of the great events of the postwar period. Lynn E. May, Jr., the executive director of the Historical Commission, carefully read the manuscript with a scholar's eye and did his best to improve my layman's knowledge of historiography. John Warren Steen, author, editor, teacher, and friend, who read the rough early drafts with his high-powered editorial magnifying glass, helped me out of many a grammatical tangle. Some will probably say that I should have taken all of his suggestions.

Other extremely helpful readers included a small specially appointed group of Administrative Subcommittee members: W. Dewey Presley, Darrell W. Robinson, Wendell Garrison, and Frank C. Ingraham, all of whom made valued and honored suggestions. Other readers included two very old and trusted friends of mine, Sam W. Scantlan, former director of missions for the Oklahoma Baptist State Convention, and Jack W. Manning, former professor of church history at Golden Gate Seminary. Finally, the Executive Committee attorney, James P. Guenther, read the manuscript looking for legal problems. All of these readers helped greatly to improve the book, yet its omissions, misjudgments, and errors should not be blamed on them.

There is one other group I want to specially mention, all of the unseen workers whose daily labors make the work of the Executive Committee possible. Over the years there have been scores of them. Some of the present ones were especially helpful in the preparation of the book were: Martha Gaddis, Ada Ruth Kelly, Gerry Dearman, Becky Jackson, Lorene Woodall, Sue Hayes, Polly House, Faye Byrnes, Brenda Adcox, and Tommy Grubbs.

It soon will be seventy years since the Executive Committee was first organized. Already, it is in the hands of the third generation of leaders. So far as I can tell, the members and the staff of today are just as dedicated and competent as the members and the staff of the other generations. As they move forward, great things will happen. In a few more years, the fourth or fifth generation will celebrate the Executive Committee centennial. Things will be different, but the kingdom of God will be the same, and the work will go on.

ALBERT MCCLELLAN

CONTENTS

1

Organization in Early Baptist Life
1624-1845

"What are Southern Baptists?" A student addressed this question to W. W. Barnes, a church history professor at Southwestern Baptist Theological Seminary.[1] The teacher took the opportunity for incidental teaching. He did this frequently, sometimes concluding with a whimsical illustration. Some of the more text-bound students called these digressions "chasing rabbits." For those who really listened, they were unforgettable learning experiences. The professor discussed Southern Baptists as people, point of view, and organization. He said that these were useful concepts for understanding but that he liked to think of Southern Baptists as movement—the movement of a people of God through centuries across America.

This happened about the time Southern Baptists were securing their first tiny foothold in California (1936) and only about two years before thirteen infant churches organized the Southern Baptist General Convention of California (1940).[2] Dr. Barnes surely knew the prophetic significance of those events and accepted them as continuing evidences of the movement. In 1942, the California Convention was approved for cooperation with the Southern Baptist Convention, 260 years after the 1682 organization of the church at Kittery, Maine, that in 1696 was transplanted to become the first Baptist church in the South.[3] Nineteen forty-two was a milestone year in the geographical movement of the denomination, marking the time when the Southern Baptist Convention as an organization at last spanned the continent.

That expansion would not have been possible without the long

11

slow spiritual coalescence of Southern Baptist people that started with the planting of the first churches in South Carolina (c. 1696), Maryland (1742), Virginia (c. 1715), and North Carolina (1727). Overcoming the handicaps of primitive communication systems, of meager organizational structures, and of serious doctrinal differences, Southern Baptists gradually came together in character and mission. By 1845 there was sufficient unity to give the denomination the prospect of becoming a national body. That year the Southern Baptist movement became an institutional reality with the organization of the Southern Baptist Convention. Given the general circumstances of America and the special character of institutions, as the new Convention moved forward from 1845, an executive committee became more and more probable.

In 1942 W. W. Barnes was writing a history of the Southern Baptist Convention planned for release three years later as part of the Convention's centennial celebration, and he was asked by the Executive Committee to include an account of its work in his book.[4] This request was appropriate because only against the sweep of the whole denominational development can the Executive Committee be correctly understood. In unique ways, it is the product of the singular polity that developed as Baptist people struggled to make the New Testament principles of freedom and responsibility work in diverse, sometimes hostile, and increasingly complicated environments. The Executive Committee is part of the fascinating Southern Baptist movement and makes its own special contribution to the formation of the Baptist future.

Historically, Southern Baptists emerged out of the presence of the Holy Spirit in the struggles of God's people as they have sought to combine freedom with responsibility. They are the blending of diversity, not into uniformity, but into relatedness; and, as the churches in the Book of Acts, their coalescence is not the coalescence of total agreement but of common mission. The size and extent of the coalescence is far beyond the dreams of the 1845 founders. Millions of people, thousands of churches, hundreds of associations, and dozens of state conventions have combined their energies and their resources to create a family of mission programs, seminaries, colleges, homes for children, homes for aging, publications, state papers, conference centers, and an array of supporting services. Impressive and productive as it is, this massive coalescence has not forgotten its simple, basic, democratically oriented polity. From the beginning, missions has been the mainspring of Southern Baptist growth in cooperation; but still, the founders allowed plenty of room for other enterprises. The proliferations have helped create the undeniable need for an executive committee.

Flowering of Organizational Seed

The dates of Baptist history belong together in a continuum of spiritual and social growth, and some dates are related in special ways. Three are important for this study: 1845, the organization of the Southern Baptist Convention; 1917, the establishment of the Executive Committee of the Southern Baptist Convention; and 1927, the restructure of the Executive Committee. One led to the next, and all were the results of seed planted long before by Richard Furman (1755-1825), thought by some to be near the top among all Baptist leaders in the South.[5] Furman was a Charleston pastor whose youthful patriotism during the American Revolution led Lord Cornwallis to offer a reward of 1,000 English pounds for Furman's capture. Also a dedicated evangelist and avid denominationalist, Furman's ideas about Baptist organization were far ahead of his time. He knew how to wait on their fulfillment. For example, he attempted to secure the incorporation of the Charleston Association; and when that failed, he led the association in 1792 to create the General Committee for the Charleston Baptist Association Fund to aid in the education of ministers. The committee functioned in ways suggestive of present-day state convention executive boards, such as holding property, raising money, and fostering programs.[6]

By 1814 Furman was one of the most respected and influential leaders among Baptists in America. Impressive and effective, he was chosen that year as the founding president of the Triennial Convention, the first national Baptist convention in America. Although the delegates accepted him, they rejected Furman's plan for organization. He wanted a system of boards directly responsible to the convention; they opted for semiautonomous societies. Furman died in 1825, but his ideas of Baptist interchurch organization remained very much alive. They were the central organizing principles of the South Carolina Baptist Convention in 1821 and the Southern Baptist Convention in 1845.

In some ways, the three dates (1845, 1917, 1927) are the sequential steps in the maturation of the first seed of local church cooperation planted by English Baptists early in the seventeenth century. From their beginning, Baptists have believed that, in order to survive and to do the work of Jesus Christ in the world, the churches must live in active association with each other. Growth came slowly, moving forward by trial and error, and was often handicapped by internal differences and opposition. The early leaders could not see very far ahead. Even Richard Furman realized only a part of his dream during his lifetime. There was a rationale in Furman's ideas that persisted in the minds of early Southern Baptists and that led to the creation of the Executive Committee and that eventually led to an Executive Committee for the Southern Baptist Convention. It was often an uneven and troubled path.

Even in 1917, the organization of the Executive Committee was not easily accomplished. "Antiboard" feelings stirred up by the Landmark Movement of the nineteenth century were still held by many Southern Baptists; and while the majority was in favor of full organization, a minority was against it. People in favor saw the Executive Committee as essential for successful church interdependence; people in opposition saw it as a threat to church independence. The farseeing leaders who prevailed may not have known it at the time, but they stood in that long line of distinguished systematic-minded leaders extending back three hundred years to the day Baptists first emerged into history.

More than the leaders of 1917 may have understood, they were being pushed forward by the spirit of the times. Soon after the American Revolution, all kinds of group relationships, both religious and secular, began to develop. These included some that are well known to later generations, such as the American Bible Society (1816), the National Education Association (1857), and the American Red Cross (1881). The movement reached a climax in the first half of the twentieth century. Simultaneous with the latest of these new associated relationships was the integration of American business corporations and super companies, including General Motors, General Electric, and General Foods. Organization and planning were the hallmarks of the times.

Responding to rising concepts of group structure and moving steadily forward in organizational understanding was both logical and certain for Southern Baptists. By 1917 social, economic, and political forces were radically reshaping life in America, resulting in a massive shift of relationships. These had first started about the time the steam locomotive was invented (1829) and had reached a climax in the automobile mass production assembly lines.

Moreover, Baptists were part of the great migrational movements that had begun sweeping across America in the middle of the eighteenth century and that by the beginning of the twentieth century had pushed large numbers of people into almost every corner of the vast new country. Increasing population, geographical expansion, rapidly developing mobility, and accelerating communication required better ways for people to work together. In quick succession, the rivers, the steam engine, the telegraph, the high-speed printing press, the postal system, the telephone, the radio, the motion picture, the automobile, and the modern highways made their impacts. Successful coping required new kinds of organization. By about 1910, there were feverish moves throughout the land to reorganize everything, including the Southern Baptist Convention. But, without question, anything done organizationally among the Baptists required careful consideration of basic Baptist commitments in church and denominational polity.

From their beginning, Baptists have been both independent and interdependent; and viewed in the light of their long history, one does not seem possible without the other. They are as much linked together as freedom and responsibility. Because of the historic emphasis Baptists have placed on independence, they are at times uncomfortable with interchurch organizations; yet, because of an equally historic emphasis on interdependence, Baptists are always moving toward organizational relationships. In an open society, independence may not be costly; but in a closed society, it can be extremely costly. The latter was true for the English Baptists for most of the tightly bound seventeenth century. The first Baptist church in England (c. 1612) was fiercely independent. The founding pastor, Thomas Helwys, dared to put its sentiments for freedom in a pamphlet addressed to King James.[7] He said:

> (We) profess and teach that in all earthly things the king's power is to be submitted unto; and in heavenly and spiritual things, if the king or any in authority under him shall exercise their power against any they are not to resist by any way or means, although it were in their power, but rather to submit their lives as Christ and his disciples did, and yet keep their consciences to God.

This was Helwys's way of saying: Yes, we will be loyal citizens, and even die for the king, except that in matters of faith our allegiance is to Christ and to Him alone. Helwys was imprisoned for his conviction and three years later became one of the early Baptist martyrs for religious freedom. Early Baptist convictions concerning religious liberty have since been a mark of true Baptist churches. The leaders quickly learned that, to preserve their freedom, they had to bring their churches into mutual association with each other. Interdependence became as much an ideal as independence, though perhaps not as often discussed. At first, cooperation was mainly in the informal meetings of leaders; but as the number of churches grew, the issues of interdependence required more formal organization. At first there were organized associations, then unions and conventions, and finally executive boards and executive committees. As these new forms were added, the leaders took care to keep always a balance between the congregational freedom and the group responsibility of the churches.

Beginning of Baptist Interdependence in England

The journey was long from the first simple interchurch relationships around 1626 to the sophisticated restructuring of the Executive Committee in 1927. The march began when the five known congregations of British General Baptists[8] formulated a letter to the Independent Waterlander Mennonites of Holland exploring the possibility of some kind of congregational affiliation.[9] The effort was not successful due to doctrinal differences, one of which was the strong isolationist views of the Holland Independents. So it was that, within fourteen years of the appearance of the first Baptists on English soil, five infant churches counseled together in primitive association, although the meeting was only specific in issue, temporary in duration, and without a recorded name.

The second significant effort was more auspicious and occurred in 1644. The seven Particular Baptist churches of London formally approved the First London Confession and included well-formulated declarations of independence and interdependence.[10]

> XLVII. And although the particular Congregations be distinct / and severall Bodies, every one a compact and knit Ci / tie in it selfe; yet are they all to walk by one and the same / Rule, and by all meanes convenient to have counsell / and help one of another in all needful affaires of the Church, as members of one body in the common faith / under Christ their onely head.

This brief statement was significant for its influence on future Baptist denominational organization for many reasons. (1) It was developed by representatives of seven cooperating churches. (2) It fully recognized the independence of the churches. (3) It was the first formal statement of interdependence known to have been approved by the vigorous and aggressive Particular Baptists churches. (4) The statement became the organizational norm for the rapidly expanding Particular Baptist movement. (5) It had the immediate effect of securing a common understanding of relationships among the scattered churches of the area. (6) It provided a point of reference to guide the associations that soon developed throughout

England and Ireland. (7) The statement stood as a kind of official norm during the formative years until replaced by the broader and more theological statement in the Confession of 1677. (8) It was a clear statement of denominational polity that has been a pattern for Baptist church relationships ever since.

In the 1640s, formally organized associations began to appear in English Baptist life. Baptist leaders had observed that civil leaders in several English counties,[11] to defend themselves from "royalist plunderings," had formed local groups (associations) to raise money and militia. That movement was so successful that Parliament reorganized the British army along the same lines. The idea of associations as a form of self-rule appealed to the Baptists, especially to the leaders and members in the new churches in Wales and Ireland, which were composed principally of former soldiers in the British army and of their converts. They saw the associations as a means of banding the tiny churches together for strength and as a means of churches keeping in touch with other churches, yet without loss of independence.

Unlike the informal General Baptist association of 1626 and the ad hoc Particular Baptist association of 1644, these new associations seem to have possessed primitive organizational continuity. In October 1652, Baptist churches in the Berkshires of England organized by "drawing up a formal constitution, as was now quite a fashion."[12] In a relatively short time (a period of forty years), the Baptist churches of England had exploded from a single congregation with one point of view to many churches in several associations with two points of view—Particular and General.

Particular Baptists were local and informal. Whitley said that they "did not attempt in this period to carry organization further: fraternal intercourse was maintained, but not between the Associations as such; no general Association to link all together was projected, nor any central staff, nor any one unifying document."[13] With General Baptists, the situation was different. They developed both formal staffs and unifying documents and launched the first national organization of Baptists.

In 1654 "many of the Messengers, Elders and Brethren, belonging to severall of the Baptized churches *in this nation*"[14] met in London "to consider how and which way the affairs of the Gospell, so farre as it concerns them, might be best promoted."[15] This national meeting was attended by pastors ("elders"), associational evangelists ("messengers"), and laymen ("brethren"). In 1660 the General Baptists met again "and published a Confession that was accepted as a bond of union for more than forty years."[16] Whitley said, "The General Baptists thus have the credit, within half a century of their appearance in England, of having worked out an articulated constitutional system, with officers told off for extension work, which was the object of the organization."[17] Whitley described the organization as "crowning the system of Associations."

These first national assemblies of a Baptist group seem to have had at least six things in common with today's unions and conventions: They (1) met formally on stated occasions, (2) were comprised of pastors, laypersons, and staff persons, (3) were formally organized with a constitutional system, (4) existed for the purpose of church extension, (5) published a temporary norm, and (6) appeared at the time not to interfere with the independence of the churches.

The term, *messenger* had a technical meaning different from later Southern Baptist usage. It developed out of a desire to evangelize all the towns and villages, and it was based on the New Testament pattern of commissioned persons for mission work, persons such as Paul, Silas, Barnabas, Tychicus, and Priscilla and Aquilla. Early Baptists in England appointed such messengers to work at evangelization and church development. "Thus the Messenger came to be a regular officer, not of one church, but of a group of churches; every such group came to realize its duty to support a missionary."[18] One need not look far in Southern Baptist life to discover this same office at work in local associations from the pioneer days to the end of the twentieth century. The title has changed, but not the task. In Southern Baptist life, those who performed this organized deputation work were first called associational missionaries, and more recently, associational directors of missions. Even current Southern Baptist vocabulary echoes with terms used long ago. Whitley tells of Thomas Collier who, when the Western Association was organized in 1654, had for eight or more years been "planting churches" as the "general superintendent of all the work in the district."[19] Both the terms *planting churches* and *district,* are used today in Southern Baptist local associations, and the term *general superintendent* sometimes applied in the past to the office of the state convention executive secretary.[20]

Beginning of Baptist Interdependence in America

Very early in their history, Baptists in America began working together informally. The first effort was the work of Roger Williams and John Clarke on behalf of religious liberty. The fact that in the beginning there were two clusters of churches, one in New England and another one around Philadelphia, indicates silent but almost certain cooperation. We can assume from how Baptists in England were relating to one another and from purely human considerations that members of those early American churches, particularly pastors, kept in close touch.

The first formal organization on an interchurch basis was the Philadelphia Association in 1707. Even before 1707, the churches had been convening annually on an informal basis. The purpose of the Philadelphia Association was to mediate and execute designs of public good.[21] Historian Robert G. Torbet said that the association's founding purposes may have been (1) careful investigation of itinerant ministers who offered themselves to the churches, (2) advice concerning doctrinal matters, and (3) consultation on vexing social problems.

General Baptists[22] may have also been meeting in Rhode Island in association as early as 1705, and some think as early as 1670.[23] Walter B. Shurden said, "It appears to have attained the functions as an association by 1729. For this reason the General Yearly Baptist Meeting . . . should be considered the second, if not the first, association in America."[24]

The Charleston (South Carolina) Association, often cited as the second to be organized in America, was constituted in 1751. Its purpose was to promote "understanding and fellowship among members along with consultation to promote harmony and peaceful progress."[25] This was the first general (not General) Baptist body in the South, seventy years before the founding of the first state convention in 1821 and ninety-four years before the founding of the Southern Baptist Convention in 1845. Sandy Creek (North Carolina), in 1758, was the first Separate Baptist association to be organized. Termed an "advisory council," its founding purposes centered in the need to hold together the churches under Separate influence for whom evangelism, church planting, revivals, and missions were extremely important.[26] The purposes of the Warren Association (1767) in New England included a sustained battle for religious liberty and separation of church and state. One of its first acts was the appointment of a Grievance Committee and the commissioning of Isaac Backus to press the cause of religious liberty upon members of the Continental Congress.

Another important early association was the General Association of Separate Baptists in Virginia that was organized in 1771.[27] The group adopted twelve rules that now appear, in the light of the practice of hundreds of Southern Baptist associations, to have been organizational compass points for the future. Five of the rules pertained to the association itself: (1) it was only an advisory council, (2) it could bar transgressing churches from sitting in the association, (3) it held the right to withdraw fellowship from noncorresponding churches, (4) it governed by majority rule, and (5) it made use of circular letters for keeping in touch. Seven of the rules defined some of the rights and responsibilities of cooperating churches: (1) isolated congregations could petition an ordained minister to constitute them as a church, (2) only ordained ministers could be invited to administer the *sacraments* and conduct ordinations, (3) churches in distress were encouraged to seek the counsel of sister churches, (4) itinerant ministers were to be recommended by the churches, not the association—and examined by a presbytery, (5) churches were to use their own liberty in covenanting, (6) church discipline was a local church prerogative, and (7) the terms of communion were fellowship in the same faith and order.

Step by step, Baptists were becoming more formal and more systematic. These twelve rules suggest: (1) a sharpening of the understanding of polity that balanced independence with inter-dependence, (2) a clarification of the duties of the association with respect to the churches, (3) an understanding that the association had the right to determine its own membership, and (4) operation on the basis of democratic principles.

Occasionally these early associations experimented with ideas not found to be practical in application or consistent with developing Baptist ideas. The General Association of Separate Baptists in Virginia ordained Samuel Harris, its best-known leader, as an *apostle.* "His work was to pervade the churches; to do, or at least see to the work of ordination, and to set in order things that were wanting and make report to the next association."[28] Other apostles were appointed by the Northern District; but, for reasons not hard to see, the experiment was short lived. The apostles reported unfavorable response, and it was decided that the office "did not belong to ordinary times." No more apostles were appointed. Early Baptists in the South were clearly people-oriented denomination. Even Baptist polity reflected the spiritual instincts of the people.

The General Association of Separate Baptists in Virginia dissolved in 1783 and called for a General Committee to be made up of representatives of all four existing Virginia Baptist associations.[29] The call met favorable response, and the General Committee was formed in 1784—a significant forward step in Southern Baptist coalescence. During the first three years, the General Committee was concerned mostly with church and state matters. The American Revolution had brought a measure of freedom; but as yet, full freedom had not been attained, and churches and pastors were still being persecuted. Organizationally, the new committee was a faint shadow of state conventions yet to come. Its membership was from the whole colony, its agenda concerned the welfare of the churches, and its work changed from year to year as new issues and problems developed.

In 1792, under the leadership of the resourceful Richard Furman, the Charleston Association in South Carolina established a committee that also foreshadowed the future. Furman had previously attempted to secure the incorporation of the association. Failing in this, he secured a definite status for the "General Committee for the Charleston Baptist Association Fund" that had been established in 1791. The South Carolina historian, Joe M. King, described the incorporation rules as follows:[30]

> (1) adopting the above name; (2) calling for an annual charity sermon to be preached in each church and the collections then taken, together with any other donations, to be applied to the education of pious young men for the ministry and for other religious and public uses if the churches approved; (3) limiting the committee membership to one delegate chosen by each of the member churches of the Charleston Association to meet at the same time as the association and to be renewed annually; (4) requiring the annual election of a president, secretary, and two assistants to transact business between sessions of the General Committee, the president to arrange for the education of candidates, and an annually elected treasurer to pay the bills on his order; (5) fixing the conditions under which candidates might receive aid; and (6) proposing to take over the property of extinct churches for the benefit of the fund.

Clearly this group carried out some executive committee or executive board functions. The incorporation rules were tightly packed with nuances for the future. Note that the General Committee (1) held and dispersed funds, (2) made rules pertaining to its work, (3) held property, (4) had stated officers who were constitutionally provided, (5) was a committee of the Charleston Association, and (6) was incorporated with all the rights and obligations of incorporation.

Reaching for National Interdependence

Two other American organizational events climaxed the first two centuries of Baptist interdependence in America. Both were important for future Baptist organizational efforts, especially for Southern Baptists. The first was *the organization of the Triennial Convention.* It occurred in 1814 when Baptists from North and South met in Philadelphia and formed The General Missionary Convention of the Baptist Denomination in the United States of America for Foreign Missions.[31] The new venture was the result of two thrusts in Baptist life: (1) a feeling expressed as early as 1767 that Baptists needed a national presence[32] and (2) a growing interest in foreign missions stimulated by Luther Rice (1783-1836).[33]

Luther Rice was not the first missionary firebrand who came South. There were others in a line going back to William Screven (c.1629-1713), the Maine shipbuilder, who led his Kittery congregation in an early day "bold mission thrust" to transplant in South Carolina. Next was Oliver Hart (1723-1795) who emigrated from Philadelphia to Charleston in 1750. Hart was soon followed by the two great Separates, Shubal Stearns (1706-1771) and Daniel Marshall (1706-1784), both from New England, who settled in the North Carolina Piedmont in 1755. Then came John Gano (1727-1804) from Pennsylvania for two periods of missionary service, in North Carolina beginning in 1756 and Kentucky beginning in 1787. But it was Luther Rice, aided by Richard Furman and William Bullein Johnson (1782-1862), who fired the hearts of Baptists in the South and who made the Triennial Convention an organized reality in the life of the Southern churches. The fervency of these pioneer leaders and their commitment to organization pushed inevitably toward a regional organization for missions.

The second organizational event with a bearing on the future was the appearance of *the first state Baptist convention* in the South—The Baptist State Convention in South Carolina, established in 1821. It included a "state board" of ten members and a statement of purpose that provided for other boards yet to come. Richard Furman was elected president. Surely, the respected old leader must have been stirred to see the fulfillment of one of his dreams. Baptists were making progress. In orderly ways, they were combining administrative commonsense, democratic procedure, and spiritual purpose and, in the process, enhancing interdependence without losing independence.

By 1845 nine Southern state Baptist conventions were organized: South Carolina (1821), Georgia (1822), Virginia (1823), Alabama (1823), North Carolina (1830), Missouri (1834), Mississippi (1836), Maryland (1836), and Kentucky (1837). The Baptists were exploding from one frontier settlement to another, pushed along by two tremendous forces: evangelism and missions. They were out to proclaim the glad tidings of the kingdom of God, certainly in the homeland, and hopefully to the whole world. Fervent evangelism, a heritage of the Separate Baptist tradition, kept them moving from one community to another, converting sinners wherever they stopped. Decency and order in organization, a heritage of the Charleston tradition, gradually infused their assemblies with decorum and efficiency. Dedication to missions—a heritage from William Carey, Adoniram Judson, and Luther Rice—inspired them with a world vision and led them deeper into organized relationships. Nearly all Baptists of the times were evangelizing witnesses, but not all were missionaries. There arose in the denomination a considerable antimission spirit that troubled the fellowship for several generations.

Coalescing into Reasonable Unity

In some Baptist communities, organized missions were vehemently opposed, even to the point of churches expelling members who preached and practiced missions. Daniel Buckner, a Baptist pastor in East Tennessee, was dismissed by his church for preaching missions at about the time Rice was at work in the South. Buckner's wife asked to be dismissed with her husband and was told that the church had nothing against her. She answered, "If I were a man I would preach missions just as my husband has done, and as I hope and pray my sons may do."[34] Two of those sons did become preachers of missions, one pioneering in Texas and the other in Indian Territory. When Henry Frieland Buckner (1818-1882) departed Tennessee 1848 by riverboat for the distant West, his aging mother stood on the landing and wept. She said, "Go my son, and the Lord be with you always. Our Saviour says, 'Go ye into all the world' and it is as much my duty to give up my son as it is any other mother. I thank God I have a son to go to the Indians." In spite of the opposition, the denomination's mission conviction was strong enough to move it closer and closer to a mission organization unique to the South.

A regional Baptist self-consciousness was gradually forming, and it was aided by two serious issues that could have destroyed the Baptists under less dynamic circumstances. One was *slavery* and the other was *Campbellism*. Fortunately, instead of destroying the Baptists, the issues were catalysts to blend them into greater solidarity. Many Baptists in the South were slaveholders, among them even ministers. As passions mounted, slavery became a point of sharp differences between Baptists of the North and the South. A climax came in 1844 when the American Baptist Home Mission Society, by a vote of 123 to 61, declined to appoint Southern slaveholders as missionaries.[35] Stunned, the Baptists in the South were caught in the vast web of Southern regionalism. Painfully, Southern Baptist moved toward a separate mission organization.

Slavery was a national issue that affected all of the states. Campbellism was a regional phenomenon that affected principally Baptists in the Midwest and the upper Middle South, especially the ones living in Kentucky and Tennessee.[36] The controversy began about the time sentiment was developing among Baptists for foreign missions. Campbellism started when Thomas Campbell, a seceded Presbyterian, joined a Pennsylvania Baptist church and began fervently preaching doctrines similar to Baptist beliefs, yet different in not-so-subtle ways: more literal, more legalistic, and more imperious. Alexander, a son of Thomas, joined his father in the movement and preached with even greater power and persuasion.

About 1836 the group influenced by the Campbells separated from the Baptists to form the Disciples of Christ. Believing their cause to be a reformation, the Campbells and their fellow ministers considered Baptist churches legitimate fields of conquest. The struggle moved to the West and strewed its fire in communities heavily populated by the Baptists. Thousands defected; in some instances, whole churches with their pastors. Even some Baptist church buildings became Disciples property, among them the meetinghouse of the First Baptist Church of Nashville, Tennessee.[37] The movement appeared at times to overwhelm Baptist life in the affected areas, but Baptist ideas of freedom and grace were too deeply rooted for easy conquest. Steadily, the churches revived with even more vitality, so that in most of the communities where Campbellism prevailed, Baptists regained the dominance.

Other forces at work in America that were influential in bringing Baptists in the South closer together included: (1) improved transportation, made possible by the first successful steamship in 1807 and the first railroads begun about 1830, (2) improved communication, including rapidly expanding local newspapers, the rapidly improving United States postal system, and the advent of the telegraph in 1837, (3) a growing Southern agricultural self-consciousness stirred up by the industrial North, (4) a developing institutionalization of the denomination as seen in state Baptist conventions, Baptist colleges, and Baptist newspapers, and (5) immigration patterns that assured Southern oriented church leadership in most Southern frontier communities.

In 1845 it had been 149 years since the Kittery Church was planted on southern soil (1696), a long period of spiritual and social growth for the Baptists. Stimulated by a growing regional self-awareness and prompted by the feeling that fellow Baptists in the North did not understand them, many Baptists of the South were strongly inclined to separate from the Triennial Convention. Virginia Baptists were the first to act. The Board of Managers of the Virginia Foreign Mission Society issued a call for the formation of a new convention.[38] The Baptist *movement* in America was in constant formation. By 1845 it had gained momentum and stability sufficient to launch a sophisticated organization that earlier had not been possible. On May 8, 1845, 327 delegates from eleven states assembled in the meeting house of the Baptist church in Augusta, Georgia, to organize a new national Baptist body. The constitution was approved on May 10; and from that day, the Southern Baptist Convention was increasingly recognized as a major American denomination.

The launching was a significant step in the continuing journey of Baptist interdependence. The first step of that journey was taken long ago when a few struggling seventeenth-century English Baptist churches looked to each other for strength and encouragement. By no means was the infant Southern Baptist Convention a total coalescence. The party differences were too great for sustained unanimity. Perhaps it was an uneasy coalescence, but at least it was a formalizing of hope for organized cooperation and a promise of things to come. In time, it became strong and aggressive enough to bridge the nation.

Notes

1. AM. The author was a student present in the classroom. W. W. Barnes was a tall North Carolinian with a gentle way of speaking. His intelligent, friendly eyes sometimes seemed to be part of his teaching.

2. Floyd Looney, "Southern Baptist General Convention of California," ESB, V.I, p. 219. The first church was organized at Shafter on May 10, 1956, to the day, exactly ninety-one years from the SBC organization.

3. Robert A. Baker and Paul J. Craven, Jr., *Adventure in Faith*, pp. 68-70.

4. ECM, June 17, 1942, p. 37.

5. Winston C. Babb and Lynn E. May Jr., "Richard Furman," ESB, 1958, I, pp. 518-520.

6. Joe M. King, *A History of South Carolina Baptists*, pp. 66-67.

7. Thomas Helwys, "A Short Declaration on the Mistery of Iniquity," quoted by W. T. Whitley, *History of British Baptists*, p. 33.

8. The first English Baptist churches believed in a "general" atonement, meaning that Christ died for all and not merely for the elect. About twenty-five years later, a group appeared more Calvinistic in doctrine, believing that Christ died only for the elect. They were called Particular Baptists.

9. Whitley, pp. 50-55; cf. A. C. Underwood, *A History of English Baptists,* pp. 50-51.

10. "Confession of Faith of those Churches which are commonly (though falsely) called *ANABAPTISTS"* as quoted by William L. Lumpkin, *Baptist Confessions of Faith,* pp. 168-169.

11. Whitley, pp. 90-92.

12. Ibid., p. 91.

13. Ibid., pp. 92-93.

14. Ibid.

15. Ibid.

16. Ibid., p. 93.

17. Ibid.

18. Ibid., p. 88.

19. Ibid., p. 91.

20. Carl Goodson, "Missouri Baptist General Association," ESB, V. II, p. 912.

21. Robert G. Torbet, *A History of the Baptists,* p. 212.

22. The General Baptist movement was not strong in America; and generally the early Baptists did not magnify qualifying labels, though most were in sympathy with the Particular Baptists of England.

23. Walter B. Shurden, *Associations Among the Baptists in America, 1707-1714,* p. 18.

24. Ibid. Shurden accepts the 1729 date, but cites other authorities who offer earlier dates.

25. King, p. 62.

26. G. W. Bullard, "Baptist State Convention of North Carolina," ESB, 1958, p. 1,991. Separate Baptists appeared in New England during the Great Awakening. They were formed when members of Separate Congregational churches began to question infant baptist.

27. Lumpkin, pp. 98-102.

28. Garnett Ryland, *The Baptists of Virginia,* pp. 87-88; quoted from Robert B. Semple.

29. Ibid., pp. 126, 122-123.

30. King, ibid., pp. 66-67.

31. The long title was abbreviated to "Triennial Convention" because the group met every three years.

32. Raymond B. Parker, "Triennial Convention," ESB, 1958, II, pp. 1427-1428.

33. Ibid.

34. E. C. Routh, _The Story of Oklahoma Baptists_, pp. 32-33.

35. W. W. Barnes, _The Southern Baptist Convention, 1845-1953_, p. 24.

36. R. Paul Caudill, "Campbellism," ESB, 1958, I, p. 228; cf. Robert H. Spiro, Jr., "Disciples of Christ," ibid., pp. 364-365; Don B. Harbuck, "Churches of Christ," ibid., pp. 289-290.

37. Lynn E. May, Jr., _The First Baptist Church, Nashville, Tennessee, 1820-1970_, pp. 36-40.

38. Barnes, pp. 26-32.

2

The Executive Committee
as an Outgrowth of Baptist Polity
1846-1916

Someone asked W. W. Barnes, "When did the Southern Baptist Convention really begin?"[1] He said that it was like the beginning of a major highway, dated more by generations than by years. First, there was the wilderness road that became a county road. Time passed, and the state decided to make the county road a highway. More time passed, and money was appropriated for the purchase of additional right-of-way. Then slowly came the graders and the bridge builders. Months and years went by, and the road was paved. Next were the fences and the markers, and, at last, the day of dedication. Barnes said that the present form of the Southern Baptist Convention was a very long time in development.

This dynamic view presents the Convention as energy and movement, always changing, yet not changing. As a highway emerges, the landmarks are fairly constant. Old surveyors' benchmarks are the same, rivers and creeks retain the old names, and the mountains and valleys are still on the maps. It may seem that the workmen are different, for they ride in different vehicles, dress in different clothing, and have different names; but in subtle ways they cling to the traditions of their fathers. Among Southern Baptists, visions and methods may differ from one generation to another, but the commitments and the causes are generally constant.

Scholars like W. W. Barnes, immersed in their study of Baptist ascent, sometime reflect on such paradoxes and contradictions of history as the loss of purpose in the midst of success, the decline of leadership in times of prosperity, and the infusion of alien ideas out of keeping with basic character. Other contraditions and paradoxes which are noted are the defense of the Baptist name without understanding of the Baptist spirit, the frenzied revival of old vocabularies in changing times, arrogant effort to subvert spiritual grace with creedal law, and the substitution of personal grace with institutional sophistication. Southern Baptists have been threatened with all of these, yet remarkably, they have overcome them and moved forward. They have relied upon the Holy Spirit for unity, always remembering their heritage and always willing to undertake new challenges. They have been sustained by their awareness of God's leadership. In some ways, their unique national organization is an outgrowth of their ancient democratic principles.

This is true of the Executive Committee of the Southern Baptist Convention. First organized in 1917, and restructured in 1927, it was new in its particular form, but not new in the work assigned to it. When William Bullein Johnson rapped his gavel on the pulpit of the "meeting house of the Baptist Church in Augusta"[2] on May 8, 1845, it was more than a call for order of the assembly; it was a high summons for a special kind of work and a unique way of working that would take Southern Baptists into a triumphant future and eventually would bring forth the Executive Committee.

In 1845 the word *executive* was not often used, but the work it embraced was commonplace in organized groups. Today, the word most often applies to the title or the office of a person primarily responsible for work assigned by a group. Sometimes it is used, as in "executive session," to describe a closed meeting or, as in "executive decision," in reference to an administrative policy. Applied to a managing group such as a board or a committee, the word means "designed for or relating to execution or carrying into effect."[3] The key idea is "carrying into effect." In an organization, *executive* implies "vested authority or deputed powers," and it suggests a source or a "prior determination of what is to be done."[4] The emphasis is on carrying out an assignment on behalf of an assigning source. The concept of an executive committee in Southern Baptist life took shape over a long, long time.

Beginning of an Ordered Legacy

The first two meetings of the Southern Baptist Convention became procedural models for the future, patterns by which the Convention would work until about 1915. The first delegates[5] who gathered at Augusta in 1845 and at Richmond in 1846 apparently assumed five principles for the conducting of the Convention's work: The Southern Baptist Convention (1) controls its dependent agencies, (2) is a parliamentary body, (3) may address any need or question it wishes, (4) uses committees in the decision-making process, and (5) delegates the expediting of any task it chooses.

These principles were at work in the first two Southern Baptist Conventions of 1845 and 1846. The members acted fully, took vigorous steps, and made assignments to persons, committees, and agencies. And when the Convention adjourned, those who were assigned tasks acted as executives on behalf of the Convention by carrying into effect that which had been delegated to them. This suggests that from the beginning the executive function has been a factor in Southern Baptist polity.

1. *The Southern Baptist Convention controls its dependent agencies.* This assumption is in keeping with the single most important legacy received from Richard Furman and William Bullein Johnson: The Convention is in complete control of its dependent groups, either by direct action during sessions or by constitutional provisions between the sessions. According to Article V of the 1845 Constitution:[6]

> To each Board shall be committed, during the recess of the Convention, the entire management of all the affairs relating to the object with whose interests it shall be charged, all which management shall be in strict accordance with the constitutional provisions adopted by the Convention, and such other instructions as may be given time to time.

This gave the Convention the right to instruct an agency, a practice that was begun the very first year of the Convention's existence. In 1845 it "instructed" the Foreign Mission Board "to communicate with the acting Board of the Baptist Triennial Convention, in reference to any claim we may have upon that Convention, or any claim which that body may have, or think they have upon us,"[7] and "to enter into any equitable and prudent arrangement, with the acting Board of the Baptist General Convention, to take a portion of its Missions under the patronage of this Convention." The Convention also "instructed" the Board of Domestic Missions "to take all prudent measures, for the religious instruction of our colored population." It recommended that the same board "direct its effective attention to aid the present effort, to establish the Baptist cause in the city of New Orleans." Very wisely, as the Convention gained insight and experience, it limited itself in the exercise of its constitutional authority, choosing instead to operate under the executive principle by delegating its powers to the boards.

2. *The Southern Baptist Convention is a parliamentary body.* From the very beginning, its annual sessions were democratically oriented business meetings, conducted in strict parliamentary fashion. It was popularly perceived as a deliberative body, and most of its work was done in five or six days. By twentieth-century standards, the deliberative pace was slow and tedious, but there were reasons for it. The Convention was a new enterprise, and the leaders were cautiously finding their way into the future. Agency responsibility was not well understood. The limited agenda and the small size of the annual meetings made extensive deliberations possible. The lack of precedents and prior experiences called for careful thought when facing demanding, delicate, and complex problems. Leisurely paced meetings lasting almost a week allowed more time for group involvement in problem solving. Limited communication facilities and difficult travel conditions necessitated that as many decisions as possible be made while the Convention was in session.

For nearly four decades, the Convention continued as a fully deliberative body, devoting most of its time to business, and debating every question, many of them at great length. As the years passed and Convention attendance increased, it became very difficult to maintain the early deliberative character. During the first twenty-five years of the twentieth century, some leaders frantically tried to keep the meetings as fully deliberative as they had been at the beginning. But overwhelmed by huge crowds and mammoth meeting rooms, the Convention abandoned its former ways and surrendered to more modern methods. It did not, however, abandon its parliamentary character.

3. *The Southern Baptist Convention has the right to address any need the body wishes.* In 1845, and especially in 1846, the Convention acted in ways that suggested wider denominational interests ahead. Its founding purpose was missions, but with all that has been added since, it is difficult for some modern Baptist minds to understand how deeply the commitment to missions was written into the hearts of the organizers. They believed that the most important thing on earth was "the Redeemer's Kingdom,"[8] and they understood that kingdom to be worldwide in scope. They knew that missions was the front line of attack and that it was the Convention's first business to sponsor mission work, both foreign and domestic. Nevertheless, the organizers were persons of great vision who left the door open for other causes yet to come. They wrote in Article II of the Constitution that "It shall be the design of this Convention to promote Foreign and Domestic missions, and other important objects connected with the Redeemer's Kingdom."[9]

Very little was said that first year in Augusta about Christian education or Christian literature; but considering the interests of the members[10] in the work of their state conventions, it is likely that these causes were at least in the edges of their concerns, even at Augusta. They wisely refused to close the door on future possibilities. The prospect of an unlimited field meant that in the future the annual Convention would be faced with a very heavy and involved agenda that would require a different kind of organization. Of course, in 1845, that was a long way ahead.

The agenda did indeed expand over the years, with many of the new items related to the old causes and some of them, to the new causes. Following is a partial listing that displays the wide range of expanding Convention interests:

1851: Creation of a Bible board.

1863: Discontinuance of the Bible Board and creation of the first Sunday School Board.

1871: A financial claim of Mrs. William Cooper against the Sunday School Board.

1872: Transfer of agency invested funds to the SBC treasurer for consolidated investment.

1873: Consolidation of the Sunday School Board with the Home Mission Board. Approval of Southern Baptist Seminary's move to Louisville, Kentucky, and of its effort to raise $500,000 for that purpose.

1874: Request that state conventions and general associations cooperate in promoting SBC plans and programs.

1887: Authorization of the Home Mission Board to employ an assistant to the corresponding secretary.

1891: Study of the plan for state and associational representation to the Convention. The creation of the second Sunday School Board.

1896: Widespread criticism of the president of Southern Baptist Seminary.

1899: Study of Sunday School Board business methods.

1902: A study to provide means for preserving order in the Convention hall.

1903: Change of the name of the Convention.

This miscellaneous listing barely touches the hundreds of subjects considered by the Convention in annual sessions in its early years. For many of the items considered, committees were appointed, sometimes several committees for one item. From its founding, the Convention asked small groups and individuals to help do its thinking and to implement its decisions.

4. *The Southern Baptist Convention uses committees in the decision-making process.* In the early years of the Convention the wide use of ad hoc committees was a useful tool for achieving consensus and moving forward. Essential for the deliberative process as then practiced, it

now seems to have been a system without a plan. As the Convention agenda expanded and as the annual attendance increased, the wide use became almost an excessive use. The practice began in 1846, when by motion seven committees of reference were appointed to review seven different aspects of foreign missions and five committees to review five different aspects of domestic missions.[11] These were in addition to six other committees, making a total of eighteen, a heavy load for the 162 members present.[12] The use of committees of reference to review and make recommendations on the reports of the boards was continued intensively until 1915[13] and in a limited way until 1928.[14]

Many of the issues before the young Convention were complex and elusive and were frequently surfaced without full information. They could not be appropriately referred because they did not fit into the chartered purposes of the existing agencies. The Convention, lacking a neutrally positioned central group to study the less important issues, resorted to the special committees composed of faithful and dependable Baptists. But without supporting staff work and sometimes with strong bias for or against an issue, they were often handicapped in what they could do. By the end of the century, leaders were searching for better ways of conducting the work not only for making the decisions but also for expediting the decisions.

5. *The Convention delegates the expediting of tasks.* This assumes that a responsibility can be temporarily or permanently assigned by the Convention to a group or a person. The executive principle is inherent in the right to delegate. Both in 1845 and 1846, the Convention fully exercised its right of delegation in two areas: (1) *Administration.* The 1845 Convention ordered its secretaries to print five thousand copies of the proceedings, and it asked a committee of distinguished citizens to apply "to the proper authorities of the state of Georgia for the Charter of incorporation." It created the Foreign Mission Board and the Domestic Mission Board and authorized them to conduct their work. (2) *Financial.* In 1846 it ordered the two mission boards to pay for the printing and distribution of four thousand copies of the Convention Proceed-

ings. Also, in 1846, the Convention instructed its secretaries "to prepare a form of bequest, and publish with the minutes." In these actions, the Convention was assigning the expediting of its work.

Delegation was not always easy for the Convention. For many years, it withheld from the general boards the right to elect their own officers, including the corresponding (executive) secretaries. It was not until 1924 that the Convention permitted the boards to elect their own secretaries.[15] As long as the practice prevailed, the officers were nominated by the Committee on Nominations and elected at the same time the board members were elected. Southern Baptist Convention polity has somewhat changed since 1846, and all of the agencies today freely elect their officers.[16] This is one of the many ways that the Convention has constitutionally limited itself.

Executive assignments to an agency are often arbitrary and dependent upon the wishes of the Convention. They are not always covered in the formal assignment given to the agency by the Convention. At first, the lines separating Convention and agency responsibilities were dim and uncertain; but gradually through the passing decades, they have been sharply and clearly drawn. Generally, the Convention has ceased making unclear and inappropriate assignments. The discretionary spans of executive responsibility to the agencies have been clarified and extended.

Moving Toward the Twentieth Century

Even after the Civil War, the Convention continued the use of numerous ad hoc committees. At the time, few, if any, of the messengers objected. For example, in 1871, a total of eighteen committees were appointed, including eleven to review the reports of the three boards.[17] Four were charged with reviewing and recommending on various aspects of the Foreign Mission Board report, four on the Domestic Mission Board report, and one on the Sunday School Board report. The eleventh committee of reference was appointed to review the treasurers' reports of all three boards. Another committee of an unspecified number of members was appointed to plan the devotional services. The other five were general Convention committees appointed to report on credentials, time, place, and preacher, constitutional changes, nomination of board members, and the claim of Mrs. William Cooper that she was due $352.83 for services her deceased husband had performed for the Sunday School Board.[18] There were 145 people appointed, 38 percent of the 360 messengers registered.[19] The 145 did not include the members of the devotional committee, identified only as the pastors and deacons of the Saint Louis churches. Most of the committees reported during the five day meeting, some of them at length.

Debate was unlimited except when cut off by motions, which was not often done. The recommendations of the review committees were usually in the form of suggestions. Most of them called for local church support of the boards. A few were frankly aimed at board policies. The Foreign Mission Board was told that only missionaries who knew how to speak the languages of the people whom they were attempting to win should be returned to their fields. The first Sunday School Board was told not to print any more general religious literature, except that for which it already had plates, and to give its attention only to Sunday School work. Some of the recommendations may have been planted by board officials seeking Convention endorsement for unpopular policies or cherished programs.

In 1871 there were three sessions daily, except on Sunday, when no official Convention business was conducted. Two unofficial "mass meetings" explored subjects of concern to the messengers— foreign mission work on Saturday evening and Sunday School work on Sunday afternoon. As was the practice, except for the election of officers and the reports of the boards, the order of business was not set until the Convention convened. There was only one sermon, preached by a person who had been selected by the 1870 Convention. Only one devotional service was held daily, a thirty-minute "religious exercise" at the beginning of the morning session. Until well into the twentieth century, the annual Conventions were heavily weighted with business matters, and the people seemed to like it that way. But as the attendance increased and as the agenda became more complicated, the system functioned less efficiently.

The organizational system of 1845 and 1846 simply could not carry the increased load in the twentieth century. The thirty-three committees appointed in 1910 illustrate the awkwardness of the ad hoc committee system for handling serious Southern Baptist problems in the accelerated times.[20] The committees are listed as follows:

General Committees
Nominate Southern
  Seminary Trustees
Education to report to
  the 1911 Convention
Vice-presidents
Nominations for Boards
Enrollment
Women's Work
Free Annuals for Pastors
Apportionment of
  Undesignated Funds for
  Agencies
Systematizing and
  Safeguarding Endowments
Communication of the
  Home Mission Society
Problem with
  International Sunday
  School Union
Temperance
SBC History
Denominational Press for
  the 1911 Convention
Order of Business for
the 1911 Convention
Arrangements for the 1911
  Convention
HMB Reference Committees
Mountain Schools
Cuba and Panama
Cities and Foreigners
Work Among Negroes
Frontier Work
Church Building Fund
Evangelism
Finances and Outlook
Laymen's Work
Work in New Mexico
SSB Reference Committees
General Work of the
  Board
Lesson Texts
Young People's Work
FMB Reference Committees
Pagan Missions
Papal Missions
Editorial Work
Field Work and Finances

This listing further illustrates the wide range of the Convention's growing agenda and the complicated structure it had developed for handling the work. The use of so many committees created problems: (1) They were in some instances assigned complex issues without full information. (2) They consumed too much of the Convention's time in reporting. Twenty-nine of the committees had to do their work and report to the Convention within a six-day period. (3) The committees of reference for board reports were barriers between the persons responsible for the boards and the Convention. (4) Too many committees were keeping the Convention preoccupied with mechanics, when it should have been concerned with message. (5) The four committees appointed to plan for the 1911 Convention pointed to the need for standing committees to work between sessions. (6) There still was no general committee to gather up the loose ends. Too much time was spent admiring the library, and there was little time left to study the books.

The mass meetings, also popular with those who attended the Convention, began to take on new importance. Begun in 1846, when an informal Sunday night gathering was held on behalf of domestic missions and pledges for five hundred dollars were secured for "the destitute in our own country,"[21] the mass meetings were soon established as permanent features. The Convention began to use them extensively in the 1850s. The records are not clear that these were at first officially related to the Convention. Occasionally in the proceedings, the secretaries recorded them as they recorded other activities. Other times they mentioned them as if they were something apart from the official sessions. Frequently, the Convention appeared to adjourn to the mass meetings. Many of the mass meetings were held on Sundays when the Convention was not in session. Different Baptist concerns were considered, at first informally and without stated speakers, but later, carefully ordered and with selected speakers. The Convention at times appeared to utilize mass meetings to discover and even to mold consensus. Slowly, with each annual session, the Convention itself became less and less a deliberative body and more and more a series of mass meetings.

There was reluctance to abandon the old, deliberative ways. The people understood their simple methods and believed that they worked well for their organization. The deliberative character of the Convention fostered feelings of importance for what was happening. Debate was welcome, both for practical and entertainment values. The oversized committee structure furnished outlets for the more active and involved messengers. It is also probable that some liked the system because they could not visualize anything different. For most of those present, the Convention surely was the biggest event of the year, and anything better was unthinkable. The deliberative sessions gave some of the messengers a sense of participation in the inner life of the Convention. For a few, they were entertainment.

Not all messengers were pleased. By modern standards, the early sessions were not well managed. For many years, the order of business was informally developed after the convening of the Convention. Since there were few public halls, the Convention met in small church buildings without adequate facilities for the physical needs of the messengers. The sessions could be hot and crowded.

In 1884 an order of business committee was appointed by the president to function for that session.[22] This became a regular annual feature of the Convention. In 1909 the committee appointed that year was continued to 1910 "to arrange the order for the next session." A problem had arisen with corollary meetings, and those in charge of them were requested "not to arrange for their separate meetings prior to the assembling of the Convention."[23] The committee was instructed to plan carefully for the 1910 session to assure that all were treated fairly on the Convention program. This was the beginning of the standing Committee on Order of Business.

Besides the Convention arrangements and the Convention program, there were other points of criticism. Some messengers were persistently critical of the way boards were organized. In 1880 George E. Brewer of Alabama failed in an effort to secure the consolidation of the two mission boards "in view of lessening the expense of prosecuting the work, without impairing its efficiency."[24] The finances of the boards suffered for the lack of effective money-raising plans. Issues like these pointed to the need for a more systematic approach for handling the details of Convention business. In 1908 a timid forward step was taken when the Convention approved an Apportionment Committee for setting state goals for church contributions to home and foreign missions, a modest arrangement that operated until the Seventy-Five Million Campaign was begun in 1919.[25] This committee was suggestive of the dawn breaking for the Cooperative Program and the Executive Committee.

Changing the Convention Procedures

By 1912 the number of reference committees for board reports had dropped to eleven. Registration that year was 1,228, twice times what it had been in 1900. The world was in turmoil. Just ahead was World War I, a mammoth social and political upheaval that would reshape all Western society, Southern Baptists included. Against this background, the Convention was about to make changes in procedure that would endure at least for most of the century. The changes were signaled by two resolutions offered back-to-back in the 1912 annual meeting, one of them reactionary and one of them forward looking. S. A. Smith of Louisiana, gazing wistfully at the past, said in a motion that the "Convention has been, is, and must remain both a deliberative body and a great mass meeting . . . the buildings furnished from year to year, more or less, force the Convention to destroy one feature or the other."[26] He asked for a committee to make things right.

The second motion was by J. C. Massie of Tennessee, who also called attention to the difficulties in maintaining the Convention as a deliberative body. He proposed a plan for the Committee on Order of Business to follow in planning the 1913 Convention. The plan consisted of a balance of addresses, reports, and open forums.[27] The Convention approved Massie's proposal, in highlighting the mass meetings, incorporating them gradually into the annual meeting format. The Convention changed radically in the next fifteen years. After 1912 it was never again to be the small, intimate, clubby annual sessions of most of its first sixty-seven years. The resolutions of Smith and Massie signaled the future.

The real difference came from a motion offered the following year by John E. White of Georgia as the last order of the fourth day, on Saturday evening, May 17, 1913.[28] It was the tiny procedural mustard seed that grew into an enormous organizational tree. White moved that "a Commission of seven judicious men . . . make a careful study and thorough examination of the organization, plans and methods of this body, with a view to determining whether or not they are best adapted for eliciting, combining, and directing, etc." The motion also named President E. C. Dargan as chairman. One can only imagine what happened after that Saturday evening session to make certain that Dargan would appoint the right seven "judicious" men, and John E. White would offer a second motion when the Convention reconvened on Monday morning. Astute as Dargan was, he did not need much prompting to see that White's motion was directed constructively toward the future.

The leaders knew that some of the messengers carried long-standing feelings that the boards should be consolidated, especially the two mission boards. Possibly, the corresponding secretaries of the boards went directly to Dargan and White. Both men were prominent pastors in Georgia and were widely known for their denominational loyalties and broad personal sympathies; they would have been open to appeals for balance and reason. It would have been logical for the corresponding secretaries to have approached Dargan first because he was president of the Convention and the better known of the two, having served for many years as professor at Southern Seminary. Or, if the corresponding secretaries did not take initiative, it may have been that the chairmen of the boards appealed to Dargan and perhaps also to White. John F. Purser, chairman of the Home Mission Board, was a Georgian and presumably close to both men. J. B. Hutson, chairman of the Foreign Mission Board, would have been counted on to fight for its integrity. The alert and systematic-minded Edgar E. Folk, chairman of the Sunday School Board, would have been sensitive to the problems involved.

At any rate, when the Convention reconvened on Monday morning, seven good men were appointed: E. C. Dargan and John E. White of Georgia, J. B. Gambrell of Texas, W. W. Landrum of Kentucky, William Ellyson of Virginia, G. C. Savage of Tennessee, and C. P. Senter of Missouri. A few minutes later, White offered his second motion, adding the four agency heads: E. Y. Mullins of Southern Baptist Seminary, B. D. Gray of the Home Mission Board, R. J. Willingham of the Foreign Mission Board, and J. M. Frost of the Sunday School Board. The appointees were judicious men, indeed. It would be difficult to find in Southern Baptist history another blue-ribbon committee surpassing this one in competence.

Named in the originating resolution as "The Commission of Seven Judicious Men," it soon acquired another name, "The Efficiency Commission." This was the first in a series of committees from 1913 to 1927 that effected radical change in the Southern Baptist Convention—change that brought the Executive Committee into existence and that made possible its present eminence.

The Efficiency Commission's nine-page report in 1914 made benchmark recommendations that were approved by the Convention. They are summarized as follows:[29]

> *On the Convention Order of Business:* The Commission, concerned about the way the Convention conducted its sessions, and especially about the confusion generated by multiple committees reviewing agency reports, recommended:
> (1) That board reports be presented in prepared speeches, using one speaker for each board, that the official reports be printed for distribution, and that time be left for discussion.
> (2) Committees of reference on board reports were declared no longer needed. [The Commission did not specifically recom-

mend their discontinuance. Though gradually reduced, they
were still used until 1928.]

(3) That morning sessions be left open for reports of committees and boards, evening sessions for inspirational addresses by
selected speakers, and afternoon sessions for committee work
and for other types of meetings.

On Publicity: Noting the generous space given Convention news
by newspapers and wire services, the Commission recommended:

(1) That boards and committees prepare and submit to the
secretaries printed copies of reports and other materials for
distribution to the press.

(2) That a press representative be appointed annually by the
president. Several years passed before the full implementation
of these actions relating to the press.

On the Work and Relationships of Boards: The commission reported
that it had concluded that the present plan for the three boards
should be continued and that their locations be left unchanged:
"Their methods of office administration are businesslike, and
that the Southern Baptist Convention is justified in its confidence in their fidelity to the large concerns committed to their
trust." The Commission recommended and the Convention
approved that the general Boards and the seminary be instructed:

(1) "To maintain affectionate relations with each other, keeping
in view the unity of their common cause and the necessity of
their cooperation."

(2) "In keeping with the By-laws of the Convention, to seek and
maintain the closest possible connection with the State
Boards," and to maintain "effective connectional organizations" between the churches, state conventions and associations.

(3) "To undertake to reach more definite and uniform agree-

ments with the State Boards with respect to the expenses of collection in the several States."

(4) "To seek the cooperation of State Boards before introducing special agencies for the purpose of collecting money in the states."

(5) To carry out a proposition recommended by state executive secretaries concerning remittances of funds being held by the state boards.

On Convention Finances: Noting "splendid advances" in Convention finances, the report recommended:

(1) That the Convention have a financial budget.

(2) That the Convention apportion Southern Baptist agency needs to the states and that the states be requested to apportion needs to the associations.

(3) That the people be asked to give regularly to Convention causes as well as to local church expenses.

(4) That the Boards continue the practice of having public accountants audit their funds and that these reports be made available to the Convention.

On Christian Union and Denominational Efficiency: A closing section of the Commission report said that Southern Baptists could attain highest efficiency in the propagation of the gospel by the Convention "by preserving a complete autonomy at home and abroad, unembarrassed by entangling alliances with other bodies holding to different standards of doctrine and different views of church life and church order."

The Efficiency Commission also proposed bylaws implementing some of these ideas. All were approved except the one that listed the agencies as separate entities, an indication that some messengers were still unsettled on the question of the consolidation of boards. It may also have been that some of the messengers strongly committed to the consolidation of the boards were temporarily voting their reservations because of the membership of the four agency executives on the Commission. On the point of consolidation, the Efficiency Commission did not make a specific recommendation in its main report. It merely said that it had concluded that the present plan should be continued. The bylaw listing the agencies as separate entities was postponed by the Convention for consideration at the next annual meeting.

In Southern Baptist life, a rule of escalation seems to be that if a group wants to expand the work of a commission or committee, first, give it an important sounding name, then, ask for an extension of its life, and finally, secure an open-ended agenda. This is what may have happened in this group in 1914 when the Convention approved motions in 1914 to continue the Efficiency Commission for a second year and for it "to consider any matters for the general good of the Convention."[30] In this instance, the maneuver produced changes that were considered revolutionary for the times. In 1915 the postponed bylaw was again approved as submitted.[31] The Convention also approved recommendations of the Commission which included the following:[32]

(1) That the Sunday School Board remain independent of the other boards.
(2) That the two mission boards remain separate.
(3) That no secretary or other employee of a board be a trustee of any board.
(4) That the boards be responsible for fixing the salaries and the conditions of work for employees.

This last recommendation was a statement clarifying one aspect of the Convention's policy on the delegation of powers, another example of how the Convention wisely restrains itself in the use of its constitutional authority. The future of the Southern Baptist Convention was written into almost every line of the two reports of the Efficiency Commission. It is reasonable to suppose that much of the thinking on this Commission was done by Mullins and Dargan. It bears in its style and language the hallmarks of both men. Most of the commission's recommendations are still in effect in the Southern Baptist Convention, and many of them are preserved in the Convention Bylaws and Business and Financial Plan.

With a highly respected, blue-ribbon commission doing a comprehensive and thorough two-year study and with the Convention clearly writing board separation into its bylaws, the long-standing question of board consolidation should have been settled. But to the probable consternation of all who had been involved in the commission, board consolidation was raised again in 1916 in a different way. M. H. Wolfe of Texas proposed a constitutional amendment that would create "one strong Executive Board which shall direct all the work and enterprises fostered by this Convention."[33] The same motion included a provision for its reference to a committee of eleven.

This new committee was appointed by President Lansing Burrows who had intimate knowledge of Convention and agency problems due to his long experience as recording secretary. The committee included E. Y. Mullins, John E. White, and E. C. Dargan who had been members of the Efficiency Commission. The next day, the chairman, M. H. Wolfe, reporting for the committee, asked permission to postpone its report to 1917. The reason: "Changes in the Constitution are too vital and too fundamentally related to our work to be made without full time for consideration of all the bearings of the proposed changes."[34] Among those discussing the motion to postpone were George W. Truett and E. Y. Mullins, who later were presidents of the Executive Committee, and Austin Crouch, who later was the first executive secretary of the Executive Committee. A new era was approaching, and it would bring changes that the people who voted for the 1915 and 1916 reports may not have dreamed possible. The old voices were still being heard, but new voices were now speaking that would be heard again and again over the next three decades.

Notes

1. Classroom lecture at Southwestern Baptist Theological Seminary, 1938.
2. SBC, 1945, p. 7.
3. *Webster's New Collegiate Dictionary*, 1973.
4. *Webster's Dictionary of Synonyms*, 1951.
5. For many years *delegate* was most often used for members of the body. The original Article III stated that the "Convention shall consist of members who contribute funds, or are delegated by religious bodies contributing funds."
6. SBC, 1845, pp. 1-19. All 1845 and 1846 references may be found on these pages.
7. Ibid., p. 15.
8. SBC, 1845, p. 3.
9. Ibid.
10. From this point, the word delegate will be substituted with either *messenger, member,* or *participant.*
11. SBC, 1846, p. 7.
12. SBC, 1983, p. 467.
13. SBC, 1914, p. 70.
14. SBC, 1928, pp. 41, 43, 70, 74; cf. SBC, 1929, p. 2.
15. SBC, 1924, p. 56.
16. SBC Constitution, 1983, VI. 4.
17. SBC, 1871, pp. 18-21.
18. Ibid., p. 30. The committee recommended that the Convention recognize the justice of Mrs. Cooper's claim and that the Sunday School Board be instructed to pay it.
19. Ibid., 1983, p. 467.
20. Ibid., 1910. pp. 7-60.
21. Ibid., 1846, p. 19.
22. SBC, 1884, p. 12.
23. Ibid., 1909, p. 36.
24. Ibid., 1880, pp. 15-16.
25. SBC, 1908, p. 22.
26. SBC 1912, p. 77.
27. Ibid., p. 78.
28. Ibid., 1913, p. 70-73.

29. SBC, 1914, pp. 69-78.
30. Ibid., 1914, pp. 69-78.
31. Ibid., 1915, p. 43.
32. Ibid., pp. 22-25. Cf. pp. 42-43.
33. Ibid., 1916, pp, 18, 30, 57.
34. Ibid., p. 57.

3

The Early Years of the Executive Committee
1917-1926

The Wolfe proposal addressed an old issue, one that had been talked about from the beginning of the Southern Baptist Convention and had officially surfaced in 1880, when the Convention approved a bid by George E. Brewer of Alabama for a committee to study the expediency of consolidating the two mission boards. Saving money was the primary reason that Brewer had given for the proposed merger. He had said that the "local Boards are engaged in supplying the destitution at home."[1] Like many loyal Baptists, Brewer believed that the Home Mission Board and the state mission boards duplicated each other. Brewer also had said that "the work among the Indians in the Territory and the Chinese of California . . . bears as much resemblance to the work of the Foreign as the Home Board." It was a long-time common perception that the two boards faced identical problems on the mission fields and used identical methods in their work. The Convention agreed with the Committee to reject Brewer's bid for consolidation because "much land yet remains to be possessed by the Convention."[2]

The issue did not disappear. Extremists, influenced by the Landmark movement and convinced that all mission work should be done directly by the local churches really wanted to do away with boards. Others, moderate in their views, were honestly convinced that there were too many boards and that they should combined. By 1916, for fifty years or more, it had been often an issue always in the halls, but rarely on the platform. Wolfe was not an extremist. Whatever his intention, it was not to destroy the denomination.

The Wolfe proposal addressed a new issue, the creation of "a strong Executive Board" under which all Southern Baptist Convention affairs could be placed. On the surface, the motion appeared to strike at the basic operating polity and principles that guided the Convention. But was that really what Wolfe had in mind? Perhaps, or it could have been something else. He was a very successful and generous Texas businessman, widely respected for his interest in denominational affairs. He had already served as a vice-president of the Southern Baptist Convention, and that same year he would be elected president of the Baptist General Convention of Texas. His intention may have been to look beyond mere consolidation of the boards to an entirely new way of conducting Southern Baptist affairs. His business experience pointed in that direction. It included the presidency of a bank, the founding two important cotton brokerage companies, and membership on the board of directors of the Texas Power and Light Company.

No doubt, Wolfe was sincere in proposing consolidation under a strong executive board, yet he may have been trying to bring the Convention into the twentieth century by a means which appeared to him to be logical and desirable. If indeed merger-minded, Wolfe may have been also struggling with the question of how to rid the Convention of its horse-and-buggy mentality in the dawning day of the automobile. If he were not thinking this way, many dedicated leaders were, including E. Y. Mullins and E. C. Dargan. Whatever the intent, Wolfe's motion contained flaming red flags that excited the leadership of the Convention. Some leaders saw the flags as disaster; some, as opportunity.

Lansing Burrows was president of the 1916 Convention and held the right to appoint all of its committees. A wise old Dutchman who had been secretary of the Convention from 1882 until 1914 when he was elected president,[3] he was also the ingenious originator of the early Southern Baptist system of gathering and preserving church and associational data. Burrows was not an outstanding presiding officer, but he knew Convention polity as well as anyone, and he certainly understood Convention organizational dynamics.[4]

He could be counted on to appoint a balanced committee. When the names were called, Wolfe was chairman, and after him, four prominent Convention leaders: Joshua Levering, E. Y. Mullins, E. C. Dargan, and John E. White. Although not as prominent, the other members were also distinguished for their denominational accomplishments.[5] The committee's preliminary report in 1916 was made under the name of "The Committee on the Revised Constitution." It was later called the Consolidation Committee. Whatever Mr. Wolfe's convictions, there is little doubt that the committee was largely influenced by Mullins and Dargan, and perhaps also by White. All three had served on the Efficiency Commission of 1913-1915 and had proven themselves as thoughtful and aggressive leaders, with superb knowledge and understanding of Baptist problems.

Mullins was near the apex of his long and productive career. After graduation from The Southern Baptist Theological Seminary in 1885, he had served churches in Kentucky, Maryland, and Massachusetts; and for a short time he had been an associate secretary at the Foreign Mission Board. He had been called to the president's chair at the seminary in 1899, at the end of the bitter struggle between former President W. H. Whitsitt and his critics. In 1900 Mullins was well received when he briefly addressed the Convention for his first time and was subsequently asked to preach the Convention sermon in 1901.[6] His affable, open manner and his skill in delineating complicated issues and in making clear penetrating statements immediately drew him into Convention affairs. He served on many committees and was frequently involved in debate. At the time he was appointed to Wolfe's Consolidation Committee, Mullins was probably the most widely known leader in Southern Baptist life and possibly the most respected.

E. C. Dargan (1852-1930), almost as widely known, had received his education at Furman University and The Southern Baptist Theological Seminary. After pastorates in South Carolina, Virginia, and California, he became professor of preaching at Southern Seminary, serving with distinction from 1892 to 1907, during which time he became established as a prolific author. His most enduring books

were the massive two-volume *A History of Preaching.* Dargan served
on numerous Convention committees, and in 1911 he was elected
Convention president. At the time he was appointed on the Consolidation Committee, he was in the last year of a ten-year pastorate in
Macon, Georgia. There would be little doubt about his commitment
to Southern Baptist principles and no doubt that, with Mullins, he
was thinking far into the future. Many other Southern Baptist leaders were looking ahead and trying to focus on the challenges inherent in what appeared to many to be impossible Southern Baptist
Convention problems.

There was some uneasiness in the minds of the messengers as
they looked toward the 1917 Convention in New Orleans. In April,
before the Convention met in May, J. B. Gambrell, Texas, an astute
denominational statesman and popularly known among close
friends as "Uncle Gideon," submitted an article to state Baptist
papers that appealed for unity in addressing the future. Gambrell's
wide reputation and exceptional credibility were based on a lifetime
of solid performance. As a Civil War hero, state mission secretary
in Mississippi and Texas, president of Mercer University, editor of
the *Baptist Standard,* and professor at Southwestern Baptist Theological Seminary, he was in a position to be heard with some notice.
Anticipating a stormy Convention, he wrote, "We need a great big
Convention in New Orleans, but that cannot be unless we go there
with a big Spirit, to do big things. I am tired of religious parades.
In the tremendous times we are in, tameness, Laodiceanism, pid-
dling away time and opportunity with trivialities will leave us in the
shallows. The Convention must pull in on the main track, get up
steam, and move on. I put the emphasis on steam."[7] The wise, old
wit mixed his metaphors, but he made his point: The keys for success in Convention enterprise are mission and energy, not quib-
bling and nit-picking, a timely message for the Baptists of any
generation. The Wolfe proposals to merge the boards and to create
a strong executive board under which all the work would be placed
were two of the pressing issues that were disturbing the people
expecting to attend the New Orleans Convention.

World War I was raging, and America was ready to fight. Three concerns were on the lips of the Baptists, *Kaiser Bill, consolidation,* and *centralization.* For a year the state papers had been debating the Wolfe proposal. The respected E. E. Folk, editor of the Tennessee paper, wrote following the appointment of the "Consolidation Committee" in 1916, "To have only one board would certainly tend to centralization, if it did not lead to it."[8] No doubt, world tensions that had driven America into the conflict had also contributed to Baptist unrest.

When the Southern Baptist Convention convened in New Orleans on May 16, the United States had been in the war since April 6. With troops mobilized and families disrupted, the nation was in turmoil. Some of that unrest was surely present in the Athenaeum when Lansing Burrows, the immediate past president, called the Convention to order. Six men were nominated for the Convention's highest office; and when the votes were counted, "Uncle Gideon" had been elected president.[9]

Opening the Door to the Future

On the first afternoon,[10] M. H. Wolfe presented the report of the Committee on Consolidation of Boards.[11] As soon as Wolfe had read his report, a substitute motion was presented by J. F. Brownlow, Tennessee, questioning the legality of the boards. Brownlow wanted: (1) the boards to surrender their charters, (2) the Convention to operate only under the original charter, (3) the boards to transfer their property to the Convention, and (4) the Convention to appoint a board of directors to manage the Convention's affairs.[12] Brownlow's motion was radical surgery, of the kind that the original Wolfe motion appeared to have intended. In the minds of some, this must have seemed like a threat to the life of the Convention. The debate continued for a long time, with Brownlow keeping the floor for one hour, refusing to surrender it to anyone except to a questioner. The debate ceased when someone moved to adjourn because of "the lateness of the hour." Later, in what was

likely a classic effort of leadership to secure consensus, Brownlow
and five other persons were added to the committee.

The next day, Wolfe reported again. Without debate, the Convention acted on the Consolidation Committee's original report.
On the old issue of consolidation, it approved the following: "In
view of the diversity of opinions concerning the best method of
conducting our work, and the distressing conditions in our country,
resulting from the world war, we recommend that the Boards of the
Convention remain separate as at present."[13] This met with approval, especially among the friends of the boards.

On the new issue of a strong Executive Board, the Convention
also approved a second recommendation:

> Recognizing, however, that there is a strong sentiment in favor of
> greater unity in the general direction of the Convention's affairs, and
> believing that some improvement in the methods of conducting the
> work would be attained by the creation of a standing committee of
> the Convention to act for the body between its sessions in ways
> hereinafter set forth, we recommend that an executive committee of
> seven, representing the different parts of the territory of the Conven-
> tion be elected annually by the Convention as are its standing com-
> mittees.

In the very next order, Brownlow also reported for the committee, calling for a special study of the legal status of the boards.
Brownlow's question had been divided, and the original report
saved—with the committee's blessing. It is not difficult to see the
hands of Mullins and Dargan in the compromise.

The next morning, on motion of E. C. Dargan, the body approved
a new Convention Bylaw Six incorporating the duties of the new
Executive Committee as recommended by the Consolidation Committee: (1) "To act for the Convention during the interim . . . on
matters not otherwise provided for," (2) "to have oversight of arrangements for the meeting of the Convention, with authority
. . . with the President . . . to change if necessary the time and place
of meeting," (3) "to act in an advisory way on matters of policy and

cooperation arising between the Boards . . . only on request," (4) "to hold meetings at such times and places as it may select," (5) "to make report (sic) . . . and receive instruction at each annual meeting of the Convention." It was also limited in the scope of its duties: "The Committee shall have no further duties except as other things may be committed to it by the Convention itself."[14] Another door was opened to the future—but only barely opened. It would not be fully opened until 1927.

The most important new feature to emerge from the work of the Consolidation Committee was that the Convention now had "an Executive Committee" and not an "Executive Board." This distinction made the new organization unique in Baptist interdependent life. It softened current fears of a monolithic Convention structure. Still, the plan provided for a way to tie up many of the loose ends. Moreover, it placed in the center of the Convention's plan of operation a neutral administrative group without authority over the agencies. The new arrangement temporarily satisfied nearly everyone. Some board leaders, however, had questions about how to limit the power of the Executive Committee, questions that had been only partially answered with new Bylaw Six.

As it developed in the next ten years, the new Executive Committee had very little power. There were five primary weaknesses: (1) It was not broadly representative, having at first, only seven members, (2) it was pauperized from the beginning and forced to live on handouts from the agencies, (3) it was without staff to keep its agenda moving forward between sessions, (4) its place in Convention life probably was not clearly understood by either the messengers or their leaders, and (5) it still was regarded with some suspicion.

To some it was an ugly duckling; to others, a bird of promise—though with its limitations, certainly not a peacock. Fortunately, there were more optimists than pessimists. R. H. Pitt, the widely read editor of the Virginia *Religious Herald*, wrote, "The Executive Committee recommended by the Committee on Consolidation will furnish a link long needed between the Convention and its constituency. The duties and responsibilities and functions of this committee are limited carefully."[15] E. E. Folk, the year before, when contemplating the power of the proposed "Executive Board," had written, "With our Baptist independence and freedom we do not believe that this Secretary could become a Pope in the sense of exercising authority over the denomination. If he should forget that he is servant of all and should attempt to become boss he would soon feel the wrath of Southern Baptists."[16] Most Baptists wanted to give the Executive Committee a chance to succeed; but they wanted it to succeed within the bounds of traditional democratic Baptist polity.

Working with Limited Agenda

M. H. Wolfe was named the first chairman of the Executive Committee. Also, from the Consolidation Committee, two others were appointed, E. C. Dargan, and Z.T. Cody. However, Dargan did not complete his term because after a long and distinguished career as pastor, seminary professor, historian, and preacher, he accepted a call that year to the chair of editorial secretary of The Sunday School Board, thus forfeiting his eligibility.[17]

Before the 1917 Convention adjourned, the Executive Committee received three specific assignments: (1) "To receive proposals from cities desiring the 1919 meeting" of the Convention,[18] (2) to bring the bylaws and constitution "into harmony with the sentiments of the Convention," and[19] (3) to study the problem of funds for the boards, referred to the Convention by Baptists in Maryland.[20] The Executive Committee made its first Convention report in 1918. On the Constitution and Bylaws, it proposed extensive changes, all of which were approved.[21] These were the first of a long line of constitution and bylaw changes that the Executive Committee in the years ahead would recommend to the Convention. On the Maryland Memorial, the Executive Committee reported at length, but without any forward movement toward solving the Convention's financial problems.[22]

In 1919 the Executive Committee did not report, though it had assignments from 1918 and the chairman was a registered messenger;[23] yet five significant changes made it less an ugly duckling. On motion of W. J. McGlothlin:[24] (1) General membership was based upon state conventions, not upon regions, (2) the Convention boards were each given a membership, (3) the president and secretary of the Convention were made members, (4) the Executive Committee was liberated to advise the agencies when differences should arise without having to be requested by one or more of them, and (5) as a result, the membership was broadened, and its influence extended. The appointment of board memberships made the Executive Committee's presence in Convention life a little more acceptable to board leadership. The way was opened for easier financial support for the Executive Committee, though adding the Convention board representatives may have weakened the Executive Committee for any role it might have had in advising the agencies. Happily, the hesitations of the previous two years soon disappeared.

Increasingly, the Executive Committee handled significant assignments, except in 1926 and 1927, when the activities of other important committees somewhat reduced its agenda. Beginning in 1919, three other Convention developments spotlighted the need for a really effective Executive Committee and led to the 1927 restructuring.

Leaping Ahead in Three Giant Strides

1. The first of these developments was *the Seventy-Five Million Campaign* that seemed to erupt spontaneously in the 1919 Convention, but no doubt was founded upon the countless money-raising schemes that had aborted and upon the rising concern of Southern Baptists for the financial well-being of their agencies. Also, America was beginning to crawl out of its rural past into the coming urban complex that would reshape the nation. The new word on the lips of most Americans was *progress,* which meant that everything must move ahead. Caught in the spirit of the times, Baptist leaders also believed that somehow the denomination must firmly take hold of

the future. Among the concerned leaders was J. B. Gambrell, seventy-nine years old in his third term as president of the Southern Baptist Convention. "Uncle Gideon" went to Atlanta for the sixty-fourth session with the future very much on his mind. When he arose to give his presidential address, he was facing over 4,000 messengers, twice as many as had ever attended any previous Convention.[25] The mood was much better than it had been two years before in the noisy New Orleans Convention.

The old soldier spoke in patriotic appreciation for the end of the war and the victory that it had brought. He said, "It is pleasant to reflect that this Convention and our people stood firm for those principles and measures necessary for the world's deliverance from tyranny into a higher civilization."[26] He quickly shifted to his main emphasis: "Baptists are the friends of liberty, both civil and religious, the world over." He moved from liberty in general to liberty for the souls of soldiers and presented his view of how Baptists had been forbidden to witness for Christ in the military camps. He quoted a secretary in the War Department who had said, "The whole desire of the department is in the interest of breaking down rather than emphasizing denominational distinctions."[27] Gambrell, as well as most Southern Baptist leaders, was strongly against any kind of organic church union. He concluded this part of his address by saying, "During the recent past all kinds of winds of doctrine and no doctrine have been blowing strong, and the air has been loaded with dust, chaff, and other light dry things. Well-paid men, paid in part by Baptist money, have gone hither and thither telling us that the old doctrines are no longer suitable for the new age and that we need a new church."[28] Then tying it together he said, "We should keep on agitating till the true doctrine of religious freedom is ingrained afresh in the American mind."[29] Finally Gambrell came to his appeal for forward movement of the denomination:

> Let us gird up our loins and go forward. Baptists have always flourished by meeting issues bravely. It is my deep conviction that this Convention ought to adopt a program for work commensurate with

the reasonable demands on us and summons ourselves and our people to a new demonstration of the value of orthodoxy in free action.

The Convention responded by authorizing a Committee on Financial Aspects of Our Program to find new ways of financing the work.[30] Two days later, the Convention approved a campaign to raise seventy-five million dollars in five years, to be promoted and distributed under the leadership of the Executive Committee.[31] Later, the Convention approved a motion substituting a committee composed of one from each state to plan the campaign and distribute the money raised.[32] This motion appears to have pushed the Executive Committee out of major involvement.

The next day, a second substitute motion by A. J. Barton, Louisiana, further confused the role of the Executive Committee. He moved: "We do not now regard this [the Executive Committee's involvement] as an adequate provision for the accomplishment of this great task"[33] and called for a commission of fifteen to be appointed by the president for the purpose of conducting the campaign. The motion was approved. It placed the struggling Executive Committee in further jeopardy.

When the Seventy-Five Million Campaign Commission (Campaign Commission) was named, George W. Truett was chairman. Its membership consisted of two former Convention presidents, three future presidents, and other distinguished leaders. Whatever had been the intention of the Convention when it voted the Barton proposal, the commission itself felt that it should confer with the Executive Committee and did in fact hold joint meetings to settle important questions of policy and distribution.[34]

The Campaign Commission began its work by appointing the forceful Lee R. Scarborough, president of Southwestern Baptist Theological Seminary, as general director. A relative newcomer in organized Baptist life, he set to work with great energy. A year later, Scarborough, by then widely known as a persistent and effective leader, reported that Baptists indeed had come through with "a program of work commensurate with the reasonable demands" made upon them: *over $92.6 million pledged on a goal of $75 million.* At the moment, it seemed a triumph for organized mission work. There was bright optimism in the hearts of the leaders, something they would not feel again for twenty-five years.

Why was the Executive Committee stripped of campaign leadership? With a few, it may have been a fear that the Executive Committee was gaining too much power. More likely, it was because of a low profile of the Executive Committee in the life of the Convention. Whatever the reason, it was ironic that Barton opposed an arrangement for the very group that some of his friends eight years later would think that he should head as its first executive secretary.

By 1923 it was clear that Southern Baptists would not reach the Seventy-Five Million Campaign objective. By 1924, the last year of the campaign, only about $58.6 million had been received toward the $75 million goal.[35] In some ways, Southern Baptists were worse off than before the campaign, for both state and SBC agencies had borrowed against the $92.6 million goal and were painfully in debt. There they would remain for the next nineteen years—severely crippled and almost decapitated for counting too much on the future pledges. Moreover, the money-raising apparatus used before the campaign had fallen to pieces and could not be put back together again. To these problems the Executive Committee would devote most of its energies for a long, long time. For this reason, it has been popular to say that the Seventy-Five Million Campaign failed. But did it fail? Surely not, for the following reasons:

(1) It demonstrated that Southern Baptists could work together cooperatively in a great organized money-raising plan.

(2) It brought together for the first time the organized forces of the Southern Baptist Convention, the state conventions, and the local associations into an effective partnership in cooperative promotion.

(3) It led Southern Baptists to begin intensive use of three modern and efficient tools for local church finance—the church budget, the every-member canvass, and weekly giving.

(4) It pinpointed state leadership as the group most responsible for leading the churches to adopt better stewardship programs.

(5) It proved that Southern Baptists, if forced into debt, could come through with banners flying.

(6) It combined all the conventions and their agencies into one gigantic program of cooperation and proved that the Southern Baptist denominational program is the good Baptists do for each other and for the world in working together for Jesus Christ.

(7) It reinforced the already existing feeling in the churches that the Southern Baptist Convention provided a worthy channel through which they can witness to the world.

(8) It erected a solid base of cooperation and responsibility on which the Cooperative Program could be established. Indeed, it may have been the beginning of the Cooperative Program.

The Seventy-Five Million Campaign surfaced complex problems that pointed to the need for a fully efficient Executive Committee with a full-time staff: (1) The tendency of state conventions to divide and distribute independently to the SBC agencies, the undesignated gifts intended for Southern Baptist Convention causes, (2) a clearer understanding of how undesignated funds were to be divided between the Southern Baptist Convention and state Conventions, (3) the right of the Southern Baptist Convention to approach directly the churches on behalf of its causes, (4) a better understanding between the Southern Baptist Convention and the state conventions on respective promotional responsibilities, and (5) a satisfactory method for dividing the Southern Baptist Convention portion of undesignated funds between the agencies. All of these problems were waiting for some person or group to suggest really workable plans for eliminating Southern Baptist Convention business confusion. Some of these problems would take years for solving.

In 1923 the Executive Committee had secured approval of the Convention for a committee "to study the question of unifying and correlating the work of the Convention activities."[36] In 1924 a majority of the members recommended that the agencies be left alone.[37] A committee minority brought by N. T. Tull of Mississippi recommended that in view of the continued growth of the agencies and the lack of a general board to coordinate the work, that four boards be formed: (1) *A Southern Baptist Publishing House* to handle all printing and publications, (2) *a Southern Baptist Social Service Board,* combining hospital, ministerial retirement and relief, and social welfare, (3) *a Southern Baptist Mission Board combining home and foreign mission work,* and (4) *a Southern Baptist Education board* combining all Sunday School Board work except publications, Convention interests in higher education, work with laymen, the Woman's Missionary, and various other programs. The two reports caused hardly a stir in that extraordinary Convention, and both motions were laid on the table. Surely, in the division of the committee, one urgent need did not go unnoticed, especially by informed leaders—a neutral, fully functioning Executive Committee must be given responsibility for solving the knottier Convention problems.

2. When the Seventy-Five Million Campaign stumbled to a shortfall and appeared to fail, there was a second giant stride forward, *the formation of the Cooperative Program.* In 1923, in response to a suggestion of the general director of the campaign, L. R. Scarborough, the Convention approved a Committee on Future Program to develop "a general outline of plans for the next forward movement of Southern Baptists."[38] This committee, under the chairmanship of the radiant M. E. Dodd, developed the Cooperative Program details and presented them to the Convention at Memphis in 1925. Dodd was bold and bald, an intensely happy man of ideas and action, noted for his forceful preaching and his unique dress. Always impeccably attired, he invariably wore a vest with white piping, which some said was his idea of a clerical collar. He had the knack of making everything he said and did seem important, an ability that may have helped him sell the twelve-page report to the Convention. As vital as the report may have seemed at the time, the state papers reveal that it was only barely noticed. Some may have felt that it was just another plan destined to failure. More likely, the

the Baptists gathered at Memphis were innundated with a cascade of other issues . . . more than they could easily assimilate.

That same Convention, 1925, was when the first *Statement of Baptist Faith and Message* was adopted. It was also the time that Southwestern Baptist Theological Seminary was transferred to Southern Baptist Convention ownership. Other concerns were prohibition and evolution, with plenty of talk about both issues. If there was indifference toward the Dodd report, it may also have been due to the general lack of understanding of the proposed Cooperative Program, especially how it differed from the Seventy-Five Million Campaign.

3. The third stride forward also took place at the Convention in 1925: *the creation of the Business Efficiency Committee.* In the midst of all the confusion, for a very few minutes, attention focused on an olive-complexioned, bald man who wore a good-natured scowl but who was known among his friends as a pleasant, sagacious observer of people and events. Austin Crouch, looking more like a dignified banker than the successful pastor of the First Baptist Church, Murfreesboro, Tennessee, quietly arose to make a motion long overdue. He asked for the appointment of a committee "to study the business methods of the Convention and make recommendations to the Convention next year."[39] Just another stern face to most people, he certainly was well known to President George W. McDaniel of Richmond, for they had been young men together in Texas, along with George W. Truett, J. M. Dawson, Pat M. Neff, Jeff D. Ray, Prince E. Burroughs, S. P. Brooks, L. R. Scarborough, and others. When the Convention voted, it approved a Business Efficiency Committee of fifteen members, with about half laymen and none denominationally employed.

The chairman was Austin Crouch, not always recognized by the messengers, but certainly noticed by the agency executives. In 1924 he had succeeded in getting an amendment attachment to the report of Dodd's Future Program Committee requiring that all agencies "sharing in funds raised for South-wide objects, shall be required to make annual financial statements of assets and liabilities and of receipts and disbursements to the Southern Baptist Convention."[40] It was probably one of the most important parts of the Future Program Committee's report that year and the handwriting on the wall for untidy fiscal accountability. Crouch was not striking at any known dishonesty but at careless bookkeeping and reporting methods. He knew that it was a problem much more complex than one simple motion, and his Business Efficiency Committee was ready to tackle it. The committee was armed with authority from the Convention "to secure any facts or information desired from any and all Convention agencies."[41] Austin Crouch, a rare combination of talent and dedication, had come to the front and was about to make his unerasable mark on the way the Southern Baptist Convention conducts its business.

Notes

1. SBC, 1880 pp. 15-16.
2. Ibid., pp. 25-26.
3. SBC, 1983, p. 468.
4. A. J. Holt, "Our Convention Presidents," WR, June 1, 1927, p. 7.
5. SBC, 1916, pp. 30, 57. See Appendix 1 for a list of Executive Committee officers, 1917-1984.
6. SBC, 1900, pp. 24, 47. Cf. SBC, 1901, p. 15.
7. BR, April 19, 1917, p. 1. Gambrell was also frequently described as the great commoner among Southern Baptists.
8. Ibid., June 1, 1916.
9. Among the nominators was Austin Crouch, who nominated his old friend, S. P. Brooks, president of Baylor University
10. SBC, 1917, pp. 30.
11. SBC, 1916, p. 60. The new name was used by George W. Truett, when he moved that a matter be postponed pending the report "on the resolution relating to the consolidation of the three boards.
12. *Baptist and Reflector,* May, 1917, p. 4.
13. SBC Annual, 1917, p. 34.

14. Ibid., pp. 47-48.

15. *Religious Herald,* May 31, 1917, p. 10.

16. *Baptist and Reflector,* June 1, 1916, p.8.

17. Dargan served in his new position as editorial secretary of the Sunday School Board until he retired in 1927, at age seventy-five.

18. SBC, 1917, p.98.

19. Ibid., p. 109.

20. Ibid.

21. SBC, 1918, pp. 16-18.

22. Ibid., pp. 104-107.

23. SBC, 1919, pp. 2, 167.

24. SBC, 1919, pp. 72, 75-76.

25. SBC, 1983, p. 468. Registration at New Orleans in 1919 was 4,224, twice what it had been in Asheville in 1916 when it was 2,125.

26. SBC, 1919, pp. 17-23.

27. Ibid., p. 19.

28. Ibid., p. 21.

29. Ibid., p. 22.

30. Ibid., pp. 52, 62.

31. Ibid., pp. 73-74.

32. Ibid., pp. 81-82.

33. SBC, 1919, p. 122.

34. ECM, February 20, 1920, p. 6. From SBCA in the library of the SBC Historical Commission.

35. ESB, II, 1,1197.

36. SBC, 1923, p. 72.

37. SBC, 1924, pp. 32-35.

38. SBC, 1923, pp. 70-71.

39. SBC, 1925, p. 45.

40. SBC, 1924, p.69.

41. SBC, 1925, p.45.

4

The Restructuring of the Executive Committee
1926-1927

Nineteen hundred and twenty-seven was a peak year in American life. The national economy was booming, and the country generally was looking forward to better times. Al Jolson was singing "Sonny Boy" in the first talking picture, a marvel that awakened the dreamers to thoughts of technical invincibility.[1] Some were saying that talking pictures soon would come into homes through radios. The phrase, "Nothing is impossible for science," was often heard on the lips of youth. World War I was fast receding into history and the political and economic troubles of Germany seemed far away. Yo-yos were jumping up and down on their strings and in another year or two would be in everyone's hands. Cows were still the same; but for most people, the creamery had replaced the barn. Milk in glass bottles with cardboard stoppers and ice on the leather-covered backs of strong men were being delivered from horse-drawn wagons to the kitchens of millions of homes. But that was changing, for trucks were abundant on the streets, and refrigerators were fast taking the places of iceboxes. The Model T Ford that had replaced the horse and buggy was itself about to be replaced with the Model A Ford. Self-service grocery stores were peeping around the corner even in small towns. That year, Charles A. Lindburg dared to fly alone across the Atlantic Ocean in *The Spirit of Saint Louis,* earning the name of Lone Eagle and signaling the beginning of serious air travel. There was a lightness in the air, and some Americans with bulging bank deposits were singing, "It Ain't Gonna Rain No More."

But not all the Baptists were singing. Tired from doctrinal infighting and from hanging on the edge of denominational bankruptcy, some of the leaders were wondering what modern Moses would lead the denomination out of the organizational and fiscal wilderness in which it had been wandering since the Seventy-Five Million Campaign shortfall.

Searching for Financial Stability

Although many Baptist leaders were aware of the problems, only a few had their hands firmly on the future. One of the few was the quiet Tennessee pastor, Austin Crouch, who believed he knew a way for the Convention to move forward. He was working at the problem, encouraged by some of the strongest men in the Southern Baptist Convention, among them the Convention president, George W. Truett. The two had been young men together at Baylor University and later pastors together in Dallas. Crouch was hoping to move the Convention from its past financial chaos into unprecedented orderliness. His ideas were so simple as to seem commonplace. It was difficult for thoughtful Baptists to escape his logic.

It went like this: BECAUSE, (1) Southern Baptists have the resources and have proved their liberality, (2) the Convention has lost credibility due to its general organizational and fiscal disorder, and (3) the relations of the state conventions and the Southern Baptist Convention have somewhat deteriorated; THEREFORE, the Southern Baptist Convention needs to take steps, (1) to improve its own fiscal responsibility, (2) to make the agencies fiscally accountable, and (3) to improve its relations with the state conventions.[2] Armed with these insights, Crouch had succeeded in 1925 in getting Convention approval for the Business Efficiency Committee.[3] During the months that followed, as chairman, he led his committee through the study of hundreds of pages of fiscal information submitted by the agencies.

His direct and simple way of thinking enabled Crouch to focus on the essentials. The Business Efficiency Committee reported in 1926 to the 4,268 messengers assembled at Houston.[4] For the first time, the Convention had a clear picture of the financial condition of its agencies all in one glance. It also had a brief understandable plan for crossing its swelling Jordon.[5] The report that Crouch made to the Convention is still an excellent model of thorough information and concise recommendations. The strategy was to take one small step at the time, leading the Convention first to approve the principles and a year later to approve the structure. The committee made four recommendations, summarized as follows:

(1) Convention commitment to use of budget control.

(2) Convention commitment to have a central fiscal agency.

(3) Convention commitment to agency accountability for the care and use of trust funds and designated gifts.

(4) Continuation of the committee to complete the fiscal survey of the fiscal activities of the agencies, to further develop the concept of the fiscal agency, and to propose necessary changes in the Constitution and Bylaws.

In essence, all the committee asked was that the Convention commit itself to sound business principles and to give the Business Efficiency Committee a year to work out the details. This meant the people would have ample time to consider the plan's merit and to decide upon the final commitment. Basic in Crouch's personal frame of reference was a rock-hard honesty. He was intent on leading the denomination beyond mere bookkeeping accountability to unquestioned financial integrity. Crouch presented his report on the first morning as the last major order before the preaching of the Convention sermon. A motion was quickly made to reset the discussion of the report as a special order for 12:00 on the second day. After the sermon, the Convention adjourned for lunch.

That afternoon, E. Y. Mullins exploded a bomb.[6] In 1924 he had been appointed chairman of the important Committee on Representation to study requirements for Convention membership. In 1925 the committee did not meet because of the illness of the chairman. But in 1926 Mullins reported for his committee with one of the most circumambient documents ever set before Southern

Baptists. In the skillfully worded report, Mullins pushed "representation" far beyond what surely must have been in the minds of the messengers when the committee was established in 1924. Embedded in the report was a convincing logic, even if under the circumstances the report appeared to some as impertinent. A. J. Barton, general director of the Cooperative Program Conservation Commission, later wrote Mullins, "The report you submitted was both a surprise and a disappointment to me, as I believe it was to a large majority of the members of the Convention . . . I could not see how your committee, which was appointed to consider one thing and one thing only, namely, possible changes in the basis of representation, could interpret its function so broadly as to bring a report recommending the complete upset and reorganization of the Convention itself."[7]

The logic of the Mullins report was much more sophisticated than the logic of the Crouch report, and it left no detail uncovered. It is summarized as follows:

> SINCE, Convention attendance has increased ten times since 1895, and now is averaging 5,559 in attendance,
> - it is burdened with a great many committee reports (fifty-four in 1925),
> - there must be limitation of speakers,
> - the reports are long and wordy,
> - there is an absence of advance knowledge about important issues,
> - the Convention meets three to five days,
> - out-of-proportion local attendance may lead to unbalanced judgments,
> - new proposals with popular support that conflict with established programs,
> - there is a tendency of the boards to start new programs without Convention approval,
> - conflict and confusion exist because of the lack of coordina-

tion between the Southern Baptist Convention and state mission boards;

AND SINCE, various "remedies" have been suggested for correcting these problems:

• limit messengers to one thousand,

• divide the convention into three separate conventions,

• divide the territory into three regional inspirational conventions with the Convention proper meeting every three years in a representative body of 250 or 300 members,

• let the Convention meet triennially, and create an Executive Committee of 300 to be responsible during the interim,

• extend the time to an entire week, reduce the number of subjects discussed, use better methods to publicize proposed recommendations in advance, and return the power of committee appointment to the president;

THEREFORE, the Committee on Representation recommends:

(1) Reaffirmation of the financial basis of representation.

(2) No change in the present basis of representation.

(3) "In order to meet many of the present needs of the Convention and to promote its efficiency we recommend the following changes in the present organization of the Executive Committee of the Convention."

Then followed nine short paragraphs detailing the reorganization. Two described the membership and officers of the Executive Committee. Seven outlined proposed Executive Committee duties. They are divided and summarized as follows:[8]

• Previously assigned: Act for the Convention ad interim in matters not otherwise provided for in its plan of work.

• Previously assigned: Oversee arrangements for the meeting of the Convention with authority to change, if necessary, the time and place.

• New: Represent the Southern Baptist Convention in negotiations with state conventions on all matters of common interest.

- New: Recommend to the Convention the allocation of funds to the Convention agencies.
- New: Develop with state conventions arrangements for the handling of SBC funds raised in the states and other related matters.
- New: Review and recommend agency budgets to the Convention.
- Previously assigned: Adjust differences between SBC agencies and between SBC agencies and state agencies and other cooperating bodies. A new feature of this duty was the adjustment of differences between the agencies and the state conventions.
- New: Employment of an executive secretary as the head of the practical work of the committee and have associated with him a promotional committee.

The report contained four other recommendations specifying new ways of forming the committees of the Convention and improved ways of making agency reports. Finally, the Committee on Representation asked the Convention not to act upon the report until a year had passed, in order to give ample time for consideration. Whatever else there was of importance in the Mullins report, the messengers probably saw and remembered only one thing, the proposal for a restructured Executive Committee. The Mullins report and the Business Efficiency report were not identical, but they did overlap. Both focused on the sensitive subject of the Executive Committee, both appeared to want a strengthened Executive Committee, and both wanted the Convention to take a year to make up its mind.

What was the motivation of Mullins and his committee? Perhaps, an intention to aid the Business Efficiency Committee in obtaining a good response to its proposals, but more likely a sincere effort to lead the Convention to correct problems that had been experienced by most of its leaders. Was there collaboration? Most likely not, though there may have been some intercommittee communication. Charles W. Daniel, pastor, First Baptist Church, Atlanta, and a close friend of Austin Crouch was a member of the Mullins Committee and may have been a link in communication. Mullins and Crouch were both independent-minded men capable of strong self-generated initiative.

Mullins's interest in the Executive Committee was at least ten years old because he had been a key member of the Consolidation Committee that had recommended the formation of the Executive Committee in 1917. Also, as president of the Convention (1922-24), he had served as a member and *ex officio* chairman of the Executive Committee. The report of the Executive Committee in 1924, the last to be made over his signature as president, included a lengthy document on the relationship of general Baptist bodies and a recommendation that the Executive Committee "be instructed" to take steps for securing better understanding between the Southern Baptist Convention and the state conventions.[9] Mullins was a systematic person and fully alert to business problems. He also understood denominational problems.

What effect did the Committee on Representation have on the report of the Business Efficiency Committee? In the long run, considering the prestige of Mullins, it probably made final passage of its 1927 report easier; but for 1926, it may have caused some people to wonder about motives; and perhaps, it slightly dulled the luster of the Business Efficiency Committee report.

The next day, when time arrived for consideration of the Business Efficiency report, after remarks by Crouch, the Convention approved a motion by J. F. Love, Virginia, to refer the entire report back to the committee, "for further consideration and perfection with the understanding that the Convention is not committing itself to any of the recommendations made by the committee."[10] Immediately a second motion by E. P. Alldredge of Tennessee was passed, instructing the two committees "to hold joint sessions and work out together all proposed changes in the Executive Committee which are to be submitted to the Convention at its next session." And after that, a third motion approved by the Convention hinted of some reaction to the confusion caused by the overlapping reports. Offered by W.O. Carver, Kentucky, it asked all other committees not to include in their reports any matters involving reorganization of the Convention. Tempers may have been a bit frayed.

Restructuring the Executive Committee

The 1927 Convention opened with an address by President George White McDaniel, a spirited appeal for the reorganization of the way the Convention handled its business. Immediately, Eugene Levering of Maryland proposed a committee "to consider the address of Dr. McDaniel, just delivered, and, in connection therewith, other matters related thereto."[11] Then followed a list of thirty prominent Southern Baptists to be named the committee. The motion was approved. McDaniel's address no doubt stirred the Convention to action, but in some minds it may have created a suggestion of crisis, possibly in the mind of Austin Crouch himself. Later, he, McDaniel, and Pat M. Neff were added to the list of members. Neff, a prominent lawyer and a former governor of Texas was a long-standing friend of both Crouch and McDaniel. It is possible that Crouch insisted on these additions to assure all points of view were fully represented on the committee and to inform the committee accurately concerning the work that had been done by the Efficiency Committee. McDaniel and Neff were both political heavies whom he could count on to help carry his side of the debate.

Many years later, Crouch told Merrill D. Moore that in the evening before the Convention had opened, President McDaniel came to his hotel room to discuss his presidential address and the Business Efficiency Committee's report.[12] The next day, McDaniel used much of Dr. Crouch's material, without credit, which may have been by design. The committee appointed to consider the president's address reported reasonably in harmony with the intentions of the Crouch committee. On some minor points, the committee was not in agreement. After several amendments, a motion was offered to refer the report and its amendments to the "the committee raised in the last section of the Report on Business Efficiency."[13] This was a committee to survey the agencies and make suggestions for merger.[14] Although the question of merger was still alive in the Convention, in 1928, this new Efficiency Committee made only two proposals for merger. It recommended: (1) That the Inter-Board Commission be merged with the Sunday School Board. This was a group that sponsored work among students on college campuses. (2) That the Education Board be discontinued and that its assets and liabilities be transferred to the Executive Committee.[15]

The 1927 report of the Business Efficiency Committee was amended and adopted. The report consisted of fifteen pages of solid information concerning Southern Baptists Convention finances and a comprehensive blueprint for fiscal recovery.[16] Without doubt, Austin Crouch was its architect, and it was a remarkable achievement for one relatively unknown. But Austin Crouch was a remarkable man, gifted in ways that Southern Baptists were yet to discover. One of his abilities was graciously to assimilate constructive ideas from others, which he surely did in approving the suggestions of the Mullins Committee for the the restructuring, most of which are still found in revised form in the Convention bylaw governing the Executive Committee.

In the strengthening of the Executive Committee, another step was taken in Southern Baptist organizational growth. Not needed or possible in 1845, the Executive Committee's time finally arrived in 1917 and 1927, when the complexity and maturity of the Southern Baptist Convention made it necessary. The founders in 1845 had made room for it with the phrase, "and other important objects connected with the Redeemer's kingdom."[17] It was the final and essential step in the the Convention reforming process begun by the Business Efficiency Commission (1913-1915).

Launching the Restructured Executive Committee

The enlarging, expanding, and strengthening of Executive Committee duties were summarized and made binding by a new Convention bylaw that specified the committee's membership, officers, and duties. The duties as approved and included in the bylaws were:[18]

(1) To act for the Convention ad interim in matters not otherwise provided for in its plans of work.

(2) To have oversight of arrangements for meetings of the Convention with authority to change, if necessary, the time and place of meeting.

(3) To act in an advisory way on matters of policy and cooperation arising between the agencies of the Convention, or between the agencies of the Convention and cooperating state agencies.

(4) To represent the Southern Baptist Convention in all negotiations with state conventions, and state boards, and other cooperating bodies in matters of common interests. The Executive Committee shall be the authorized agency of the Southern Baptist Convention to conclude all agreements with cooperating state agencies for the conduct of necessary arrangements as to handling of Southwide funds raised in the various states, and all other related matters.

(5) To recommend to the Convention an operating budget for the Convention year, and to recommend the percentages of Southwide funds to be allocated to each cause of an agency. The Operating Budget shall include all agencies of the Convention.

(6) To present to the Convention a consolidated financial statement of all the agencies of the Convention. The statement shall show the Assets, Liabilities, and the Debts of the agencies.

(7) The Executive Committee shall notify the agencies of the Convention of all actions or instructions of the Convention relating to the work or other matters of the agency or agencies involved, and shall report to the Convention whether such agency or agencies have carried out the wishes of the Convention.

(8) To hold meetings at such times as may be necessary or

advisable for the transaction of the business committed to it by
the Convention.

(9) To make reports of its proceedings to the Convention at
each annual session, and to make any recommendations it may
desire concerning the affairs of the Convention, or concerning
the affairs of the agencies of the Convention.

The Convention bylaws added an unnumbered paragraph, de-
scriptive of powers that are considered by many to be the heart of
Executive Committee authority:

> The Executive Committee shall have no authority to control or
> direct any agency of the Convention. But the Executive Committee
> shall have full authority to study the affairs of the agencies of the
> Convention, and to make suggestions, when deemed advisable, to the
> agencies, and to report its findings to the Convention, and to make
> any recommendations to the Convention concerning any matter
> whatsoever.

These bylaws contain nearly all of the duties suggested by the
Committee on Representation and presented to the Convention by
E. Y. Mullins in 1926.

It is most difficult to say which of the duties have been most
significant in shaping the character and the agenda of the Executive
Committee. Five were especially formative in the years immediately
following 1927. These were that the Executive Committee was authorized: (1) to act ad interim in all matters not otherwise provided
for, (2) to study, advise, and recommend concerning the affairs of
the agencies—on its own initiative, (3) to negotiate on behalf of the
Southern Baptist Convention with state conventions concerning
matters of common concern (including the handling of SBC funds
by state conventions), (4) to have the custodianship of all Southwide
funds, and (5) to have the responsibility for recommending allocation of undesignated funds to the agencies.

The Committee on Representation also reported in 1927, but
without any reference at all to the Executive Committee. The report
was presented by Charles W. Daniels, Georgia. Though the Con-

vention met that year in Louisville, President Mullins, still the chairman of the Representation Committee, was not present. He had been ill with bronchitis since late spring and remained in poor health until the end of his life.[19]

Mullins managed to be present at the 1928 Convention, "a lively and effective figure in all its proceedings."[20] It was his last Convention, and he made the most of it. Those who watched him said, "He seemed electrified, swaying things with a high spiritual power. The spirit, indeed, was rapidly taking control of the body." On November 23, 1928, at high noon, "He passed over, and all the trumpets sounded on the other side."[21] For a quarter of a century, he had carried the Southern Baptist Convention in his heart and had helped keep its doors widely opened to the future. He was for the times probably the Convention's most consistent and influential leader. Included in all of the many things for which he is remembered must be his significant part in (1) helping first establish the Executive Committee in 1917 and (2) helping give the Executive Committee its new strength and new significance in the life of the Convention in 1927.

Assessing the Changes

What did the Convention really do in adopting the 1927 report of the Business Efficiency Committee? (1) It pinpointed responsibility for developing an orderly financial program. To do this, it was necessary to merge the Commission on Cooperative Program with the Executive Committee, a step not too popular with some leaders. (2) The Convention ridded itself of the burden of too many poorly informed committees. In this step, it at last emerged from its town-meeting simplicity, which had been a severe handicap for more than a quarter century. (3) The Convention provided a way to secure successful uniting of state Baptist conventions and the Southern Baptist Convention into a truly cooperative partnership. As it turned out, this was one of the restructured Executive Committee's most immediate and difficult tasks. (4) The Convention lighted a tiny ray of hope for relieving the galling burden of debt that was

crushing the agencies. It did this by providing a systematic approach
to problem solving, something it would often need to employ in the
years ahead. (5) The Convention helped to prepare Southern Baptists for the yet unseen financial and social upheaval of the 1930s.

What was the response in the state conventions to the new Executive Committee? Generally favorable. L. L. Gwaltney, editor of the
Alabama Baptist, wrote, "The new Executive Committee, in our judgment, is going to work well. It is in line with what our people are
used to both in the associations and states, and it merely means that
the same idea has been enlarged so as to meet the needs of the
Southern Baptist Convention. When one now talks about the Executive Committee, he will be using the language of Zion."[22] M. H.
Wolfe, the layman from Texas who eleven years before had attempted to secure "a strong executive board" and who was the first
chairman of the 1917 Executive Committee, was delighted. He circulated a lengthy article to state Baptists papers in which he said,
"Southern Baptists in the recent Convention at Louisville, Kentucky, evidently struck the right track . . . completely revolutionized
denominational policy."[23] He was pleased that "soft peddlers" did
not stampede the Convention into rejecting the Business Efficiency
Committee's report.

Meeting for Organization and Work

Strengthened and restructured, the Executive Committee met
briefly in Louisville during the Convention and elected George W.
Truett as its temporary chairman. Six weeks later, it convened in
rooms at The Sunday School Board in Nashville. Truett was elected
the "president."[24] Hight C Moore was elected the secretary and
treasurer. After the appointment of a nominating committee—and
some delay—Austin Crouch was elected executive secretary. The
minutes of the Executive Committee do not mention any others who
were considered by the committee. Years later, Crouch recalled that
there were several, among them Dr. A. J. Barton, general director
of the Cooperative Program Conservation Commission that had
been absorbed into the Executive Committee.[25] The election of the

executive secretary was in executive session. According to Crouch, this was because of confusion over voting rights. Some of the state secretaries and agency heads present assumed that, being members of the "Promotional Agency," they were privileged to vote on the executive secretary, which the elected members denied.

R. H. Pitt, editor of the *Religious Herald,* in reporting the election of Crouch, said, "We had supposed that Dr. Barton, as a matter of course, would be chosen for the new position. Other counsels seemed to have prevailed in the Committee."[26] Just before the meeting of the Executive Committee in June, J. W. Storer, writing to Crouch from his study in the Grove Avenue Baptist Church in Richmond, said, "A. J. B. has no business at the head of this new Executive Committee, if it is to clean house and function. He just has not that thing which in another sense the young folks call *IT.* Too smooth, too familiar with the old long, long trail a wandering, too committed to the old army game. And the boys in the brush who may not have much platform presence . . . just won't have it."[27] Though not considered a national leader at the time, J. W. Storer knew well that what Crouch, Mullins, Dillard, and many other Convention leaders wanted was to break out of the old structural restrictions of the past. Storer evidently felt that Barton was too tradition-bound to accomplish it.

Storer's comments were probably not meant to be disrespectful of Barton, who for many years had been a loyal, perceptive, talented, and cooperative Southern Baptist. It is also known that Barton did not have the support of E. Y. Mullins. In a lengthy letter to Mullins, written in August of 1926, Barton had complained about the anticipated report of the Business Efficiency Committee. "My deep conviction is that the Convention as organized is in admirable shape to go forward and that it would be unwise and hurtful to attempt so to enlarge the power and functions of the Executive Committee to make the Executive Committee a sort of overlordship over the several boards. A wheel within a wheel will not work well with Southern Baptists."[28] After some delay, the ailing Mullins wrote in a blunt reply, "Letters from the eastern, western and southern sections of the Southern Baptist Convention . . . have convinced me that the most positive movement now current among us is for abolishing the Cooperative Commission. I am thoroughly convinced that you are mistaken in your attitude toward the new functions which will be recommended for the Executive Committee . . . As proposed, it is in the strictest and most literal way, in perfect harmony with every Baptist tradition and principle. What has amazed me is that you apparently have not been unable to grasp this."[29] Sick as Mullins was from a prolonged attack of respiratory problems, he was not too sick to speak forthrightly.

Before coming to the Conservation Commission, Barton had been a pastor in several states and an employee of conventions in Texas, Louisiana, and Missouri. He had been active in Southern Baptist Convention affairs and had developed great skill as a parliamentarian and debater. Also gifted as a writer, he was deeply concerned with temperance and social service issues. For many years, he wrote the annual report for the Social Service Commission. Barton continued in diligent cooperation with the Convention and died in 1942, after having attended almost every session of the Convention for fifty years. Something of Barton's loyalty to the denomination is glimpsed in the letter he wrote to Mullins when word had gotten out that the Business Efficiency Committee was considering discontinuing the Conservation Commission, "If the Convention thinks the Cooperative Commission ought to be abolished, then by all means I want the Convention to express its judgment and abolish it."[30]

At the time of his election, Austin Crouch was fifty-six years old, a man well prepared in experience, talent, and disposition for the task ahead of him. As a pastor and denominational worker, he knew Convention life and especially did he know Convention leaders. Reared as an only child in his father's general store near McKinney in North Texas, he understood business. He was a very patient man. He could wait and wait and wait, sometimes losing his battles, but more often winning them. He sometimes won even after he had lost. Crouch had an orderly mind and could see the most complicated problems in their simplest forms. Never a popular platform person, he was gifted, however, in personal relationships; and it was through personal relationships that he accomplished many things for Southern Baptists. He was a very tough man who would not bend under pressure. His toughness rested on more than his personal temperament. He never entered a situation without being clear on two things—the Convention rules and the basic facts. If one did not serve his purpose, the other one would; and most of the time he was master of both. In the minds of both friends and foes, there was a mystical quality about his little black book of financial data that he always had with him. Crouch did not think of himself as a great leader. If he had been asked about his role, he might have said that he was a minister of Christ searching for ways to establish and assure total financial integrity in the Southern Baptist Convention for the sake of the gospel.

The first president of the restructured Executive Committee was in his first term as president of the Convention. George W. Truett was renowned for his statesmanship and leadership, but it was his preaching that attracted the multitudes. His voice was like honey and lava melded into burning words that were penetrating and unforgettable. Beyond his spoken words always was his pure spirit. If ever a man lived out "this one thing I do" for the cause of Christ, it was George W. Truett, whose great unction poured forth from his sincerity, his seriousness, and his conviction. Besides all this, he was a very practical and loving man, never strident, never obtuse, and never divisive. He was not a perfect man; and as all other men, he could make wrong judgments. He was sometimes impatient and sometimes aloof. Still, he was a very great man, one of the greatest ever to cross the Baptist horizon. When he was elected to head the Convention, J. E. Dillard wrote of him, "We need at this time a great heart, a great brain, and a strong hand. We have them. Dr. Truett showed himself a master of assemblies, and he loves every cause fostered by our great denomination."[31] In his day, thousands of deacons laid their ordaining hands on hundreds of young ministers and whispered, "You will be the next Truett." How many of those young men in any way approached his greatness?

Notes

1. *Information Please,* 1983, p. 116.
2. The author was closely associated with Dr. Crouch from 1949-1957 and had many enlightening conversations with him concerning the beginning of the Executive Committee.
3. SBC, 1925, pp. 9, 45.
4. SBC, 1983, p. 468.
5. SBC, 1926, pp. 18-29.
6. SBC, 1926, pp. 31-34.
7. Letter from A. J. Barton to E. Y. Mullins, August 10, 1926. p. 1 (The I. J. Van Ness papers, SSBA).
8. One duty as recommended has been divided into two parts for clarity.
9. SBC, 1924, pp. 24-26.
10. SBC, 1926, pp. 57-58.
11. SBC, 1927, p. 17.
12. "Oral Memoirs of Austin Crouch," interview by Merrill D. Moore," c. 1950 (SBCA).
13. Ibid., p. 57.
14. SBC, 1927, pp. 72, 88.
15. SBC, 1928, pp. 54-56.
16. SBC, 1927, pp. 55-72.
17. SBC, 1845, p. 3.
18. SBC, 1927, pp. 68-69. cf. pp. 12-13.
19. Isla May Mullins, *Edgar Young Mullins,* pp. 196-199.
20. Ibid., p. 204.
21. Ibid., p. 213. By John Bunyan. Inscribed in bronze on the tomb of Edgar Young Mullins, Cave Hill Cemetery, Louisville, Kentucky.
22. AB, June 9, 1927, p. 3.
23. RH, June 9, 1927, pp. 4-5.
24. ECM, June 21, 1927, pp. 2-6.
25. Oral Memoirs of Austin Crouch."

26. RH, July 7, 1927, p. 11.

27. Letter from J. W. Storer to Austin Crouch, June 9, 1927, p. 1 (SBCA).

28. Letter from A. J. Barton to E. Y. Mullins, August 10, 1926, pp. 4-5 (The I. J. Van Ness papers, SSBA).

29. Letter from E. Y. Mullins to A. J. Barton, January 18, 1927, p. 1 (The I. J. Van Ness papers, SSBA).

30. A. J. Barton to E.Y. Mullins, March 7, 1927, p. 2 (The Van Ness papers, SSBA).

31. AB, May 19, 1927. p. 7.

5

The Stabilization of the Executive Committee
1927-1933

In commending the reorganization of the Executive Committee, M. H. Wolfe said, "When we go off on some sidetrack, the ditch is always just ahead."[1] The members of the committee certainly understood his metaphor, for all of them were accustomed to traveling by train. They knew the tedious experience of waiting in a hot coach on a rickety old railroad sidetrack in sight of the ditches for another train to slowly pass. For years, the Convention had been involved in shattering doctrinal disputes and devastating debt. Gifts to missions had steadily declined. The leaders, pondering these problems in the summer of 1927, were thinking that the Convention must return to its mainline commitment of eliciting, combining, and directing the energies of the people for the preaching of the gospel. If not, then surely, the ditches!

By the end of its second meeting, the new Executive Committee had dealt with twenty-eight different agenda items. Most of them were routine organizational and personnel matters. Four of the twenty-eight needed immediate attention: Southern Baptist Convention and state convention relationships, the dying Education Board, a Convention financial plan, and Executive Committee involvement in stewardship and Cooperative Program promotion. Other serious problems that surfaced later were the Carnes defalcation, the strengthening and clarification of the Cooperative Program, and Southern Baptist debt. To some Baptists, these were not mainline issues, but to Truett, Mullins, Crouch, Scarborough, Van Ness, and dozens of others, they were not only mainline issues but also challenging problems that had to be solved. The future of the Executive Committee and the Convention depended on their solution. Solving them proved more difficult than it appeared in the summer of 1927. Five of the problems could be temporarily settled in a few years, two would take much longer.

Keeping On the Right Track

1. One of the first problems considered was Southern Baptist Convention and state Baptist conventions relations. By 1845 nine state conventions were already in the area embraced by the Southern Baptist Convention.[2] Tensions first appeared when the Domestic Mission Board announced plans to send missionaries into territory claimed by state conventions. As a result, until the early 1880s, the future of the Home Mission Board was uncertain. Lacking was a set of principles upon which cooperative relationships between the conventions could be consistently and constructively built. The problem came to public attention in the report of the Efficiency Commission in 1915 when it recommended that the Convention ask all Southern Baptist agencies "to maintain and promote the internal peace and harmony of the denomination to the end that waste by friction may be avoided."[3] E. Y. Mullins was a member of the commission, and the language of its report suggests his unique way of thinking. Nine years later, Mullins, as president of the Convention, was also chairman of the Executive Committee when its 1924 report again brought the problem of interconvention relations to the attention of the Convention. One statement in that report clearly enunciated the basic premise of cooperation: "Since no Baptist body has authority over any other, there can be no question of dictation on either side,"[4] The report also called for a conference of state and SBC representatives to resolve differences. It is probable that Mullins had a strong hand in the formation of the report, and possible, that he wrote it.

No further initiative was taken, and the matter lay dormant until the report of the Business Efficiency Committee in 1927 that called for the Executive Committee immediately "to clarify all principles

involved in our Co-operative work with all other bodies."[5] This led
to an Executive Committee subcommittee of nine—three from the
Executive Committee, three from the agencies, and three from the
state conventions—assigned to formulate definite recommendations. E. Y. Mullins was one of the three agency members.[6] The
report as approved by the 1928 Convention was so basic that it was
reaffirmed in 1956—exactly as originally written—by the Southern
Baptist Convention.[7] Its essence is reflected in the following key
paragraphs.

> All Baptist general bodies are voluntary organizations, established
> by individuals who wish to cooperate for some common end or ends
> in the kingdom of God. This Convention is not an ecclesiastical body
> composed of churches, nor a federal body composed of state conven-
> tions. Churches may seek to fulfill their obligation to extend Christ's
> kingdom by cooperating with these general organizations, but always
> on a purely voluntary basis, and without surrendering in any way or
> degree their right of self-determination. These associations, unions,
> or conventions vary greatly in form, in size, in purpose, in territorial
> extent and in conditions of membership. But they are all similar to
> churches in the fundamental principle of their organization and life
> in that each is independent of all others in its own work, free, frater-
> nal, autonomous, or self-determining in its own sphere and activities.
>   There is no relation of superiority and inferiority among Baptist
> general bodies. All are equal. All make their appeal directly to in-
> dividuals and churches. Each determines its own objectives—finan-
> cial or otherwise—and allocates its own funds to the interests
> promoted by it. Each defines and fixes its own sphere of activities. But
> all is done with due consideration and regard for the functions of
> other Baptist bodies.

The principles set forth in the document establish equal rights of
access by the related and cooperating associations and conventions
to the churches. Approval of the report by the Convention did not
settle all of the problems, but it did provide a sound basis for their
solution in the years ahead. E. Y. Mullins surely had a hand in
developing the statement. The clear, logical, language reflects the

thought of the veteran Southern Baptist statesman. It was his third effort to get something done about interconvention relationships and his last major service for the denomination. He died the following November.

2. The problems of the SBC Education Board made a back door entrance into the agenda when the 1927 Convention referred to the Executive Committee a resolution concerning New Mexico's Montezuma College. From the Executive Committee's point of view, it proved to be a big bee with a big stinger. A year later, the Executive Committee unexpectedly received the whole Education Board beehive, honey included. The Education Board was created in 1919 as a successor to the Education Commission, which in 1918 had launched a fifteen-million-dollar campaign on behalf of all Southern Baptist Christian higher education, including a $100,000 matching grant, dollar for dollar, to help New Mexico Baptists establish Montezuma College in Las Vegas.[8] Encouraged by the early success of the Seventy-Five Million Campaign, the college immediately plunged into debt and disaster. Two arguments were used to push the Executive Committee into action: that the new college offered challenging mission opportunities[9] and that fifty New Mexico laymen had signed notes which if not paid would "seriously cripple these brethren if not virtually ruin them."[10] Though other solutions may have been possible, the Executive Committee chose a most difficult course by asking the Convention to approve a $250,000 bond issue.[11]

Concerning this bold move, there is an unanswered question: Should the Executive Committee have recommended and the Convention approved a $250,000 bond issue to cover the distress of a single state convention? From a mission point of view, the answer is a weak: perhaps. For under the circumstances, it appeared that the work in New Mexico could not otherwise be saved. From a strictly practical point of view, the answer is: no because: (1) From the beginning the Executive Committee has not been involved directly in program areas belonging to the agencies. (2) Also, from the beginning, the Convention has committed itself to do its mission work through its agencies. (3) During the debate on the Convention floor, someone asked a very practical and penetrating question: "If the Convention rallies to underwrite a state convention in this matter, will there not arise numerous other occasions to underwrite other state conventions?"[12] And, (4) was a Baptist college in the state essential to the future of the work? Some did not think so. Many messengers were uneasy over the commitment.

Where was Austin Crouch when the project was discussed? Probably very much present but not willing to risk the future on this one issue. Or, he may have considered it as fundamentally a commitment made by the Education Board and, therefore, a legitimate program matter. By the time the Convention considered the matter in 1929, the Education Board affairs had come under the control of the Executive Committee. Given his single eye for realities and his clear perception of principles, it is difficult to imagine how Crouch could let it pass without raising questions, which he no doubt did, for he was a master at indirect leadership, always involved in issues, but never obvious and overbearing.

The whole Education Board beehive came to the Executive Committee in 1928 when the Convention refused to approve the board's annual report. It was a lively time, taking a whole afternoon and most of the next morning. One state editor called it the "great debate."[13] Finally a resolution by Charles E. Maddrey, North Carolina, was adopted that discontinued the board "as now constituted," and made the Executive Committee the board's "successor in law."[14] The Executive Committee found itself responsible for the properties and programs of Ridgecrest Assembly in North Carolina (the honey in the hive), the Umatilla Assembly in Florida, and the Nuyaka School and Orphanage for Indians in Oklahoma.

The programs were more easily handled than the properties. The Sunday School Board agreed to operate the summer assembly at Ridgecrest.[15] The Home Mission Board took temporary responsibility for the program at Nuyaka[16] and then a group of Oklahoma Baptists assumed its care.[17] Florida Baptists were asked to operate the Umatilla Assembly for a time.[18] This left the Executive Committee free to look after the finances and the maintenance of three properties. In 1928, at the time of the transfer, they had a book value of about $799,929 and a debt of $345,000.[19]

Why was the Education Board discontinued? In 1928 some Southern Baptists were unhappy about the proliferation of agencies, which they felt interfered with the basic mission purposes of the Convention. They balked when the Education Board acquired too quickly too many properties with too much debt; and still not satisfied, it asked for more. The leaders had cautiously suggested other acquisitions, such as an additional seminary, a university in Washington, D.C., and permission to study Southern Baptist theological education.[20] Also, from the day of the Seventy-Five Million Campaign, undesignated gifts for the seminaries had been forwarded through the Education Board to the seminaries.[21] This may have raised in some minds the fear that the Education Board might make a bid for the control of the seminaries. Most Southern Baptists approved the discontinuance of the Education Board, but some did not. J. E. Dillard told Alabama Baptists that it was "the biggest blunder" of the 1928 Convention.[22] This was understandable, for Dillard had been the acting corresponding secretary for the Education Board in 1920.[23]

In the transfer of the properties, the Executive Committee acquired numerous financial and legal problems. With little funds coming in and interest payments coming due, growing debt was a major concern. Maintenance and insurance added to the burdens. The Great Depression which began in 1929 compounded the problem. By 1931 the Education Board debts had climbed to $375,000, not including the New Mexico bond issue for Montezuma College.[24] To meet the demands, the Executive Committee authorized the officers to borrow up to $150,000 for the "maturing obligations of the Education Board."[25] It must have been with some embarrassment that the Executive Committee in 1934 had to ask The Sunday School Board to pay the interest due on the Education Board debts.[26] The Sunday School Board was already paying most of the Executive Committee expenses. In the heart of the depression, keeping the Southern Baptist train off the financial sidetrack was almost an impossible task. Though distressed at times, the officers were never apologetic. It was a long, uphill battle. The picture was a little improved near the end of 1934 when Austin Crouch was able to secure refinancing of the Education Board debts at a lower rate of interest.[27]

The property management problems were gradually eliminated. After some hesitance and the unraveling of several knotty legal problems, The Sunday School Board agreed to assume ownership of Ridgecrest in 1944,[28] having operated it for the Executive Committee since 1928. The Nuyaka School and Orphanage was operated through lease agreements until 1935; and then, unable to find satisfactory leaseholders, the Executive Committee at last voted to sell the property in 1937.[29] The Umatilla property was operated by Florida Baptists for a few summers and later offered to the Florida Baptist Convention. After some delay, the offer was declined.[30] The property was later deeded to Stetson University.[31] In its management of Education Board problems, the Executive Committee gradually established its reputation for skill in fiscal matters. This was an accomplishment that went a long way toward rebuilding the confidence of the Nashville banking community in Southern Baptist ability to manage properly its fiscal affairs.

3. Another challenge before the new Executive Committee centered in the question: How can an agency be kept from sinking into financial disaster? This question had been very much in the minds of the members of the Business Efficiency Committee who recommended the restructuring of the Executive Committee. They were determined to secure a sound Southern Baptist Convention financial plan, and this no doubt caused some agency executives to raise questions. The executives did not resist financial responsibility, but only wanted to be responsible in their own way, and not subject to a third party. Awareness of this resistance may have kept the new Executive Committee from immediately proposing stringent reform. Perhaps Crouch and his advisers felt that, at first, relationships had to be strengthened and confidences established.

The first faint step toward a comprehensive business and financial plan was taken in May 1928 when the Executive Committee recommended to the Convention a nine-point plan for the control and liquidation of debt. The plan itself was not effective, but one point in the plan suggested the kind of controls that could be expected in the future. It was, "That the current deficit of operations of a given year shall be the first item in the budget of the succeeding year."[32]

The next step was the appointment of a subcommittee to develop a financial plan. This stirred considerable feeling in the Executive Committee. Even after it was voted, it provoked a "prolonged informal discussion of general financial policies . . . until 11:40 P.M. when a recess was taken until 9:30 A.M., Wednesday."[33] The talk resulted in a sixteen-point "New Financial Plan" approved by the Convention in 1929.[34] The strategy for getting the plan accepted was to present it as a means of controlling debt. Though not a comprehensive business and financial plan, such as was approved in 1939 by the Convention, the New Financial Plan was a start in that direction.

The new plan brought together many of the previous Convention instructions to the agencies and combined them with some new guidelines for the agencies to use in the management of their finances. It covered such subjects as agency budgets, annual audits, handling of trust funds, remitting of funds, and special solicitations by agencies. Two interesting paragraphs attract the interest of persons familiar with definitions and procedures followed many years later.[35] The first was the introduction of the report, as follows:

> We believe that the time has arrived when the Southern Baptist Convention should adopt a policy in its Co-operative Program of attempting to provide for the approved operation budgets of its various agencies by *allocating specific sums instead of percentages as heretofore.* In order that this may be done the principle of cooperation among agencies of the Convention must be applied to the making of obligations, as well as sharing in the distribution of funds.

The arguments were clear: time had come to make Cooperative

Programs allocations on a specific dollar basis; and for the agencies to share in the allocations and distributions, they must keep their financial houses in order—by staying out of debt. These were noble dreams but almost fifteen years would pass before the budget would be placed on a specific dollar basis fulfillment. The massive debts would not be paid until 1943, and soon the agencies would be in debt again for good reasons and in reasonable amounts.

The other interesting paragraph described conditions for participating in Cooperative Program allocations:

> That, in preparing the proposed total budget, and in determining the total receipts which may reasonably be anticipated from *the Cooperative Program, designated and undesignated,* the Executive Committee shall take into consideration the following facts: (1) Total amount of the submitted budgets of the agencies; (2) total receipts of all the agencies for the past year from *the Cooperative Program, designated and undesignated;* (3) goals set by the states for Southwide causes for the next calendar year.

Strange to modern eyes is a phrase that is twice repeated, "Cooperative Program, designated and undesignated." In the early years, the Cooperative Program included designated gifts. This feature soon disappeared, probably because a designated gift to one agency is not really a cooperative gift to all agencies.

Though the Convention approved the plan, not all Baptists were happy with it. Prior to the opening of the Convention, R. H. Pitt, the thoughtful editor of the Virginia's *Religious Herald,* had publicly opposed the plan.[36] He objected to the rule that provided for mid-term adjustments in Cooperative Program receipts for those agencies that had met their Convention-approved budgets from designated sources. The opposition would not die, and in 1933 this feature was repealed on recommendation of the Executive Committee.[37] Pitt also objected to the Executive Committee being the forwarding agent between the state conventions and the agencies. Others were openly affirming. L. L. Gwaltney, editor of the *Alabama Baptist,* thought, "The most important policy of the Convention has to do with the new financial plan." He added, "Austin Crouch, the executive secretary, is responsible for the inauguration of the new plan. He has given it much thought and has exemplified great ability."[38] The plan was approved in an atmosphere of general good will and minimum controversy. Gwaltney felt, "The spirit of the Convention was excellent. The difference between the Convention just closed and the one held in Memphis four years ago is the difference in a storm-swept, turbulent sea and that of a calm one." The veteran South Carolina editor, Z. T. Cody, called it "one of the most constructive meetings of the Southern Baptist Convention ever held."[39]

Content with the favorable acceptance, the Executive Committee did not immediately attempt further major adjustments. Instead, it slowly went at the task a step at the time. In September 1929, it proposed a model budget for agencies;[40] and in December 1931, in order to be better informed, it appointed a committee "to make a careful study of the policies and budgets of all our agencies."[41] On the same day, the Executive Committee resolved "that it is the sense of the Executive Committee that it is contrary to the functions and responsibilities of the Committee to become legally involved as endorsers or guarantors of the financial obligations of the agencies of the Southern Baptist Convention."[42]

4. The Carnes defalcation. The ordinary problems were tough enough, but suddenly the Executive committee was slammed with an extraordinary one. Nothing has ever confronted Southern Baptists quite as suddenly and with as much anguish as to learn in August of 1928 that the treasurer of the Home Mission Board, Clinton S. Carnes, had stolen nearly a million dollars in mission funds and had disappeared from public view. As W. W. Barnes described the scandal:[43]

> He had a penitentiary record in the city of Atlanta, but it was not
> discovered until after the defalcation. He was an expert bookkeeper
> and accountant, and seemingly had no difficulty in securing a position
> in a firm of accountants during the period of World War I when men
> who had ability were difficult to secure. With best recommendations

from business sources and church sources the board engaged his services. By authority from the board he was empowered to borrow money from banks in different states to carry on the work of the board. He so manipulated his financial dealings that his criminal acts were committed legally in different states. When his conduct came to light, it seemed to the lawyers employed by the board that it would be next to impossible to assemble all of the various threads of evidence necessary to convict him on his different acts of thievery. Since his crimes were committed legally in different states, he could not be tried in Georgia upon the indictments for every individual act. Carnes returned to Atlanta and confessed his defalcation. He pleaded guilty to one of the indictments committed in Georgia and was sentenced to the limit of the law allowed upon that conviction. He had taken $226,126.86 from the church building fund, and $683,334.14 from the general fund of the board, making a total of $909,461.

From a Nashville newspaper wire service story, Austin Crouch learned of the Carnes embezzlement. Within a few hours, he was on his way to Atlanta to get the facts.[44] On Sunday he called his old pastor and friend, Charles W. Daniel, who was also a member of the Executive Committee. They talked; and on Monday Crouch went to the office of B. D. Gray, who at the time was seventy-three years old and in his twenty-fifth year as executive secretary of the Home Mission Board. Gray said that he had been thinking about writing the president of the Convention. Crouch admonished, "Write nothing. Wire. If you don't, I will,"[45] words typical of his direct, assured way of thinking and acting.

President Truett, who was in a meeting at Lynchburg, Virginia, went at once to Atlanta. After discussing the problem with Crouch, Daniel, Gray, and local members of the Home Mission Board, he immediately called a joint meeting of the board and the Executive Committee.[46] Convening in Atlanta on September 4, 1928, the two groups spent most of the morning and early afternoon in review of details and general discussion. At 3:00 PM, the board retired to consolidate its opinions and formulate a report for the joint session. An hour later, the joint session reconvened; and the Home Mission

Board made a short formal statement,[47] including the following significant comment:

> The Home Mission Board realizes that it is utterly unable to finance itself under the present condition. We, therefore, ask the assistance of the Executive Committee of the Southern Baptist Convention in such ways and under such conditions as the Executive Committee may suggest. We pledge ourselves to the fullest cooperation in this, no matter what it may involve.

After remarks by Charles W. Daniel, President Truett appointed a three-man subcommittee of the Executive Committee to recommend a procedure. The subcommittee consisted of three very wise and politic men: Daniel, Pat M. Neff, and J. E. Dillard. That evening the members reported: (1) expressing to the Home Mission Board "profound sympathy in the calamity that has overtaken it," (2) concurring "in the proposal made by the Home Mission Board that the Board should be at once reorganized and rehabilitated," and (3) suggesting "a committee of three to work in conjunction with a like committee from the Home Mission Board in working out to a successful termination all matters herein above mentioned."[48] The plan was immediately accepted and the members appointed. The Home Mission Board members of the joint committee were L. R. Christian (president), W. H. Major (secretary), and F. S. Ethridge. the Executive Committee members were Austin Crouch, W. L. Ball, and C. W. Daniel. Quite properly, the president of the board was appointed chairman.

The problem was eased when the Home Mission Board, aided by the special committee: (1) secured the retirement of B. D. Gray, the executive secretary of the board. He was not in any way linked to the crime; and he continued useful to the Home Mission Board for several years afterwards; (2) asked Arch C. Cree, the executive secretary of Georgia Baptist Convention to serve part time as acting executive secretary of the board; (3) reorganized completely the Board finances; (4) renegotiated with creditor banks all outstanding loans; (5) held operational costs within income limits.[49] Victor I.

Masters wrote with heroic flourish, "One clear note has been sounded by everybody—and that note is that our Baptist honor shall not be impaired."[50] An Honor Day Campaign was approved for November 11; and when the money was counted it netted the board $390,659. Taken in the very doorway of the Great Depression, the offering was the last successful effort of the kind for many years.

In the minds of some Southern Baptists, there still may be a question: Did the executive secretary and the chairman of the Executive Committee act correctly in taking initiative in this matter? Acting within its right to study and recommend, the Executive Committee asked for information and offered help. After the full facts were uncovered, when the board requested help, the Executive Committee suggested the procedure of a six-member joint committee. All that it did was in keeping with this procedure, and the board was free to accept or reject the committee's recommendations. Otherwise, the Executive Committee made no formal recommendations to either the board or the Convention. It completely informed the Convention, taking care to put the Home Mission Board in a positive light.[51] This challenge surely indicates that not only did the Executive Committee act correctly but it also acted responsibly, and by so doing it gained new maturity.

One sidelight of the crisis was that the young *Christian Index* editor, Louie D. Newton, was present in the Atlanta meeting and was asked to work with Frank E. Burkhalter in making a statement to the daily press. Beginning in 1930, Newton was a very useful member of the Executive Committee for more than a quarter of a century.

5. The first effort of the Executive Committee in the management of stewardship promotion (1927-1932) was, at best, a mixture of some success, much misunderstanding, and near failure.[52] The official story is as follows:

> For two years, May, 1927, to May, 1929, the Promotion Committee of the Convention was composed of the members of the Executive Committee, Southwide Secretaries, State Secretaries, and Editors of denominational papers. For two years, May 1929, to May, 1931, by

action of the Convention, the work of promotion was entrusted to the Executive Committee. However, in making plans for promotion, the Committee conferred with Southwide Secretaries and with State Secretaries. During these four years the regular features of promotion were carried out, such as giving information through tracts, articles, addresses, letters, and so forth, concerning the Co-operative Program; pushing the Every-Member Canvass, and so forth. In addition to other methods of publicity, the office of the Executive Committee has distributed through the regular channels 3,944,225 tracts on stewardship, tithing and the Co-operative Program; printed 26,250 wall posters (22x31 inches) for churches; furnished free to pastors 39,650 of the Pastors' Manual (62 to 84 pages); published for free distribution 159,650 copies of the Baptist Program; and supplied practically at cost approximately 9,500,000 copies of the Baptist church bulletin.

This account hides little episodes of unhappy history. The actual year-to-year operation was frustrating and unfruitful. Faced with two stubborn problems, declining gifts and increasing debts, the leaders were greatly discouraged. The usually optimistic L. L. Gwaltney told his Alabama readers in January 1929, "Denominationally, the outlook is not bright. That is, not bright with reference to institutions and boards . . . not bright, yet it is not hopeless."[53] In South Carolina the following May, Z.T. Cody wrote, "The writer has been more or less acquainted with Southern Baptist life since 1887; but has never known a time when our leaders were as perplexed as at present."[54] Gifts to missions in 1929 were about what they were in 1918, the year before the Seventy-Five Million Campaign. From 1920 to 1933 they declined 77.5 percent.[55] Plans availed very little, and sermons fell on deaf ears.

The first years (1927-1929) were the years of the "Promotional Agency," a clumsy arrangement in which SBC agency executive secretaries and state executive secretaries were "joined with" the Executive Committee as voting members when it considered promotional matters.[56] This was probably in recognition of the value of the fairly successful Cooperative Program Commission (successor to the Campaign Conservation Commission).

But the new Promotional Agency "joined with" arrangement did not work. First, there was a mixup on voting rights.[57] This was understandable because previously the important promotional group of the Convention had been the Conservation Commission that had handled stewardship and Cooperative Program promotion. Because of its staff, and its prominence, the people and even the leaders may have assumed that its general form would be continued. According to Crouch, some of the former members of that group who had been "joined with" the Executive Committee to form the Promotional Agency thought that they had full privileges, even the right to vote on the new executive secretary of the Executive Committee.

Next, perplexity over mounting debts and Cooperative Program management rendered the new Promotional Agency arrangement almost sterile. About all that it produced during its short life (1917-1929) were strategies emulating those of the Seventy-Five Million Campaign. Victor I. Masters, who had been present in the first meeting of the combined Executive Committee and Promotional Agency, later wrote:[58]

> It will be remembered that there was a good deal of confusion at that first session at Nashville. The dissatisfaction and confusion were so manifest that several members of the Executive Committee proper privately expressed the opinion that it would be desirable to call together another meeting and correct the error which had been made. . . . The Committee will need to decide whether or not the Promotional Agency—which was set up last year, being "joined" with the personnel of the Executive Committee "as constituting" a Promotional Agency—is, so to speak, a graft upon the tree of the Executive Committee that can be taken off after the sap gets into the branch before the fruit matures, or whether it is a tree with roots of its own.

Masters did not think the Promotional Agency would accomplish very much as long as the Executive Committee held the power of veto. Change was in the air, and it took place in 1929 when the Executive Committee recommended "that the Promotion Committee (Agency) be discontinued and that the responsibility for the conduct of the promotional work be entrusted to the Executive Committee."[59] Though the Convention approved the new plan, there was no noticeable improvement in the promotion of stewardship. Mission gifts further declined, the Cooperative Program was seriously questioned, and some of the SBC agency representatives were critical. D. F. Green, state secretary in Alabama, reporting a meeting of state secretaries in which the problems of the Cooperative Program were discussed, said that "heads of boards and institutions were saying publicly that the Cooperative Program had failed."[60] All was not at ease in the Baptist Zion.

The confusion led to major surgery. In 1931 a special Convention committee on memorials, appointed by President W. J. McGlothlin, recommended the establishment of a Convention Promotion Committee with a staff of its own, financed by The Sunday School Board.[61] The action was in response to McGlothlin's presidential address in which he suggested "a more effective agency for the cooperation of all the people in promotion of kingdom work."[62] As chairman of the Executive Committee, the president was certainly in a position to observe the confusion. The Convention was in the mood for a change, so it approved the recommendation. J. E. Dillard, an astute observer of the Convention wrote defensively, "Bear in mind the Executive Committee itself asked for a Promotion Committee."[63]

Why did the Executive Committee have difficulty in its early efforts at stewardship promotion? One possible answer was the lack of full-time promotional leaders. It was almost too much to ask the executive secretary to meet all of the leadership needs of the Executive Committee. At one point Gwaltney warned, "Austin Crouch, our executive secretary, is working at his task, but it is possible to place upon him more than one man can do and then we will be sure to find fault with him because he is not a half-dozen men; and that's the way it goes."[64] By disposition, Crouch was not a promoter. He was not fond of travel, and he was not the kind of platform personality who fired the masses. As skilled as he was, he probably knew no more what to do about the mammoth task of promotion than most other Southern Baptists.

Another answer was the limited office staff. During this period, only one professional was assigned to stewardship promotion. From 1927 to 1929, the position was held by Frank E. Burkhalter, a highly competent lay journalist who was disposed to the academic by training and interest and not the kind of personality needed for public platform promotion of stewardship. Burkhalter had been employed to direct publicity for the Seventy-Five Million Campaign and had stayed on to work for the Cooperative Program Conservation Commission and finally for the Promotional Agency. In 1929 Burkhalter was succeeded by Walter M. Gilmore who also carried heavy responsibility as Convention press representative. One person, no matter how competent, could not do everything that needed to be done.

The third and most likely answer was that in 1931 Southern Baptist agency and state convention leaders were not quite ready to work together with the Executive Committee in promotion. That would come one or two hard knocks later.

One of the hard knocks was that the new Convention Promotion Committee worked no better than the previous Promotion Agency and Promotion Committee that had been related to the Executive Committee. In fact, it did not work as well, though possibly through no fault of its own. The times were against it because of (1) a deepening depression, (2) churches in debt and unable to pay even the interest of their loans, and (3) declining mission gifts. With 1933 the low point in Southern Baptist mission giving, the new Convention Promotion Committee did not have much of a chance to prove itself. Even a few months after it was created, "There was a feeling on the part of many people . . . that the two committees . . . were unnecessary because they felt that one could do the work of both."[65]

Another hard knock was that the great and gifted Charles E. Maddrey who was asked to be the general director of the Promotion

Committee was called to the equally urgent challenge of leading the
Foreign Mission Board before he could take hold of the task.

So in 1933, for the fourth time in six years, the Convention voted
on promotion, this time to return it to the Executive Committee.[66]
This was a sign that in spite of the Executive Committee's doubtful
moments, it was at least making headway against its opposition
toward the maturity it needed for survival.

Leading Through the Storm

The stormy years of 1927-1933 were perhaps the most difficult
the Executive Committee has ever known, though the ones that
followed also brought many anxious moments. For a long time, the
thing that most bothered Austin Crouch was the possibility that the
Executive Committee would be voted out of existence before it had
full opportunity to prove itself. He felt that the people did not
understand its nature and its work. They associated it with centralization, which in Crouch's mind was as far from any Southern Baptist
leader's intention as it was from the possibility of the Convention's
approval. He believed that one of the motivations in the clamor for
separation of the Promotion Committee in 1931 was the hope that
separation would destroy the Executive Committee.[67]

Crouch thought, perhaps with some justification, that he was the
focal point of much of the criticism and that this was due to his
determination to enforce impartially the rules the Convention had
applied to the agencies. He was the kind of person sometimes described as "tough but fair," yet occasionally accused of being more
unfair than fair. Even some members of the Executive Committee
may have wanted to limit his position. Hight C Moore, who had
been the Executive Committee treasurer since 1917, decided in
1932 to nominate Crouch in his place. After brief consideration, the
Executive Committee referred the nomination to the Administrative
Committee. When it reported, Moore was again treasurer.[68] Not
until 1951, when Crouch briefly served as interim executive secretary between the terms of Duke K. McCall and Porter Routh, was
he authorized to sign checks as treasurer. There may not have been

any personal resistance of Crouch as treasurer, for it was a common practice of the times for organizations to have both elected executive secretaries and treasurers. Baptists especially were very cautious in vesting too much power in a single office.

Hight C Moore was one of the brightest stars in the life of the early Executive Committee. A beaming man, his love for the denomination was as broad as his love for people. Gifted as a writer and editor, he performed masterful services as recording secretary for the Convention. Over the years, he had fallen heir to a variety of duties in connection with the annual Convention. In 1933 he realized that the time had come to change this awkward procedure. He laid before his brethren a carefully formulated list of proposed new Executive Committee duties, covering most of the things he had been doing. These included: (1) keep all Convention files and annuals, (2) distribute messenger enrollment materials, (3) arrange travel discounts for messengers, (4) provide needed Convention clerical help, (6) provide services for the Committee on Order of Business, (7) pay all bills, (8) publish and distribute the Convention bulletin, and (9) keep all correspondence files between sessions.[69]

In approving the new duties, the Convention added one more seal of approval to the Executive Committee. By no means was it the most important, for many previously assigned duties were much more meaningful. But for the average messenger, the "new duties" were visible and understandable; and they further enhanced the general acceptability of the Executive Committee.

Prominent leaders also had important roles in generating acceptability. Two of the most helpful after 1927 were George W. Truett (1927-1930) and W. J. McGlothlin (1931-1933). McGlothlin served as professor of church history at Southern Seminary for twenty-five years and as president of Furman University for fourteen years. He was broadly educated with graduate degrees from Southern Seminary and the University of Berlin. Scholarly in temperament and distinguished in bearing, he was also a practical man and a force behind several Convention innovations and forward movements.

His nine published books indicate a man fiercely loyal to his denomination.

Austin Crouch had none of the public charisma of Truett or McGlothlin, but he had a unique charisma of his own. It beamed best in small groups and one-on-one conversations. Behind it was an unquenchable love for the denomination and a compelling dream for the Executive Committee, two causes for which he regarded himself as expendable. In his old age, one of his proudest memories was of the support Mrs. Crouch gave him through the harried and uncertain years. For some reason he called her "Little Jap," and each year when he would leave home for the annual meeting of the Convention, they would embrace and agree that if worst came to worst, they still would have each other. As he walked away from her toward the train, Little Jap knew that he carried his resignation in his pocket and that he might not have it when he returned home. His reasoning was, "If they attack the Executive Committee they will see the executive secretary as its symbol. I will then publicly submit my resignation and the Executive Committee will be saved." Happily, he never had to use it.[70] He was spared to work on numerous demanding problems facing the Executive Committee. Two of them were the payment of Southern Baptist Convention debt and the administration of the Cooperative Program.

Notes

1. RH, June 9, 1927, pp. 4-5.
2. SBC, 1983, pp. 422-423.
3. SBC, 1914, pp. 77.
4. SBC, 1924, p. 25.
5. SBC, 1927, p. 71.
6. ECM, January 11-12, 1928, p. 20.
7. SBC, 1928, pp. 32-33; cf. SBC, 1956, pp. 56-57. See Appendix 2 for

complete text of the report: "Relation of Southern Baptist Convention to Other Baptist Bodies."

8. SBC, 1918, p. 100.

9. SBC, 1927, pp. 107-108.

10. ECM, June 27, 1927, p. 9.

11. SBC, 1929, pp. 63-64.

12. WR, May 16, 1929, p. 9.

13. BC, May 21, 1928, p. 19.

14. SBC, 1928, pp. 52-54.

15. ECM, March 5-6, 1929. pp. 48-49.

16. ECM, May 7-8, 1929, p. 63.

17. ECM, May 15, 1931, p. 111.

18. ECM, June 29, 1928, p. 29.

19. ECM, June 14, 1928, p. 31.

20. SBC, 1920, pp. 101-102.

21. SBC, 1920, p. 114.

22. AB, May 24, 1928, p. 7.

23. SBC, 1920, p. 509.

24. ECM, March 5, 1931, p. 101.

25. ECM, June 10, 1931, p. 119.

26. ECM, January 11, 1934, p. 166.

27. Ibid., p. 184.

28. R. L. Middleton, "Ridgecrest Baptist Assembly," ESB, Vol. II, p. 1166.

29. SBC, 1937, p. 40.

30. ECM, June, 16, 1937, p. 56.

31. ECM, Dec. 15, 1937, p. 60; SBC, 1938, p. 36.

32. SBC, 1928, p. 40.

33. ECM, March, 5-6, 1929, p. 56.

34. SBC, 1929, pp. 73-75.

35. Ibid.

36. RH, May 2, 1929, pp. 10-11.

37. SBC, 1931, p. 34.

38. AB, May 16, 1929, p. 3.

39. BC, May 23, 1929, p. 2.

40. ECM, September 5, 1929, p. 75.

41. ECM, December 8, 1931, p. 124.

42. Ibid., p. 125.
43. W. W. Barnes, "Carnes's Defalcation," ESB, Vol. I, p. 232.
44. Austin Crouch to Merrill D. Moore.
45. Ibid.
46. ECM, September 4, 1928, pp. 38-41.
47. Ibid., p. 39.
48. Ibid., p. 40.
49. ECM, March 5-6, 1929, pp. 52-54.
50. WR, October 18, 1928. p. 5.
51. SBC, 1929, pp. 67-71.
52. SBC, 1932, p. 54.
53. AB, January 3, 1929, p. 2.
54. BC, May 2, 1929, p. 2.
55. QR, July 1983, pp.70-71.
56. SBC, 1927, p. 69.
57. Austin Crouch to Merrill D Moore (SBCA).
58. WR, May 10, 1928, p. 10.
59. SBC, 1929, p. 75.
60. AB, January 31, 1929, p. 5.
61. SBC, 1931, pp. 60-61.
62. AB, W. J. McGlothlin, "Forty Years," May 21, 1931. p. 1.
63. AB, J. E. Dillard, "The Convention," ibid., p. 7.
64. AB, May 31, 1928, p. 3.
65. Ibid., May 26, 1932, p. 3.
66. SBC, 1933, pp. 42-43.
67. Austin Crouch to Merrill D. Moore (SBCA).
68. ECM, June 15, 1932, pp. 130-131.
69. SBC, 1933, p. 49.
70. Austin Crouch to AM.

6

Rebuilding the Denominational Dream
1933-1943

America began its slow climb out of the depression in 1933. Under a new national administration banks were stabilized, markets reopened, and some farmers saved. Some of the unemployed returned to work, even if only to lower hourly wages and less job security. On the horizon, there were promises of retirement assistance for the aging and educational opportunities for the youth. The new president, Franklin D. Roosevelt, quickly lifted the spirits of most Americans. In his presidential address in March 1933, he said, "The only thing we have to fear is fear itself—nameless, unreasoning, unjustified terror."[1]

The president's optimism was a needed note, even for the Baptists who like everyone else were uprooted and torn by devastating economic forces beyond their understanding and control. Roosevelt spoke with candor in describing the agony of the times. He said, "Values have shrunken to fantastic levels . . . the means of exchange are frozen in the currents of trade; the withered leaves of industrial enterprises lie on every side; farmers find no markets for their produce; the savings of many years in thousands of families are gone." His barren picture was one that most Southern Baptists knew very well.

The grimness was felt in the churches, where budgets often were half what they had been a few years before and where sometimes as many as one-fourth of the members were unemployed. Churches in cities and towns somehow kept going, though many of them found the way discouraging. Peeling buildings went unpainted, worn

111

hymnbooks unreplaced, floors uncarpeted, and staggering debts unpaid. Most managed to support their pastors, buy needed literature, pay their current bills, and give a little to missions. Spiritually, amid their meager circumstances, the churches survived and flourished. From 1929 to 1938 Southern Baptist church membership increased from 3,770,000 to 4,770,000,[2] a gain of one million members.

In face of the material discouragements, denominational leaders maintained great optimism. Pastors, often underpaid and sometimes not paid at all, remained faithful to the calling of the gospel. Most of them did not all blame the depression for failures in the churches or in the denomination. They believed that the cause of Christ was invincible and would always remain triumphant. The associational meetings and state conventions of the era were usually happy, hopeful assemblies where high expectations helped dispel low feelings. The ministers and the few laypeople who managed to attend them heard hopeful leaders, such as John R. Sampey, M. E. Dodd, Charles E. Maddrey, Kathleen Mallory, Mrs. F. W. Armstrong, L. R. Scarborough, and George W. Truett.

Questions for which there did not seem to be answers were often on the lips of the leadership: "How will we ever pay our debts?" "Can the Cooperative Program be made to work?" Finding answers was essential for the survival of the denomination. The year 1934 was a very important one because for the first time there was a glimmer of light at the end of the tunnel.

Searching for Ways Out of Debt

Compared with the higher living standards of the late twentieth century, the financial picture was somber. The people lived under an entirely different economy. Coffee could be bought for twenty-five cents a pound, milk for twenty cents a gallon, gasoline for fifteen cents a gallon, and bread for five cents a loaf. Labor could be secured for a dollar a day, and a room in a motel for a dollar a night. Such low prices meant little to most households because there was so little money with which to buy even the simplest of the daily necessities.

Denominational deficits had been created in the early 1920s when the agencies wrongly assumed that they could count on an annual income from the Seventy-five Million Campaign. Buildings were built, programs enlarged, and personnel added. But a sharp financial recession that pushed thousands of small businesses into bankruptcy suddenly proved the assumptions wrong. Confident of better times, the agencies borrowed against the unpaid pledges, but the conditions did not improve. "The time came when it was not possible to meet the payments. . . . One agency after another defaulted . . . loans had to be renewed from time to time, without any payment on principal."[3]

Sometimes even the interest could not be paid. There was "a deep despondency on the part of Southern Baptists. . . . Our workers were discouraged, and our creditors were clamoring for payment of loans, some even threatening legal proceedings to collect or to throw the Convention and agencies into bankruptcy." The leaders did not altogether blame the faltering economy. Some of them thought that the agencies had exercised poor judgment and others, that the people generally were not concerned. Many believed that debt could be controlled. Control of debt had been one of the motivations in the restructuring of the Executive Committee. For nearly six years, beginning in 1928, the Executive Committee debt payment plans faltered, one after another.

A Thank Offering was set for Christmas 1928. At the time, the debts of the SBC agencies were officially listed as $5,432,579.[4] State convention debts may have been even greater. The Executive Committee was to receive 5 percent of the total Thank Offering for emergency purposes. Actually it got only $2,748. When the money was counted, there was not enough to pay campaign expenses. The failure was principally due to the early fall emergency offering to aid the Home Mission Board in overcoming the losses sustained in the Carnes embezzlement. The Thank Offering was followed by a series of small maneuvers, none of them really productive.

By 1931 debts of the agencies had risen to $5,582,400, up $149,852 from the 1928 listing.[5] In the March meeting of the Executive Committee, a special subcommittee recommended a five-year payment plan. From the floor, six other plans were proposed and still another subcommittee was appointed. The Executive Committee then concluded that the best way to handle the debts was through the Cooperative Program. An emphasis plan was suggested; but in the confusion over the separation of the Promotion Committee from the Executive Committee, the plan did not materialize. In June 1931, after the separation, the Executive Committee attempted to share responsibility for payment of debts with the new SBC Promotion Committee.[6] It proposed the development of a four-year plan for liquidation of bonded indebtedness. Again, no results. Generally, the nation was in the grip of an unshakable lethargy. In the Southwest the lethargy was made worse by prolonged drought and suffocating dust storms.

When it seemed that all had failed, at least for the Baptists and their debts, hope appeared with the appointment of one more committee and the appearance of two new leaders. On May 11, 1932, the Executive Committee established a joint "refunding committee" with the SBC Promotion Committee and asked it to report on a "debt paying policy."[7] Eleven months later J. E. Dillard and Frank Tripp reported for the joint committee.[8] The plan was so simple that it must have been difficult for some of those present to take it seriously. Previous plans had aimed at doing big things; this one, at doing little things. It asked loyal Baptists everywhere for as little as a dollar a month to apply on SBC debts. Of course, the Baptists would be encouraged to give more than a dollar; but for a dollar, one could have a part in liquidating SBC indebtedness. A month later the plan was given final approval and passed on to the Southern Baptist Convention.[9] The recommendation made to the Convention was covered in twenty-four lines of clear prose—so simple that some of the messengers present surely must have dismissed it as another fruitless plan. Nevertheless, the Hundred Thousand

Club was approved, and the Convention was on its way to debt liberation.[10]

The architect of the Hundred Thousand Club was Frank Tripp, a pastor from Saint Joseph, Missouri, and a newcomer to the Executive Committee. Elected in 1932, he was immediately appointed to the joint "refunding committee." In tribute to his work, J. E. Dillard later said that Frank Tripp of Saint Joseph, Missouri "originated the idea."[11] Tripp was elected general director, and under his hand the plan was vigorously promoted. In May 1934, the Executive Committee informed the Convention that it had at last begun a successful debt-paying venture and that since the previous May a total of 20,163 Southern Baptists had pledged $360,000 to be paid in monthly installments of one dollar or more. It further said that $87,524 had already been collected. From 1934 to 1943, the Hundred Thousand Club flourished. Annual gifts for SBC debts indicate a healthy growth until the last debt was paid.

But the Hundred Thousand Club was not always an untroubled road; for, like the highways of the times, there were sharp turns and treacherous shoulders—and at one point, almost a tragic wreck. A mistake was made in strategy when the Executive Committee did not at first take the states as full partners. State conventions were expected to do the promoting and the collecting, but not to share in the receipts. For a half dozen with large debts that had also resulted from the Seventy-five Million Campaign, this was a chilling rejection. South Carolina was the first to protest.[12] It warned:

> If the Southern Baptist Convention does try to set up this club in South Carolina during this year we recommend that the General Board be called to meet at an early date to take action looking to the reduction of the percentages of our Cooperative Program funds which go to Southwide causes. While we shall regret to take this step it seems to us absolutely necessary to save the credit of the denomination in South Carolina.

Tennessee said that unless the promoters were very careful the Hundred Thousand Club would hurt the Cooperative Program. It

recommended that the Executive Committee "be asked to cooperate with our forces in doing this work, rather than bring confusion
into our State by seeking to carry out an independent campaign."[13]
Kentucky asked the Executive Committee to endorse a plan that its
general board had approved for dividing Hundred Thousand Club
funds "50-50" with the Southern Baptist Convention.[14] In the face
of all of these requests, the Executive Committee adamantly held to
its exclusive right to the Hundred Thousand Club receipts. Relationships continued to deteriorate until two things happened to
ease the problem.

First, in 1935 the state executive secretaries asked for a high-level
conference of SBC and state convention leaders "on all matters
pertaining to their cooperative relationships and their joint approach to our Baptist constituency."[15] The Executive Committee
referred the request to its Committee on Cooperation and Enlistment, but that committee did not act. Tempers flared. In the midst
of the confusion, the general director, Frank Tripp, abruptly resigned, saying that he positively refused to continue his leadership
another year "under the present arrangement."[16] Whether he was
for or against taking the states into the Baptist Hundred Thousand
Club is not presently known. Whatever the reason, his action produced a number of changes that led to an easing of relationships.

The Executive Committee appointed a Committee on the Future
of the Club,[17] and from this committee came the first full-time
director of stewardship promotion. The position was offered to
Frank Tripp, but he felt that he could not accept it; and then it was
offered to J. E. Dillard, who at the time was president of the Executive Committee.[18] Dillard accepted and began at once to work with
the state conventions, and this surely led to better understanding.
This led to the next step toward easing tensions.

In December 1936, three years after the beginning of the Hundred Thousand Club, Kentucky, Alabama, and Tennessee made a
joint effort to secure cooperation.[19] Dillard was in a position to help
in getting this done. Given his position, his sensitivity, his sympathies, and his diplomatic skills, it is a safe assumption that he was

involved at least in the background. He was as much committed to
state Baptist work as he was to Southern Baptist work. Since Alabama was included in the final petition to the Executive Committee,
he may have been involved in that state's initiative. By 1937 six of
the state conventions were full partners.[20]

James Edgar Dillard (1879-1953) was born in Virginia and reared
in Missouri. He was a graduate of Howard College and Clarksville
College. For many years, he was pastor of the prestigious Southside
Church in Birmingham. During this time he wrote a column for the
Alabama Baptist. Literally interested in everything, he included arti-
cles such as "Why Go to College," "Vacation Fiction," "Pulpit
English," "Prohibition," "Big Coons in Little Trees," "Celebrating
My Birthday," "Ping-Pong," "The Bathtub Book," "Roses,"
"Denominational Debt," "Christian Education," "The Cooperative
Program," "Missions," "The Southern Baptist Convention," and
"The State Convention." All were done in good taste. Dillard was
an exhaustless reader and often would include book reviews in his
column. Cosmopolitan in interests, he was also a practical person.
Tenacious in his pursuit of goals, his mind did not wander or his eye
look backward, traits that equipped him well for the arduous task of
leading Southern Baptist promotion. As director of promotion, for
seven years, Dillard kept an unrelenting hold on the Hundred
Thousand Club. His first goal was a debtless denomination by
1945.[21] When that appeared more than possible, he led the Executive Committee to reset the goal for 1943.[22] Whimsical in some of
his promotional methods, Dillard frequently used alliterations and
jingles to make his points. One of them that helped pay Southern
Baptists out of debt was, "Debt Free in '43, Count on Me."[23] He
sometimes humorously changed it to "Debt Free in '43, Count on
Me; J. E. D."

Edgar Franklin Tripp (1894-1975) was one of the truly creative
promotional minds among the Southern Baptist leaders of the era.
He was a man of ideas and a shaper of events. Independent, self-
confident, direct, and sometimes brusque, he was also loyal, dedicated, and cooperative. After forty years in the pastorate, Tripp was

elected superintendent of the New Orleans Baptist Hospital. While in that position, he founded the Jacksonville Baptist Hospital; and after retirement, he founded the Montgomery Baptist Hospital. It was fitting that a man of such ability would be elected to succeed J. E. Dillard as the tenth chairman of the Executive Committee.

Refunding Southern Baptist Convention Debts

Renewing the confidence of the fiscal community in the Southern Baptist Convention required two things: payment of debts and sound management of finances. In 1929 the New Financial Plan stimulated the agencies to manage their affairs more efficiently. The faithful application of the new rules and the gradual repayment of the debts of the agencies at last enabled the Convention to establish itself as fiscally dependable. This made possible the refunding of debts and a consequent saving of great sums in the reduction of interest rates.

There were seven major refundings from 1934 through 1941. These were initiated with the appointment of a subcommittee on "debt-paying policy" on May 11, 1932.[24]

In 1933 the Executive Committee could not pay the interest of the Education Board notes. At first The Sunday School Board came to the rescue, but it declined to do so on the next request.[25] Later, on account of the "serious complications" that might arise, The Sunday School Board did on February 6, 1934 appropriate $7,000 "to supplement the funds on hand for the payment of the interest in default." Likely, the "serious complications" were threats of foreclosure on the Ridgecrest property, the honey in the Education Board hive. This led Austin Crouch and the Executive Committee to concentrate attention on the $345,000 Education Board bond issue that would mature December 15, 1936.[26] With most of the corpus due, unless the note was paid or renegotiated, it would mean foreclosure. After conferences with the bondholders, the note was extended to December 15, 1941.[27] The refunding was a minor achievement, but it did establish the ability of the Executive Committee to negotiate difficult fiscal problems successfully.

Three years later the second renegotiation was initiated when Austin Crouch presented to the Executive Committee a "refunding resolution"[28] that called for a bond issue not to exceed $600,000. The money was for a variety of causes: discharging the bonds of the Education Board ($236,000), current notes held by the Executive Committee ($126,000),[29] outstanding Montezuma College bonds, ($188,000) and the balance on a pledge made by the Convention in 1920 to the National Memorial Baptist Church in Washington, D. C. ($50,000).[30] The details of this complicated negotiation took thirteen single-spaced legal pages to describe. The day after it was approved, the Executive Committee adopted a resolution commending Austin Crouch for "his tireless spirit and fine technical grasp of the many problems. . . . His judgment has been cool, calculated and correct."[31] The resolution said that even the bankers recognized his ability.

In 1940 and 1941, there were five other refundings totaling about two and one-quarter million dollars. In conversations with Crouch, Porter Routh later learned that Crouch had also assisted state conventions in the refunding of their debts.[32] This was possible because of Crouch's newfound ability and the connections he had established with banks and trust companies and because of the Executive Committee's reputation for dealing responsibly with its debt problems.

There is no doubt that Austin Crouch was the prime mover in all these events. Mrs. Raymond Rogers, whose husband was at the time one of Crouch's closest banker-advisers, remembered long conferences in her living room. She said, "Raymond, Dr. Crouch, and Dr. Dillard would talk for hours and hours on the financial problems of the Baptists."[33] Sometimes they were joined by Walter M. Hale, Jr., an officer in Nashville Securities Company, who was involved in many of the transactions. Following one of the most difficult transactions in which Hale had been involved with Austin Crouch, the banker sent to the Executive Committee, a glowing congratulatory letter,[34] in which he said:

It was Dr. Crouch who first believed it could be done, and who interested us in attempting to undertake it. The first large sale was made to a financial institution which had long dealt with Dr. Crouch and the Executive Committee, and the purchase of the issue was largely predicated on confidence in the integrity and stability of the Executive Committee and on knowledge of how its affairs were being administered.

The bondholders wanted their payments to come from the Executive Committee, not from the agencies for whom the loans had been obtained. The request was not a slap at the agencies, but a recognition of the financial responsibility of the Executive Committee and its staff. In the fourteen years since its reorganization, torn with mind-rending problems and against persistent opposition, the Executive Committee had reached full fiscal maturity.

Launching the 1939 SBC Business and Financial Plan

The New Financial Plan of 1929 was not a complete plan but probably was as much as the Executive Committee could wisely recommend at that time. In later years, Austin Crouch talked of the resistance of some of the agency heads to the idea of outside regulation, no matter how neutral the regulatory group. The reluctance was certainly understandable, for none of the agency heads wanted their causes endangered with unproven interference. Before a fully matured and fully enforceable plan could be installed, the Executive Committee needed time to prove itself as fair, consistent, reliable, and noncompetitive. As time passed, it made the right choices in that direction. Over the years, the Executive Committee:

- Established the practice of open meetings. Visitors were welcomed and their presence minuted.
- Managed carefully its own financial affairs. In 1930, it had a fifteen-point procedure for handling Convention funds.
- Used its power to study and recommend, cautiously. It intruded only when confronted with the gravest of problems.
- Avoided major overlapping competition with the agencies.

- Carried out Convention assignments, faithfully and promptly.
- Maintained a low profile, sharp enough to be seen and understood, but restrained enough not to seem out of place.
- Worked tactfully and openly with the agencies that appeared to be in violation of Convention rules.

For eight years the Executive Committee worked with the New Financial Plan. Most apparent violations were not violations at all but misunderstandings. Some of the more serious ones did not surface in official meetings. Usually, following a suggestion from Crouch, the executive of the agency in question would take steps to correct the problem. Violations were due to oversight or ignorance, not to malfeasance. During this time, the Executive Committee and its staff acquired insights and experience needed for the development of a new plan.

The next step occurred in 1937 when the Convention approved a recommendation from the Executive Committee "That the Executive Committee of this Convention be instructed to formulate plans and policies looking toward the prevention, in the future, of the incurring of debts either by this Convention or its agencies."[35] It was probable that Austin Crouch was somewhere in the background of that motion. He, no doubt, had decided that the time had come to seek Convention approval for the next step in total fiscal accountability. Debt regulation was a popular subject among Southern Baptists, and a recommendation dealing with it could not be successfully opposed.

In 1938 the Executive Committee presented a tentative Business and Financial Plan to the Convention for study. Described as a means of controlling debt,[36] it covered much more than the 1929 plan. Wisely, the Executive Committee did not press for adoption but asked for a joint review by SBC agency executives and Executive Committee members. The joint conference was held in December; and after friendly discussion and some minor changes, the plan was approved for recommendation to the Convention.[37] The 1939 Convention amended the plan with some ideas of its own and then approved it as the "Business and Financial Plan of the Southern Baptist Convention."[38]

Regarded by its framers as a major Southern Baptist benchmark, the plan was printed in the 1939 *Southern Baptist Convention Annual,* along with the Charter and Bylaws, as one of the controlling documents of the Convention. It covered seventeen subjects:

Operating Budgets	Convention Expenses
The Disbursing Agency	Cooperative Program
Special Solicitations	Distribution
Designated Gifts	Trust Funds
Gift Annuity Contracts	Capital Investments
Contingent Reserve	Audit Reports
Financial Reports to SBC	Sunday School Board
New Enterprises	Appropriations
Publications	Auditor
	Amendments

Strategically, prominent display and provision for amendment were important decisions, for in this way the Business and Financial Plan was given prominent display, making it difficult to be forgotten or ignored. The Hundred Thousand Club and the Business and Financial Plan helped to revive the confidence of the churches in the Christ-honoring possibilities of the Cooperative Program.

Strengthening the Cooperative Program

The year 1933 was the bottom year for the Southern Baptist Convention Cooperative Program. In 1932 the state conventions had forwarded $1,198,680 to the Executive Committee—$744,595 undesignated and $454,084 designated. One year later, they sent $880,489—$580,094 undesignated and $300,395 designated. A staggering 27 percent decline, it brought the worst year in a thirteen-year slide.[39] Just ahead was 1934, the turnaround year. Seldom do religious groups experience such increments of growth as fol-

lowed in the next ten years. The national economy had something
to do with the rapid increases, but it was not the sole reason. Three
things combined to make the growth possible: (1) Southern Baptist
commitment to missions and Christian education, (2) an unprecedented revival in stewardship, and (3) the coming of age of the
Cooperative Program.

Officially established in 1925, the Cooperative Program scarcely
made a ripple in that stormy Convention. Too many headline events
were taking place, such as the first "Statement of Baptist Faith and
Message," the continuing debate over evolution, and the acceptance of Southwestern Seminary into the family of Southern Baptist
institutions. Besides, due to the persistent promotion of the Conservation Commission, the churches and the states were already attempting some of the things the committee's report called for, such
as the every member canvass and local church budget; moreover,
there already existed in the Seventy-five Million Campaign a kind of
cooperative program. For some, the new plan was not really new.

Even an observer as clear-sighted as L. L. Gwaltney believed that
the Cooperative Program really began in 1919 with the Seventy-five
Million Campaign. He wrote in 1929, "After ten years its (Cooperative Program) full significance has never been grasped by half our
preachers, to say nothing about the people."[40] Gwaltney, like many
others, apparently believed that the Cooperative Program began
with the Seventy-five Mission Campaign in 1919. But, at least the
1925 plan incorporated three new things: (1) It had annual goals
and annual tables of distribution; (2) it had a new name, the "Cooperative Program"; and (3) it brought a new enthusiasm, especially
among leaders. This latter contribution was not unanimous, for, at
first, among some leaders the enthusiasm was less than had been
expected.

There were some weaknesses too. (1) Distribution of SBC funds
was left to the states. At first, they forwarded receipts directly to the
agencies and sometimes changed the suggested SBC table of percentages in keeping with their own ideas of distribution. (2) Lacking
sufficient funding and adequate leadership, the new Cooperative

Program Commission could not entirely fulfill its responsibilities. (3) The Cooperative Program Commission inherited some of the problems and procedures of the Seventy-five Million Conservation Commission. During the two crucial years of its short life, the Cooperative Program Commission simply repeated the use of worn-out materials and methods. By not striking in new places and in new ways, it failed to fuse the new Cooperative Program into the life of the denomination. (4) Relationships of the state conventions and the Southern Baptist Convention in the new program were not yet well understood. This was the situation that the Executive Committee faced in 1927, and it was made worse by the numbing realization that total gifts to combined state and SBC missions were rapidly decreasing,[41] down two million dollars in four years.

1924	$9,863,134
1925	8,255,435
1926	8,161,411
1927	7,843,652

Both Executive Committee and state leaders were inexperienced in the cooperation and relationship which the new procedure required. At first they were much more aware of the challenges and problems of cooperation than of the ways to deal with them. Eight of the more pressing Cooperative Program problems required careful attention.

1. *Changing of Southern Baptist Convention distribution tables by the state conventions.* In 1928 the Executive Committee asked the Convention to request the states, "in (the) interest of exercising the spirit of cooperation, the interest of a Cooperative Program, and in the interest of all our Convention causes, to leave the percentages of distribution of Southwide funds to this Convention."[42] The same appeal was made in 1929 with added words, "and that the Executive Committee be instructed to confer with the several states for the adjustment of this matter."[43] It was repeated again in 1930. As late as 1934, Virginia was still changing SBC percentages.[44]

2. *Right of Southern Baptist Convention access to the churches.* This

problem was eased in 1928 when the Convention approval the principle, "There is no relation of superiority or inferiority among general Baptist bodies. All make their appeal directly to churches, and to each other."[45]

3. *State conventions forwarding of SBC Cooperative Program directly to the agencies.* This ended in 1929 when the Convention approved the New Financial Plan. It included a statement that "all sums collected in the various states for Southwide objects shall be forwarded monthly by each state secretary to the Executive Committee, which shall become the disbursing or distribution agent of the Convention."[46] The next year the Executive Committee reported, "All of the states except two, are now sending all or certain of their funds for the various Southwide agencies through the office of the Executive Committee. Some of the states send designated funds direct to the agencies."[47] The practice was not altogether the blame of the state conventions. Some of the agencies apparently wanted it that way. In 1930 "The Executive secretary [Executive Committee] presented a resolution from the Foreign Mission Board requesting change in the plan adopted in May, 1929, providing that monies be sent from the offices of the state secretaries to the several Convention agencies rather than through the office of the Executive Committee at Nashville, Tennessee."[48] The Executive Committee rightly replied that the it had "no power to alter the terms of the Cooperative Program which it is working by instructions of the Convention."[49]

4. *Special solicitations that disrupted the Cooperative Program.* The New Financial Plan provided "that any special campaign by any agency for endowments, or building and equipment, or other purposes not specified in the approved budget of any agency, shall first receive the endorsement and approval of the Southern Baptist Convention, or its Executive Committee," and "any and all such solicitations on the part of any agency shall be considered a breach of the Cooperative Program."[50] Debt and decline in Cooperative Program giving placed heavy burdens on the agencies, and the best way their leaders knew to secure funds was through direct solicitations. Some

found ways to bypass the rules, but most kept pressure on the Executive Committee for permission to conduct special campaigns. Especially hurtful was the absence of similar restraining rules in some of the state conventions.

5. *Neglect by some SBC agencies of Cooperative Program promotion.* The Seventy-five Million Campaign had stopped the wide and intensive use of field agents to raise money for the agencies. The new plan required collective promotion—all for each and each for all—a principle considered by many to be the reason for its success. In 1919 most of the agency leaders were energetic in their support; but with the adoption of the Cooperative Program, some of them did not see the need for promoting the whole program. Agency neglect of field support for the Cooperative Program prompted this stern appeal in 1928: "The Executive Committee would even urge upon . . . all our southwide causes that they should go afield in every way and to every degree in harmony with the Cooperative Program of the Convention possible to stir up the conscience and quicken the souls of Southern Baptists for our common cause."[51] Some of the agencies were slow to respond.

6. *Danger that the Cooperative Program would be terminated before it had a chance to succeed.* The Cooperative Program did have its enemies, and even some of its friends had difficulty with it. Four years after the Cooperative Program was begun, L. L. Gwaltney, the editor of the *Alabama Baptist,* listed seven reasons why it "has not worked well."[52] They are summarized as follows:

(1) It allows no room for specific causes and in consequence it never stirs the emotions. (2) The doctrinal discussions, which like a firebrand had to rage until it burned itself out, claimed the attention of our people three or four years. (3) Enormous debts on nearly all of the larger churches have, and will for many years yet, decrease the gifts to missionary causes. (4) The many special collections have helped defeat the general program. (5) Many institutions have trusted in the machinery to bring in their needed funds apart from cultivation and enlisting their own clientele. (6) The spirit of restlessness, and criticism, which has been produced by one thing and one thing only—

lack of funds. This spirit has militated against our work. (7) The deplorable Carnes case.

In 1929, at a winter meeting of the state executive secretaries, it came to light that some agency executives were saying publicly that the Cooperative Program had failed.[53]

7. *Misunderstandings of what promotional costs at the state level were chargeable to the Cooperative Program at the state level.* It was understood from the beginning that state conventions should be responsible for promoting the Cooperative Program in the field and gathering the funds from the churches. The Southern Baptist Convention was quite willing for this, as long as it held the right of direct access to the churches. This was the main point of the 1929 statement on Relations of General Baptist Bodies.

It was also understood that the cost of promotion could legitimately be financed out of the funds raised. But, how much could be financed, for what purpose, and at what level? In 1930 a joint conference sponsored by the Executive Committee agreed that the state conventions could deduct, before division, certain administrative expenses "insofar as they are used for the whole program" and appropriate promotional expenses including the Woman's Missionary Union work in the states.[54] At this time, some expense items were not included, such as Baptist state papers and ministers' retirement.

Not all state conventions were represented. Consequently, the agreement was no more than a norm, and the states generally deducted what they thought appropriate. But in one of the worst years of the depression, when the SBC agency pantries were almost bare, the SBC agency executives on the edge of bankruptcy raised their voices. With the respected L. R. Scarborough as their spokesman, they presented a resolution to the Executive Committee, asking that the states "eliminate all *preferred items* in their appropriation and distributions of funds before divisions of state and SBC funds are made. Southwide funds ought not in any case be compelled to pay State debts or other items of State causes."[55] This move was prompted by the assumption that the Cooperative Program funds raised in the states should be divided fifty-fifty between the state conventions and the Southern Baptist Convention.

As a result, Austin Crouch assembled a list of the prevailing practices. He also developed a suggested contract form for specifically binding the states. In February 1934 a joint conference was held at which time a six-point agreement was reached, similar to the agreement of 1930, that again included the ideal of a fifty-fifty division of funds between state and Southwide causes. It also reaffirmed the right of the states to deduct basic administrative and promotional expenses. The agreement recommended "that the Executive Committee of the Southern Baptist Convention shall seek to establish and maintain contacts and conferences with the several state agencies with reference to working out these principles."[56] A general understanding was reached that administrative and promotional expenses in proper proportion would be deducted, including state paper publicity and WMU promotion. The proposed contract form was not successful. True contractual relationships were never really possible. The essential part of the agreement was that the conventions keep closely in touch. In later years, other items were added through mutual agreements; but generally, from the 1934 meeting, the two groups worked at the problem on the basis of respect and trust.

8. *Developing an effective promotional program for the Cooperative Program.* Promotion was essential for the program's success. After 1936 promotional leadership was much improved over the earlier years. J. E. Dillard was elected chairman of the Executive Committee in 1935 and director of promotion in 1936. His leadership made considerable difference. The promotion of the Cooperative Program began to improve, due to (1) the improved understanding of the working relationships of the Executive Committee and the state conventions, (2) the dramatic success of the Hundred Thousand Club, (3) the improving economy, (4) the lapse of time that muffled dissident voices and that enabled leaders to work comfortably with each other, (5) the realization that the Cooperative Program was,

after all, working, (6) the skillful uses of literature, (7) more interest among state leaders in cooperative promotion, and (8) better participation by SBC agency representatives.

Dillard's approach to promotion was broadly based and strategically oriented. He once stated his task "as that of helping to promote the whole program of Southern Baptists. . . . All our people in all our work."[57] He used a variety of methods: intensive publicity, unstinting field work, single-minded pursuance of goals, constant emphasis on the basics, and the utilization of the Executive Committee meetings as a means of communicating with state convention and SBC agency leaders. Through the meetings, the agency and state convention leaders most responsible for stewardship promotion were drawn into the work of the Committee on Cooperation and Enlistment in a kind of "cooperative program" of Cooperative Program promotion. Dillard was untiring in his contact in the field. In an effort to relieve Dillard's overstrained travel budget, Crouch requested the president of the Southern Railroad to transfer the free courtesy pass usually offered to the president of the Convention to the director of promotion.

By the end of 1943, Southern Baptists were paid out of debt. The total Cooperative Program, including both state and SBC causes, had increased 234 percent over 1933, rising from $1,903,615 in 1933 to $6,348,841, a gain of $4,445,226.[58] Southern Baptists had come a long way since the depth of the depression. With the denomination free of debt and with gifts to missions soaring, the Cooperative Program had at last come of age.

Moving Forward with the Times

The Cooperative Program was not all that had come of age; the Executive Committee also had at last proved itself in the eyes of Southern Baptists. No longer was it necessary for Crouch to carry his resignation with him to the Convention in fear that someone would stampede the annual meeting into voting his office out of existence. By the end of 1943, the Executive Committee had the respect of a great many knowledgeable people, enough to see it through almost any situation.

From the beginning of the Executive Committee in 1917, its officers had been among the strongest leaders of the denomination. The first was the Texas layman, M. H. Wolfe, appointed by the Convention as the first chairman. The next seven chairmen were presidents of the Convention. The early bylaws called them "presidents" of the Executive Committee, though the minutes often referred to them as "chairmen." Those who served from 1917 through 1943 were:

M. H. Wolfe, Texas industrialist	1917-1919
J. B. Gambrell, Southwestern Seminary professor	1919-1921
E. Y. Mullins, Southern Seminary president	1921-1924
George W. McDaniel, Virginia pastor	1924-1927
George W. Truett, Texas pastor	1927-1930
W. J. McGlothlin, Furman University president	1930-1932
Fred F. Brown, Tennessee pastor	1932-1933
M. E. Dodd, Louisiana pastor	1933-1935
J. E. Dillard, Alabama pastor	1935-1936
Frank Tripp, Missouri pastor	1936-1940
Charles W. Daniel, Arkansas pastor	1940-1943

Two of the chairmen, though very able, were not well known. Brown was a Knoxville pastor who served only briefly; and Daniel was an Arkansas pastor who had been first elected to the Executive Committee in 1928. Brown was greatly loved as pastor and preacher. His term unfortunately was cut short by serious illness. He is probably best known in Southern Baptist life for his preaching ability and for his support for the short-lived "Crucible Service Campaign" that appealed for people to give their old gold for the payment of Southern Baptist debts.[59]

Daniel had previously served as vice-chairman, and as chairman of several important subcommittees. A personal friend of Austin Crouch, their close association began when Crouch worked for the Home Mission Board and was a member of Daniel's Atlanta church.

"Dr. Charley," as he was affectionately known, was one of the key persons in the Executive Committee's involvement in the problem of the Carnes affair. Preeminent in the pulpit, he was widely respected as an "expository preacher without a peer in his time."[60] It was said of him that "he not only believes the Word but preaches it with peculiar insight, understanding, and power." After Daniel's death in 1951, the Convention in a memorial resolution praised him: "He was brave as a Numidian lion in fighting for fundamental principles which have determined the course of Southern Baptists. . . . Those of us who met him in the arena of debate can bear testimony that he was sincere. Those of us who had Convention-fellowship with him know that he gave himself without stint to hard work by day and by night."[61] In the years following his friend's death, Austin Crouch often spoke of "old Charley Daniel" with touching tenderness and fraternal respect. Such were the bonds of brotherhood between many of the early Executive Committee leaders who fought so bravely to keep the denomination out of the ditches and on the mainline.

The Executive Committee organization at first consisted of a chairman or president, a secretary, a treasurer, an executive secretary, and an administrative committee. Much of the work was done by the committee of the whole, which is understandable, considering that for a long time, the Executive Committee had only twenty-nine members. Like the Southern Baptist Convention for so many years, the Executive Committee frequently established special committees. Seldom were all of the members of the Executive committee present for a meeting.

Two women were elected members of the Executive Committee in 1927: Mrs. W. F. Armstrong of Missouri and Mrs. Ben S. Thompson of Georgia. Mrs. Armstrong, president of Woman's Missionary Union, was present at the second meeting and served as a valuable and respected member until her death in 1945. Mrs. Thompson was not recorded present at any of the meetings, and for some unknown reason was replaced in 1928. In March 1929, Mrs. Eugene Levering of Maryland, was elected by the Executive Committee to fill the unexpired term of her late husband. She served until 1933.

Following Mrs. Levering's election in 1929, except for Mrs. Armstrong, no other women served until 1946, when two were were elected: Mrs. George R. Martin, Missouri, and Mrs. Frank S. Burney, Georgia. During this period, Miss Kathleen Mallory (1879-1954), as executive secretary of Woman's Missionary Union, was one of the most helpful of the agency representatives. A genial and energetic lady, she worked diligently "to fully realize the relationship of Woman's Missionary Union to the Southern Baptist Convention."[62] Her work succeeded so well that the Convention in a memorial resolution years later asked all Southern Baptists to rise up and call her blessed.[63]

Executive Committee finance was relatively simple in the early years. From 1916 to 1924, its expenses were divided among the several boards.[64] In 1925 and 1926, The Sunday School Board was asked to provide up to $5,000 for each of the years.[65] From 1927 The Sunday School Board was again asked "to advance, from time to time, sufficient funds for the Committee to discharge its duties without financial embarrassment."[66] The most The Sunday School Board advanced in any one year was $37,500 in 1937, and the least was $12,000 in the deep depression year of 1932; however, in that same year, it furnished a similar amount for the SBC Promotion Committee. In addition, The Sunday School Board helped the Executive Committee with special projects, such as interest for Education Board loans, financing for the Hundred Thousand Club, and budget assistance to the smaller agencies. Besides the money received from The Sunday School Board, the Executive Committee had some income from the sales of Baptist Bulletin Service and other stewardship literature. The board and its officials always seemed willing to respond when the Convention required assistance.

The spirit behind this willingness was Isaac Jacobus Van Ness (1860-1947),[67] better known as I. J. Van Ness, the corresponding (executive) secretary of The Sunday School Board. A graduate of

Southern Seminary, he was called to the pastorate of the Immanuel
Baptist Church, Nashville, in 1890. Six years later he joined the
editorial staff of the *Christian Index* in Atlanta, Georgia. In 1900 he
became editorial secretary for The Sunday School Board and remained in that position until he was called to be the corresponding
secretary in 1917. His position and influence were such that with
one negative word from him, the board would not have been as
open as it was to requests for Executive Committee assistance. His
goodwill, no doubt, derived in part from his understanding of the
Baptist spirit.

Van Ness once wrote a book on this subject in which he said,
"How so many independent bodies can join together effectively
without sacrificing part of their independence is a puzzle to many.
It would be impossible were it not for the spirit which characterizes
our people. The Baptist spirit, at its best, makes possible this cooperation."[68] In his thinking, three things were at the heart of the
Baptist spirit: a belief in New Testament principles, a desire for the
New Testament spirit, and a proper zeal for the great purposes to
which the spirit naturally and surely leads. A denomination, grateful
for his sympathetic spirit and forceful leadership, asked his old
longtime associate, Hight C Moore, to prepare a final memorial
tribute. Moore wrote:[69]

> In his denomination he was credited with exceptional ability to dis-
> cern the trend and emphasis of opinion. Intimately identified with his
> people as in the heat of battle and closely observant as from a conning
> tower, he had rare insight of their need, their temper, their resources,
> and their possibilities. Indeed, he had in remarkable degree the dou-
> ble faculty of the wide sweep of the field glass and the deep look of
> the magnifying glass. With wonderful accuracy and facility he was
> thus able to sense a situation in its perspective and relate it to the
> kingdom of God.

Van Ness was succeeded by an equally generous man, T. L. Holcomb, as merry a spirit as ever spoke from a Baptist pulpit, a genius
in promotional strategy, and, like Van Ness, a heart wide open to

the denomination. He extended a warm affirming hand to the Executive Committee, which no doubt was a comforting joy to Austin Crouch and J. E. Dillard in the closing of their denominational ministries. For many years, when the Executive Committee was smaller, Holcomb, with beaming good-humored courtesy, invited the members and staff to have lunch with the members of The Sunday School Board at the Hermitage Hotel. Toward the end of his administration, the luncheons were held the week before Christmas and were festivals of lightness and joy. When Kearnie Keegan was present, he would be asked to sing with his clear tenor voice the high notes of "The Lily of the Valley." The Executive Committee fellowship was a rare experience that left a lump in the throat of memory. Holcomb was indeed an affable, outgoing person. Still, he could be as hard as granite in protecting the interests of The Sunday School Board; and if cornered, he could become very angry. More than once, he abruptly left a conference to walk up and down the halls until he regained his poise. Small in stature, T. L. Holcomb was a giant in Baptist life and a good friend to the Executive Committee.

With so many of the older leaders disappearing from view, it was not surprising that younger leaders were taking their places. Two of them were recorded present in an Executive Committee meeting for the first time on May 12, 1943—Duke K. McCall, the youthful president of Baptist Bible Institute, and Porter Wroe Routh, the new editor of the Oklahoma *Baptist Messenger*. Time was fast coming for a changing of the guard.

Notes

1. Basil Rauch, editor, *The Roosevelt Reader* (New York: Rinehart, 1957. p. 90.
2. "Southern Baptist Summary," QR, July 1983, pp. 70-71.
3. SBC, 1942, p. 64.

4. SBC, 1928, pp. 23, 40.

5. ECM, March 5, 1931, pp. 100-104.

6. ECM, June 10, 1931, p. 114.

7. ECM, May 11, 1932, p. 129.

8. ECM, April 12, 1933, pp. 136-138.

9. ECM, May 18, 1933, pp. 142-144.

10. SBC, 1933, p. 57.

11. AB, May 18, 1933, p. 7.

12. ECM, June 14, 1933, pp. 154-155.

13. ECM, January 11, 1934, p. 165.

14. ECM, December 12, 1934, p. 189.

15. ECM, June 12, 1935, p. 5.

16. ECM, December 11, 1935, p. 14.

17. Ibid., p. 15.

18. ECM, June 17, 1936, p. 29; December 10, 1936, p. 34.

19. ECM, December 10, 1936, p. 35.

20. SBC, 1937, pp. 41-42; cf. SBC, 1944, p. 38.

21. ECM, May 16, 1939, p. 117.

22. ECM, December 16, 1942, p. 43.

23. Ibid.

24. ECM, May 11, 1932, p. 129. This committee was popularly known as the Refunding Committee.

25. SBC, 1934, p. 41.

26. ECM, May 25, 1934, pp. 172-174.

27. Ibid., p. 173.

28. ECM, May 12, 1937, pp. 47-49.

29. The only record of Executive Committee borrowing to this date was for interest on the Education Board debt.

30. ECM, September 10, 1930, pp. 92-93; A. This provides a full description of the National Memorial Church involvement.

31. ECM, June 15, 1939, p. 95.

32. Porter Routh to AM.

33. Mrs. Raymond Rogers to AM.

34. ECM, May 13, 1941, pp. 171-172.

35. SBC, 1937, p. 43.

36. SBC, 1938, pp. 43-47.

37. ECM, December 14, 1938, p. 104.

38. SBC, 1939, pp. 41-45, 16-18.

39. SBC, 1934, p. 59; cf. SBC 1933, pp. 62f.

40. AB, April 4, 1929, p. 3.

41. QR, July 1983, pp. 70-71.

42. SBC, 1928, p. 40.

43. SBC, 1929, pp. 74-75; cf. SBC 1930, p. 83

44. ECM, January 11, 1934, p. 163.

45. SBC, 1928, pp. 32-33. For a fuller discussion of this subject see chapter 5 of this book.

46. SBC, 1929, p. 74.

47. SBC, 1930, p. 86.

48. ECM, May 13, 1930, p. 77.

49. Ibid., p. 78.

50. SBC, 1929, p. 74-75, items eleven and fourteen.

51. ECM, May 13, 1930, p. 79.

52. AB, April 4, 1929, p. 3.

53. AB, January 21, 1929, p. 5.

54. ECM, September 11, 1930, p. 96.

55. ECM, April 13, 1933, pp. 136-137. Cf. SBC, 1933, pp. 54-55.

56. SBC, 1934, pp. 48.

57. SBC, 1937, p. 33.

58. "State/SBC Cooperative Program Totals," an Executive Committee report.

59. SBC, 1933, pp. 33-34.

60. Mrs. Lucien Matthews, "Charles William Daniel," ESB, Vol. I, 347.

61. SBC, 1951, pp. 56-57.

62. SBC, 1955, p. 74.

63. Ibid.

64. SBC, 1917, p. 12.

65. SBC, 1925, p. 13.

66. SBC, 1927, p. 13.

67. J. M. Crowe, "Isaac Jacobus Van Ness," ECM, Vol. II, pp.1441-1442.

68. I. J. Van Ness, *The Baptist Spirit* (Nashville: Sunday School Board, 1914), p. 137; cf. p. 7.

69. SBC, 1947, p. 55.

7

Postwar Transition
1943-1951

In late December 1943, Southern Baptists paid their last debts, closing the door on more than two decades of denominational uncertainty. Despite the hard times, church membership had nearly doubled, from 2,887,428 in 1918 to 5,493,027 in 1943.[1] Sunday School enrollment was up about the same, from 1,729,208 to 3,322,978. Total Southern Baptist collection plate offerings substantially increased, from $17,852,929 to $63,067,085 annually. In 1918 there were 24,851 churches and in 1943, 25,790, which meant that the average church membership nearly doubled, from 116 to 213.

As important as was the 1943 victory, there was little time for celebration. During the war, the Executive Committee meetings lasted only one day. When the Convention met, it lasted only about four days. Two years, 1943 and 1945, it did not meet. All over the nation, families were savagely torn by the losses of loved ones in the fighting that raged on a dozen fronts. Weary as they were, Baptists generally remained faithful in witness and worship. They gathered regularly in their meetinghouses to celebrate the reign of the Prince of peace.

Those few who attended the Executive Committee meetings brought with them this same expectant faith. As was true during the Great Depression, the official minutes noted little of the sufferings of the times. It was characteristic of the members of the Executive Committee to look ahead with hope. In 1943 there was much to look forward to—movements and events half-hidden in the mists, includ-

137

ing the changing of leadership, the increasing stewardship, the funding of capital needs, the refining of organizational procedures, the providing for new agencies, and the ending the postwar transition. Most apparent at the beginning of the period was the changing of leadership.

Changing the Leadership

Austin Crouch was seventy-four years old in 1943 and still efficient in his work. He had overcome most of his opposition and was widely respected as an elder statesman. Many of his old associates were fading from the scene, "going down the river, one by one."[2] George W. Truett, a friend from their youth, died in the summer of 1944 and was memorialized in a Convention resolution that said, "As the visitor to St. Paul's Cathedral [London] is told, 'If you would see the monument of Sir Christopher Wren, look about you,' so if one is to measure the meaning of George W. Truett, one must look at the Baptist denomination."[3] It was a tribute that could have been applied to Austin Crouch. On the same day of the Truett Memorial, the Convention sent a telegram to Mrs. L. R. Scarborough whose husband, the old Seventy-Five Million champion, was lingering in his last illness. More and more, the executive secretary thought about passing on the torch and quietly slipping into retirement with his faithful "Little Jap." Facing the inevitable, on June 13, 1945, about a month before his seventy-fifth birthday, the "Cardinal" submitted his resignation.[4] "Cardinal" was a private name occasionally given Crouch by Louie D. Newton in tribute to his princely bearing and his rare ability.

The frailties of the flesh were showing everywhere, and the ranks of leadership were thinning. That same day the Executive Committee mourned Mrs. F. W. Armstrong, an eighteen-year veteran of the group: "because of her Christian personality, adorned by the most charming graces and lovely virtues, her fellowship in the ministries of our Master afforded us high inspiration and joy."[5] She had died since the last meeting.

The immediate response of the Executive Committee to Crouch's retirement was the appointment of a special committee to ask him to continue in service. The motion was made by Frank Tripp who sometimes had opposed Crouch but who, in spite of differences, deeply respected the old leader. But as always, Austin Crouch knew his own mind and politely declined. He told the committee that four years before he had planned his resignation to coincide with the Convention's centennial in 1945. In keeping with one of the personal values with which he had rescued the denomination from financial disorder, he kept steadfastly to his plan.[6] He was not entirely successful. Within a year, he experienced painful loss in the sudden death of Mrs. Crouch. Her friends remembered her as one of the "most energetic, gracious and tactful companions any man in public office ever had."[7] Her loss was a double blow to Crouch because soon after losing her, he virtually lost his eyesight. The stress was too much for him. Suddenly, he became almost blind, unable to read or to drive a car.

The search committee at first wavered between two Oklahoma pastors, J. Howard Williams of Oklahoma City and J. W. Storer of Tulsa.[8] But after some confusion and a split vote, it turned to Dr. Edgar Godbold, then the president of Louisiana College and previously the state secretary in Missouri.[9] After Godbold declined, the committee did the unexpected. It recommended the youthful Duke K. McCall, president of the Baptist Bible Institute. Impressed with his proven competence and his platform ability, the Executive Committee, without delay, elected him.[10] Those previously considered belonged more or less to the past; the young man, then thirty-two years old, belonged to the future.

Reared by parents noted for their piety and their devotion to missions, it was the testimony of McCall that he had been compelled into ministry by the Holy Spirit. He was educated in Furman University and Southern Seminary. Open, bright, and personable, he was recognized from his youth as a person of unusual ability. One of his early, older admirers saw him as a man of stunning articulation and superior intelligence, traits that sometimes tempted his critics to think of him as loquacious.[11] Though irrevocably committed to the

Baptists and deeply evangelical in outlook, McCall was not provincially minded. Aristocratic in bearing and a forceful presence and strong voice in any situation, he was sometimes accused of imperiousness. The people closest to McCall knew him to be decisive, disciplined, tenderhearted, and fair-minded. With him at work in the Executive Committee, the denomination began to change, all for the better.

After Crouch, the next to leave Executive Committee leadership was Hight C Moore, who for thirty-one consecutive years had been secretary of the Southern Baptist Convention. He had been one of the prime movers in shaping and preserving the Executive Committee during the frustrating years of debt and depression. Clifton J. Allen once said of him, "Dr. Moore's greatest contribution was his life of goodness and his example of faithfulness in every opportunity of service."[12] Next to go was Walter M. Gilmore, who died suddenly at seventy-six after a long day's work in his office. A Convention memorial used words of Edgar A. Guest to describe him, "To play my little part, not whine that greatest honors are not mine. This, I believe, is all I need for my philosophy and creed."[13] Then, after persistent ill health, the peerless J. E. Dillard resigned early in 1947. The Executive Committee presented him a "parchment" of honor, and the Convention stood in admiring respect. The parchment concluded, "His efficient and enthusiastic promotion of the Cooperative Program has done much to stabilize the financial structure of every . . . agency of this Convention."[14]

Gilmore was succeeded by C. E. Bryant, the youthful editor of the *Arkansas Baptist* who brought with him exceptional skills as writer and publicist. He had previously served as a reporter for the Associated Press and the Religious News Service and had contributed articles to the *Readers Digest.* When Bryant resigned two years later to work for Baylor University, he was succeeded by Albert McClellan, the editor of the *Baptist Messenger.* He was thirty-seven and experienced as pastor and denominational worker. Dillard was succeeded by Merrill D. Moore, a Nashville pastor and a member of the Executive Committee. Moore was a Mississippian and a graduate of

Mississippi College and Southern Seminary. After several short pastorates and a term as president of Tennessee College for Women,
he settled in Nashville as pastor of the Immanuel Baptist Church.
Endowed with a pleasing combination of friendliness and reserve,
he was occasionally misunderstood. Deeply respected by his associates, one of them said that Merrill D. Moore is "one of the most
totally Christian men I have ever known." Within two years, the
average age of Executive Committee professional staff was lowered
by about thirty years.

Changes in Executive Committee chairmen was another weather
vane indicating a shifting in leadership stance. The 1943-1951 era
opened under a veteran leader, Charles W. Daniel, who in 1944 was
nominated for his fifth term but was defeated by a newcomer, J.
Howard Williams, a Texan. Williams served three terms. He was
followed by John H. Buchanan, a distinguished Birmingham pastor
and an old friend of Austin Crouch. A victim of membership rotation, Buchanan was replaced as chairman by George B. Fraser, an
attorney from the District of Columbia. The trait most apparent in
Fraser was his unquestioned integrity. He served five years. Like a
carousel, the great wheel of leadership turned; and, with each stop,
some got off and others got on. After several turns, the faces were
different. The problems—many with different names—were much
the same.

Abounding in Stewardship

The leaders, both old and young, were singing doxologies of
thanksgiving for the rapidly abounding Southern Baptist stewardship. On January 1, 1944, the Convention had something rare for
it, a surplus of $38,846 left over from the Hundred Thousand
Club.[15] Ten years earlier it would have seemed a mountain of
money; but in 1944, compared with the growing needs of the
denomination, it was almost too little. Both mission boards were
facing abundant opportunities for wider scope and greater depth in
mission work. The three seminaries were harried with the prospect
of soldiers returning from the war seeking education for ministry

and of increasing numbers of women desiring seminary education. Some Baptist leaders believed that new seminaries were needed. There were urgent needs in all areas of Baptist life, including social work, women's work, men's work, youth work, ethics leadership, denominational services, and retired ministers' relief, as well as in the established areas of missions and seminary education. The state conventions were also facing challenges of homes for the aging, homes for children, colleges, hospitals, assemblies, and state missions.

Most Baptists were optimistic, but there were those who believed that after the war the nation's economy would fall apart and all the recent gains in the churches would be lost. The real leaders believed that the best was yet to come. The question most on their minds was: How can Southern Baptists take hold of the opportunity to meet the challenge?

A prophetic response to the challenge of the postwar future had come in the 1942 San Antonio Convention, when H. H. Hargroves, Texas, moved "to appoint a Committee to study the needs for world-wide expansion in Foreign Mission work."[16] The motion was approved and the Postwar Planning Committee was appointed. Its report was delayed because of the cancellation of the 1943 Convention. Meanwhile, the Subcommittee on Cooperation and Enlistment of the Executive Committee had also been looking to the future. It was under the leadership of Louie D. Newton, the chairman, and J. E. Dillard, the director of promotion.

Joint meetings of the two committees resulted in the "Cooperative Centennial Program," an emphasis for 1945, the centennial year of the Southern Baptist Convention.[17] As approved by the 1944 Convention,[18] the plan included: (1) Intensive promotion of almost everything the denomination was doing—evangelism, stewardship, education, life enlistment, missions, finance, and prayer. This was probably the plan's greatest weakness because, in emphasizing everything, it emphasized nothing. (2) The states as equal partners. Thus it avoided the mistake of the Hundred Thousand Club. The committee said,

Certainly the Southern Baptist Convention nor its Executive Committee has any right or desire to dictate to the state organizations in any way, but since the constituencies are the same and appeals for both state and southwide causes must be made to the same people it is wise if not imperative that we work together to prevent conflict and over-lapping. We should confer with the state organizations through their executive secretaries seeking a feasible and equitable plan of co-operation in this Centennial Crusade.[19]

(3) A $20,000,000 Centennial Thank Offering was set to be taken in April 1945. Whether the plan was actually developed jointly by the Executive Committee and the state secretaries is unclear, but considering the number of secretaries absent from the planning meeting, probably not.

The "Centennial Cooperative Program" failed. Promoted as the "The Centennial Crusade," the Thank Offering was barely noticed. It brought a meager $237,674 to Southern Baptist causes. Assuming that the states received about the same amount, the total may have been around $500,000, far short of the expected $20,000,000.[20] However, the collection plate dollar in 1945 increased by 28 percent, from $76,588,616 (1944) to $98,458,425 (1945); and gifts to mission increased 30 percent, from $17,300,389 (1944) to $22,490,751 (1945).[21]

Almost nothing was said in the reports about the success of the comprehensive emphases plan that included everything. Why was the Centennial Crusade not totally successful? Probably because (1) the plan was too comprehensive, like prescribing a whole drugstore for one ulcer; (2) there was still insufficient cooperation between the Executive Committee and the state conventions both in planning and promotion; (3) the pressures of wartime worries sapped the interests of the people; and (4) the momentum for promotion was lost when the 1945 annual Convention was canceled.

Although there was some disappointment with the campaign, the the leaders were encouraged when offerings for the year indicated a growing appreciation for the cooperative work. But there was still not enough money, especially for the critical needs of foreign missions. Prompted by worldwide distress due to the dislocations and sufferings caused by a war and influenced by the urging of the Foreign Mission Board, the Executive Committee asked the Convention meeting in Miami to approve a $3,500,000 world relief offering for the summer of 1946.[22] The plan was "to be in harmony with the accepted methods in each of the cooperating states. . . . All promotional literature and publicity be uniform and that it be prepared by the Executive Committee in co-operation with the secretaries, editors of state papers, and the executives of southwide agencies." The funds were to be distributed by the Foreign Mission Board as part of its mission program.

This may have appeared to some to have been a departure in procedure, for, in effect, the Executive Committee was taking responsibility for a special promotion exclusively for the work of one agency. There was no rule against it, but was it a wise thing to do? The move was probably justified because it was for world relief and mission rehabilitation purposes. The need was urgent, and the appeal was widespread. Frank Tripp was again part of the planning group.[23] The result was a concise single-barreled, understandable plan that was approved June 11. It aimed at a blitz offering by September 30.

The offering was successful, which must have been reassuring to Duke K. McCall, in office since the first of January.[24] The total amount raised was $3,743,300. Cooperation between the state conventions and the Southern Baptist Convention was at its best. McCall reported, "Every state adopted a goal, and nearly all of them reached and some far exceeded their goals." He also announced that "the states have adopted tithing goals, the total of these being more than one million." This was called "a good beginning." The long-lookers had set their eyes on a stewardship performance greater than the official goals; and by securing the promise of tithers, they had pushed their success far into the future.

Giant strides were made in the Executive Committee's approach to promotion. Every year brought better understanding of Southern

Baptist Convention and state Baptist convention relationships. Leaders gained new insights on planning and communication of plans. Through trial and error, and stimulated by a determination to make cooperation work, the leaders gradually developed by 1951 a method by which the conventions could work together in the joint promotion of stewardship without overlapping and friction. The general features of the method were:

(1) The Southern Baptist Convention Executive Committee and the state conventions jointly planned stewardship promotion in cooperation with SBC agencies. Staff leadership for the planning was furnished by the Executive Committee.

(2) The Executive Committee provided the general promotional materials available to the state conventions and to the churches at nominal prices.

(3) State Conventions supplemented the general literature with specialized publications of their own.

(4) State conventions through the offices of the state executive secretaries were primarily responsible for the field promotion of stewardship.

(5) The state secretaries were generally responsible for maintaining contact directly with the churches, though the Southern Baptist Convention retained the right of access to the churches.

(6) Executive Committee staff was available to assist the state convention staffs in field promotion. It worked directly with individual churches and associations if invited, or if it was developing or testing methods for use in the churches and associations.

(7) Planning was done in joint promotion conferences, which at first had met only on demand, but later met annually and semiannually. Staffing was provided by the Executive Committee.

These understandings had begun to take shape in the 1940s under the leadership of J. E. Dillard and Merrill D. Moore, with significant assistance from Frank Tripp and Louie D. Newton. Both

Austin Crouch and Duke K. McCall provided policy-making guidance and cooperation. The purpose of the Executive Committee's role in promotion was more precisely defined when the name of the old Committee on Cooperation and Enlistment was changed to Promotion Committee.[25] It was during this period that Louie D. Newton made some of his most important contributions. He was a man of unusual personal presence, all the more impressive because of his broad, appealing smile and his sincere common touch. A skillful debater in a day when debate rather than conversation shaped Executive Committee decisions, he usually sat in the same chair, near the front and to the right of the podium, ready to face the crowd and join in all of the discussion. Tall and masculine in temperament, it was easy for him to hold the platform against opponents, though in manner he was most courteous. His speeches were homespun and indirect but effective, and he was on guard against the possibilities the Executive Committee's assumption of Convention prerogatives and agency rights. Deeply interested in the denominational program as it touched the churches, he took special joy in his membership on the Promotion Committee, and on its predecessor, the Committee on Cooperation and Enlistment. For nearly two decades, thousands of churches displayed brightly colored banners with the words: "Every Baptist a Tither." One legend is that the banner came into existence when a small committee was attempting to find some new promotional approach. Newton grasped his pen, wrote the words, and said something like, "That is the poster," and so it was for perhaps a million printing impressions and twenty years of exposure.

Upon becoming director of promotion in 1947, Merrill D. Moore approached the task with the energy and vision of one oriented to modern promotional and advertising methods. Very early, he helped to refine the understandings for the joint promotion of stewardship, taking care to make state conventions equal partners in the planning as well as in the expediting of plans. Moore began the regular use of annual and semiannual promotion conferences. These included, for the first time, the associates of state secretaries who were carrying stewardship promotion responsibilities. During this period, Moore began the study of the methods of professional fund-raising companies. He wanted as soon as feasible to incorporate some of these methods into church building fund campaigns for Southern Baptist churches. Among the projects that he introduced for local church use was TEV (Tithers' Enlistment Visitation), an educational approach to the every member canvass.

In the postwar years, the use of stewardship literature in the churches dramatically increased. In 1951 the Executive Committee alone produced a total of 4,801,871 copies of twenty-four different items that were distributed mostly through the offices of the state secretaries.[26] The Baptist Bulletin Service circulated 674,300 copies weekly through 4,000 churches. The *Baptist Program* was published ten times during the year and was sent without charge to 23,000 church and denominational ministers. These materials were supportive of the Cooperative Program and were generally used by the churches to inform members on the work of the Southern Baptist Convention.

The lure of new programs and methods and the increasing preoccupation with building larger and better church meetinghouses had not turned attention from world needs. Southern Baptists still could respond to a lofty mission challenge. On Thursday evening, May 20, 1948, M. Theron Rankin, the new executive secretary of the Foreign Mission Board, in making his annual report to the Southern Baptist Convention said, "Six million Southern Baptists cannot continue to answer the world call with six hundred missionaries and an average per capita gift of seventy cents a year. The God in whom we believe, the faith which we proclaim, and the need of the world all call for ADVANCE."[27] The Advance Program became immediate reality, not only for foreign missions but also for home missions. In June, Rankin carried his concern to the Executive Committee; and from that day until the middle 1970s, the Advance Program became one of the basic financial and promotional concerns of the Executive Committee. Even in the 1970s and 1980s when the term *advance* ceased to have significant promotional impact, Executive Committee interests did not wane. Under the committee's leadership, the Convention still pursued advance objectives, by adapting other terms like "Mission Challenge" and "Bold Mission Thrust."

Funding the Capital Needs

Part of the forward march was to provide the institutions with a massive building and renovation program, better field facilities for missionaries, and better quarters and classrooms for seminary students. Many of the existing buildings were substandard, and others were urgently in need of modernization. The smaller agencies were asking for space in which to carry on their work. Even in the early 1940s, the denomination's leaders looked far ahead to the end of World War II and saw that once peace had come and new construction was possible, all Convention properties should be improved. Some were even dreaming of new seminaries and new assemblies.

The first move had been made in 1943 when the Committee on Cooperation and Enlistment called for a survey of "both capital and operating needs" of the agencies, "and that the same be gone over by the Executive Committee before presentation to the Convention."[28] The next move was by the Administrative Committee in February of 1945 when it made a second survey. The surveys were likely prompted by (1) growing awareness of the needs of the agencies, (2) knowledge that many churches were beginning to plan for buildings, and (3) hints from the agencies that they would soon be seeking permission to make special solicitations for capital needs.

The second survey revealed even more need than the first. Something had to be done.[29] The result was the first Southern Baptist Convention Capital Needs Program authorized in 1946, not a special solicitation but a vital part of the Southern Baptist Convention Cooperative Program. For 1946 the goal was fixed at $3,000,000, half of the expected Cooperative Program total for the year. The agencies sharing the funds were[30]

Foreign Mission Board	$1,250,000
Home Mission Board	367,900

Relief and Annuity Board	100,000
Southern Baptist Seminary	450,000
Southwestern Baptist Seminary	450,000
Baptist Bible Institute	400,000
American Baptist Seminary	45,000
TOTAL	$3,062,900

Similar allocations were voted annually through 1951, though each year more of the total Cooperative Program was needed for agency operations. By 1951 the annual amount available for capital purposes was down to $2,500,000. Agencies included had risen from seven to fourteen. The additional ones were WMU Training School, Southern Baptist Hospital, Baptist Brotherhood, Radio Commission, and two new seminaries, Golden Gate and Southeastern. The 1951 total Cooperative Program Allocation "someday" Budget was:[31]

Cooperative Program Operations	$4,500,000
Cooperative Program Capital Needs	2,500,000
Cooperative Program Advance Program	3,000,000
TOTAL	$10,000,000

The mission boards were granted the privilege of using any portion of their capital funds for operations, as needed. Most years the Advance funds were divided between the two mission boards, 75 percent for foreign missions, and 25 percent for home missions. There were strategic advantages in the Capital Needs Program. It:

(1) provided substantial funds for capital needs,

(2) enabled the Convention to wisely pace agency operations growth,

(3) went far in eliminating the need for special competing solicitations by SBC agencies, and

(4) provided the Convention a way of allocating capital funds proportionate to the needs of the agencies.

In 1927, the first offices of the Executive Committee were located in the Frost Building of the Sunday School Board, Nashville, Tennessee.

E. Y. Mullins, Kentucky, a leading advocate for a strong Executive Committee, was president (chairman) of the Executive Committee, 1921-1923.

I. J. Van Ness, Tennessee, the executive secretary for the Sunday School Board was a supportive friend of the Executive Committee, 1917-1935, during its most trying years.

Hight C Moore, Tennessee, was a member of the Executive Committee, 1927-1946. In the early years, he served as secretary and as treasurer.

George W. Truett, Texas, was president (chairman) of the restructured Executive Committee, 1927-1929. He was widely known as a prince of preachers.

Mrs. F. W. Armstrong was a member of the Executive Committee from 1927 to 1945. From 1933 to 1945, she was the president of Woman's Missionary Union.

J. E. Dillard, Tennessee, was director of stewardship promotion for the Executive Committee, 1936-1947. He originated the slogan: "Debt Free in Forty-three."

Frank Tripp, pastor of the First Baptist Church, Saint Joseph, Missouri, and a member of the SBC Executive Committee, was the founder of the Hundred Thousand Club.

Austin Crouch, executive secretary of the Executive Committee, 1927-1945, was the leader most responsible for its renewal and restructuring in 1927. Fifty-seven years old when he assumed office, he was often credited with saving the denomination from financial ruin.

Duke Kimbrough McCall succeeded Austin Crouch in 1946. He served as executive secretary-treasurer until 1951 when he resigned to accept the presidency of The Southern Baptist Theological Seminary. He later was elected president of the Baptist World Alliance to serve for the 1980-1985 term.

From 1927, the chief executives of the Southern Baptist Convention agencies regularly attended the meetings of the Executive Committee. In 1952, they were all present except one for the December meetings. Seated (left to right): Roland Q. Leavell, New Orleans Baptist Theological Seminary; M. Theron Rankin, Foreign Mission Board; J. B. Lawrence, Home Mission Board; T. L. Holcomb, Sunday School Board; Alma Hunt, Woman's Missionary Union; Porter Routh, SBC Executive Committee. Standing (left to right): A. C. Miller, Social Service Commission; Dupree Jordon, (acting), Radio Commission; Norman W. Cox, Historical Commission; Sydnor L. Stealey, Southeastern Baptist Theological Seminary; L. S. Sedberry, Commission on the American Baptist Theological Seminary. George W. Schroeder, Brotherhood Commission; R. Orin Cornett, Education Commission; J. M. Dawson, Public Affairs Committee; Charles H. Bolton, Southern Baptist Foundation; Duke K. McCall, Southern Baptist Theological Seminary; Harold K. Graves, Golden Gate Baptist Theological Seminary; Frank Tripp, Southern Baptist Hospital; Walter B. Alexander, Relief and Annuity Board. E. D. Head, Southwestern Baptist Theological Seminary, was absent when this picture was made.

Executive Committee staff leadership in 1951 was definitely on the youthful side: Left to right: Duke K. McCall, executive secretary-treasurer; Porter Routh, recording secretary; Merrill D. Moore, director of stewardship promotion; and Albert McClellan, director of publications.

In 1957, the chairman of the Executive Committee was Homer G. Lindsay, Florida, (seated right); the secretary was Elwyn N. Wilkinson, Kentucky, (seated left); and the vice-chairman was T. K. Rucker, Arkansas, (standing center). With them are Merrill D. Moore and Porter Routh, Executive Committee staff.

Typical of the Executive Committees of the 1950s was the one for 1954. Seated on the first row are: (left to right) J.D. Grey, a former president of the Baptist Convention and a member of the Executive Committee; Louie D. Newton, a former president of the Convention; W. Douglas Hudgins, vice-chairman of the Executive Committee; Mrs. George R. Martin, president of Woman's Missionary Union; Porter Routh, executive secretary-treasurer of the Executive Committee; Casper C. Warren, president (chairman) of the executive Committee; Austin Crouch, executive secretary emeritus of the Executive Committee; Mrs. Gordon Maddrey, a member of the Executive Committee; J. W. Storer, president of the Convention; Oliver R. Shields, secretary of the Executive Committee; and J. Norris Palmer, a member of the Executive Committee. One of the few such pictures known to exist.

Women were members of the Executive Committee from 1927. Many more women attended its meetings, among them representatives of the Woman's Missionary Union. (Left to right), Billie Pate, Young Women's Association promotion associate; Betty Brewer, Girls Auxiliary director; Mrs. Robert Fling, Texas, president of Woman's Missionary Union and a member of the Executive Committee; Porter Routh, executive secretary of the Executive Committee; and Elaine Dickson, Women's Missionary Society promotion associate.

In about 1954, the Executive Committee commissioned a portrait of Austin Crouch, the first executive secretary. It was unveiled at a meeting of the Executive Committee by Ruth Nelson, longtime bookkeeper for the Executive Committee. Also present was J. W. Storer, a close personal friend of Crouch and president of the Southern Baptist Convention.

Porter Wroe Routh, executive secretary-treasurer of the Southern Baptist Convention Executive Committee from September 1951 to July 31, 1979. A layman, Routh had been editor of the Oklahoma *Baptist Messenger* and secretary of the Department of Survey, Statistics, and Information, for The Sunday School Board.

Harold Clark Bennett, executive secretary-treasurer (later president) of the Southern Baptist Convention Executive Committee, from August 1, 1979. For many years a pastor, Bennett came to the Executive Committee from the position of executive secretary-treasurer of the board of directors of the Florida Baptist State Convention.

Executive Committee meetings have traditionally been open to everyone. Major questions are debated by the Committee as a whole, and sometimes visitors take part in the debate.

Three men who served the Executive Committee in the office of executive secretary-treasurer: Porter Wroe Routh, 1951-1979; Duke Kimbrough McCall, 1946-1951; and Harold Clark Bennett, 1951-.

Merrill D. Moore, Director of Stewardship Promotion, 1948-1959.

Albert McClellan, director of publications, 1949-1959; associate executive secretary and director of program planning, 1959-1980.

John H. Williams, director of financial planning, 1959-1976.

W. C. Fields was elected director of public relations in 1959, and in 1984, had served twenty-five years in that position.

Reginald M. McDonough, elected associate executive secretary and director of program planning in 1981.

Timothy A. Hedquist was elected director of financial planning in 1978.

Left photo
The Bible, the cross, and the world, are combined to symbolize the authority, the mission, and the field of Southern Baptist purpose. The great medallion was later moved to the new building at the corner of Commerce street and Ninth Avenue, North. In this picture, Southern Seminary students are displaying the signatures of their fellow seminarians signifying appreciation for the part the Cooperative Program had in their seminary education.

Bottom photo
The second home of the Southern Baptist Executive Committee was a Virginia greenstone and aluminium sheathed eight-sided building at 460 James Robertson Parkway, Nashville, Tennessee. Constructed in 1962 and occupied in 1963, it served its occupants well until they outgrew its limited space. It was so solidly designed that the contractors claimed it could be turned sideways and rolled to the Mississippi River. Perhaps the building will stand for years as a testimony both to the great strength and the continuing growth of Southern Baptists.

The Southern Baptist Convention Building at Commerce Street and Ninth Avenue, North, Nashville, Tennessee, the new home of the Executive Committee and six other Southern Baptist Convention agencies and organizations.

Testing Executive Committee Strength

A few Baptists still occasionally questioned the usefulness of the Executive Committee. Even in Nashville, where its offices were located, Southern Baptists generally did not understand either its work or its relationships. It was not uncommon in the early 1950s for its employees to be introduced as working for the executive committee of The Sunday School Board. This may have been due to the location of its offices in the premises of The Sunday School Board. General misunderstanding may have been a holdover from the early 1940s, when it was even less understood. Some Baptists still felt that it interfered with the democratic processes of the Convention. Victor I. Masters of the *Western Recorder* had written in 1940, "Free discussion of S. B. C. messengers is not wanted. It is practically destroyed."[32] While Masters was one of a few public critics, there were private critics who questioned the Executive Committee's leadership. The few remaining criticisms were not directed at the Executive Committee itself, but at its decisions.

In the spring of 1944, the Executive Committee had to decide what to do with the $38,846 surplus from the Hundred Thousand Club. Austin Crouch and the Administrative Committee saw the money as a way to begin a Southern Baptist Convention Reserve Fund for emergency purposes. A plan was presented to the Executive Committee in March that called for a goal of $4,000,000 to be started with the surplus. The fund then would grow, assisted by $5,000 monthly from The Sunday School Board, surpluses from the Convention Operating Budget, averages from the Cooperative Program, and 10 percent of the profits of Southern Baptist Hospital.[33] The same recommendation proposed to reduce mission board Cooperative Program budget allocations to support the near bankrupt old annuity plan of the Relief and Annuity Board. This was the first retirement plan created in 1917 without sound actuarial advice. Since the retirement income of hundreds of ministers who had invested in the plan was at stake, the plan was regarded as a legal and moral obligation of the Convention.

By the pre-Convention meeting of the Executive Committee in May, the plan had gathered considerable opposition. The first dissenting voices were raised by the agencies.[34] Theodore F. Adams presented a resolution from the Foreign Mission Board in opposition. Charles E. Maddrey, also of the Foreign Mission Board, asked that "the present arrangement not be disturbed." J. B. Lawrence spoke to the proposed cutting of Home Mission Board funds from 23.5 percent to 21 percent and outlined the "necessity for a greatly enlarged program of Home Missions." Kathleen Mallory "expressed her sentiments as an individual woman, and not as representing W. M. U., opposing the change in allocations of the Home and Foreign Mission Boards." Louis J. Bristow said that the charter of the Southern Baptist Hospital would not permit the donation of 10 percent of its net income to Convention agencies. After discussion and a substitute motion by Frank Tripp, the plan was referred to the Administrative Committee.

The next day the Administrative Committee reported again without any change in its recommendation. Tripp was ready with his substitute which, like his Hundred Thousand Club Plan, eleven years before, was brief and simple. A Convention Reserve Fund was not needed because the Business and Financial Plan had made the agencies responsible for their own reserve funds, and in Tripp's opinion they were fully capable of managing them. His plan called for an operating budget to cover miscellaneous needs, including—for the first time—the needs of the Executive Committee. The surplus of the Hundred Thousand Club would apply to the old annuity plan.[35] The table of percentages for the Cooperative Program Allocation Budget for 1945 would remain the same, except that money for the hospital would be eliminated and the money for the three seminaries slightly increased. When the vote was taken, eleven were for Tripp's substitute and eleven against. Charles W. Daniel, as chairman of the Executive Committee, broke the tie in favor of the Administrative Committee Plan. Tripp at once announced that he would take a minority report to the Convention, which he did later in the week; and when it was put to a vote, his plan was accepted by the messengers.[36] The Executive Committee discovered that it could survive sharp differences of opinions and even lose a Convention vote without loss of prestige.

The second testing also related to the Cooperative Program Allocations Budget. In 1946 J. B. Lawrence circulated editorials that objected to the Executive Committee's proposed table of percentages for 1947 that reduced the Home Mission Board allocation from 23.33 percent to 18 percent, a painful loss of 5.33 percentage points. He also had publicly appealed for a great increase in the Annie Armstrong Offering to offset the reduction.[37] The Foreign Mission Board had been reduced by four percentage points from 50 percent to 46 percent but did not publicly protest.[38]

The Executive Committee responded to Lawrence with a public reprimand prepared by the Administrative Committee. Lawrence explained his position, and the matter was referred to a small committee to confer further with him. Two things happened.

(1) Lawrence issued a statement seeking reconciliation:[39]

I sincerely regret that anything I have ever written has caused members of the Committee to think or feel that I was antagonistic to the Committee or that I would purposely do anything that would question the integrity of any member of the Committee itself. I want here and now to pledge my full cooperation, and to assure you, one and all, that you will never again hear a word or read a word from me that will cause you to doubt or question the sincerity of the statement I am making.

(2) The Executive Committee stayed with its recommendation, proving that it could make a tough decision involving one of the agencies and stay with it.

Why did Lawrence write the editorials? For more than fifteen years, he had been carefully building a contemporary home mission program. With the increasing availability of funds and the final payment of the Home Mission Board debt in 1943, he was making progress, especially in the far West and the North Central pioneer areas. To be stymied by forces he could not control aroused his fighting instincts.

Why did the Executive Committee find it necessary to reduce allocations to home and foreign missions? Possibly: (1) the pressure of the old annuity plan, (2) the three seminaries were faced with the welcomed challenge of hundreds of returning soldiers crowding their facilities, (3) the two mission boards had steady incomes from the two rapidly growing mission offerings, (4) smaller agencies were also growing and needed help with their programs, and (5) it may also have been that the hundred-year-old conflict between state and home mission programs was still a factor. The fairest judgment seems to be that with its eyes on the total work and resources of the Convention, the Executive Committee was endeavoring fairly and honestly to respond to all agency needs.

The third testing also involved the Home Mission Board. In 1948, because of the continued financial pressures of the old annuity plan and of the rapidly growing seminaries, the Executive Committee proposed to cut the Home Mission Board another one and one-half percent.[40] The recommendation was passed by the Convention without discussion. A few minutes later Fred Eastham, a prominent Missouri pastor and popular radio preacher who had once been director of evangelism for the board, moved for reconsideration. When the motion carried, he offered an amendment cutting the seminaries by one-half percent each, increasing the old annuity plan by one-half percent, and restoring one percent to the Home Mission Board. After discussion, the amendment was adopted. That was on Wednesday afternoon. On Friday morning, W. Douglas Hudgins of Mississippi succeeded in getting the question again reconsidered and offered a motion to approve the original recommendation of the Executive Committee. Following stormy debate, in which the eloquent Eastham was one of the leading contenders, the Hudgins motion was approved. Again the Executive Committee survived a determination to firmly stand behind a recommendation it believed to be the best course of action for the Southern Baptist Convention.

Refining the Organizational Procedures

The most important structural change in Southern Baptist life in the postwar period was the 1946 Southern Baptist Convention decision to place the memberships of the standing committees and the boards of agencies on rotation.[41] With some justification, some Baptists regarded long terms as injurious to denominational processes. Others, also standing on firm ground, believed that long terms contributed to denominational stability. The popular perception was that the long terms meant knowledge and knowledge meant personal power. Many believed that the real danger in not rotating lay in a few leaders who used the power they had gained from long membership for unwholesome control of the group. This was thought to be particularly true of agencies with nonrotating local boards of trustees. The Convention recognized this as a possibility and changed the system in 1946.

Of the members of the Executive Committee appointed in 1927, three were still serving in 1945: Mrs. F. W. Armstrong, Hight C Moore, and Charles W. Daniel. Some of the other long-term members still serving in 1946 were Louie D. Newton, sixteen years; Henry W. Tiffany, Virginia, nine years; George Ragland, Kentucky, nine years; and John H. Buchanan, Alabama, eleven years. These were able people, and their positive contributions to Southern Baptist Convention life is unquestioned. Most of the members of the Executive Committee of this period served much shorter terms. In fact, a study of the membership roles of Executive Committee members from 1927 to 1946 shows little difference in the average length of terms, before and after rotation. In the long run, rotation did not hurt the quality of Executive Committee leadership. The loss of established leaders may have made some difference, but other leaders soon emerged.

With McCall's election, there were two important structural changes in the Executive Committee. Austin Crouch had not been in charge of all the work and all the personnel. There had been a separate treasurer, at first, Hight C Moore who was a member of the

Executive Committee, and later, Walter M. Gilmore who was an employee. Also from 1936, with the coming of J. E. Dillard as the first full-time director of promotion, the Executive Committee had two executive officers, one for administration and one for promotion, both directly responsible to the Executive Committee. They made separate reports and had separate budgets. It was an arrangement common among associational-type organizations of the times, including some Baptist state conventions. At the time of McCall's election, administrative lines were clearly drawn when in the same meeting, the Executive Committee approved a recommendation of the nominating committee that said, "The Executive Secretary shall be the Executive Officer of the entire work of the Executive Committee of the Southern Baptist Convention, including the present divisions or departments of the Committee's work, or/and such other personnel or activities as may be authorized by the Executive Committee."[42] The second structural change came a year later, when upon the death of Walter M. Gilmore, McCall was elected treasurer.

Making Room for the New Agencies

The five and one-half year tenure of Dr. Duke K. McCall was relatively short but extremely busy. It was his responsibility to oversee the moving of two older agencies to full-time staff status and the assimilation of three new agencies and one new subsidiary institution into Convention life. His chief role was to lead in solving the financial problems of expansion.

The first of the older agencies to become full time was the Public Affairs Committee in Washington, D. C., in 1946; and the second was the Social Service Commission in Louisville in 1948. The Social Service Commission was renamed the Christian Life Commission in 1953.

The first of the new agencies to become full time was the Southern Baptist Foundation.[43] A foundation had been first proposed in 1927; but nothing became of it, except that the Executive Committee was recognized as the Convention's fiduciary agent. This designation included the care of Convention trust funds.[44] In 1942 Charles E. Maddrey, executive secretary of the Foreign Mission Board, in a spirited speech to the Executive Committee, described "the potential gold mine that Southern Baptists now have in soliciting bequests from their people."[45] At the next meeting, a special committee was encouraged to move ahead in planning for the foundation.[46] This resulted in a charter approved for recommendation to the Convention.[47] The proposal made to the Convention was for a foundation wholly under the control of the Executive Committee. After an amendment by L. E. Barton to make the trustees directly responsible to the Convention, the charter was approved, and a special committee was appointed "to set up the Foundation and select its members."[48] This is the only SBC agency ever originated by the Executive Committee.

The special committee did not report until 1946, due to the cancellation of the 1945 Convention. In 1946 it proposed a new charter that removed any suggestion that it had a subsidiary relationship to the Executive Committee.[49] Trustees were elected, and the executive secretary of the Executive Committee was appointed to "serve as Executive Secretary-Treasurer of the Southern Baptist Foundation, unless otherwise provided by the Directors."[50] For nearly three years, the Foundation was operated from the office of Duke K. McCall, the executive secretary of the Executive Committee. Under his leadership, all of the trust funds of the Executive Committee were transferred to the Foundation for management. Early in 1949, Charles H. Bolton of Florida was elected the first full-time executive secretary.

Beginning in 1945 and continuing for six years, many of the Executive Committee sessions were concerned with the rapidly growing interest in the establishment of new seminaries. The interest began with the appointment of the Committee to Survey Capital Needs in February of 1945. To do its work, the committee utilized subcommittees, one of which was a committee to survey Baptist seminaries. The agenda of this subcommittee was expanded to consider proposals for two new seminaries.

In 1945 the Ministers' Conference of the Buncombe Association in North Carolina had petitioned the Executive Committee to consider turning Ridgecrest into wintertime use as a seminary campus.[51] In the same session, A. F. Crittendon renewed an earlier effort of Baptists in the West by calling "attention to the imperative need for trained leaders in California."[52] Fifteen months later the "Special Committee on New Seminary," to whom the two proposals had been referred for study, told the Executive Committee "that any further action in regard to a new seminary should be taken by a committee set up by the Southern Baptist Convention." Its reason: "We do not feel that the Executive Committee should take initiative in seeking to establish a new theological seminary."[53] The Executive Committee agreed; in 1947 the Convention appointed a Theological Education Survey Committee with John H. Buchanan as chairman. Utilizing studies done by Porter Routh and James E. Dillard, this committee recommended in 1949 the creation of a new enlarged and more representative committee.[54] This new Committee on Theological Education under the chairmanship of J. W. Storer in 1950 recommended and the Convention approved acceptance of two new seminaries into the Southern Baptist Convention family of agencies, Golden Gate in California, and Southeastern in North Carolina.[55] Duke K. McCall was involved in all of the negotiations, and the Executive Committee was kept fully informed. This was necessary because it required considerable study to bend the Cooperative Program to absorb two major institutions at one time.

Why did the Executive Committee back away in 1946 from recommending the creation of the new seminaries? Porter Routh, who served as a staff person to the Survey Committee and who at the time was senior secretary of the Convention, thought it was possibly due to: (1) the need for Convention involvement in large new projects, (2) the desire to avoid unnecessary criticism of the Executive Committee from friends of the agencies heavily dependent upon the Cooperative Program, and (3) the wish to keep in a position to counsel the committee in event of strong differences of opinion.[56]

After negotiation between the Executive Committee and the Southern Baptist Historical Society,[57] and the creation of a special Convention Committee on Preservation of Baptist History, the Historical Society was officially recognized as a Convention agency and included in the list of Convention commissions in 1947.[58] A commission was substituted for the society in 1951, and its offices and library were moved to Nashville and housed in The Sunday School Board.[59]

The cry for a "western Ridgecrest" came about the time Baptists spread into the far West. Some of them said that they were tired of the long-distance trips to North Carolina, and some even claimed that the future of Southern Baptists lay in the West. In 1940 the Executive Committee asked the Convention to drop consideration of a southwestern assembly "in view of present conditions."[60] The question was revived in 1947; and on recommendation of the Executive Committee, a Southern Baptist Convention committee was appointed to study and locate a site, and to report to the Executive Committee.[61]

The majority of the special committee finally decided on a site near Harrison, Arkansas, and recommended it to the Executive Committee. The minority, however, recommended a site at Glorieta, New Mexico.[62] After brief review by the Administrative Committee, both reports were referred back to the Convention committee for more study. In 1949 the Western Assembly Committee recommended the Arkansas site to the Southern Baptist Convention, meeting in Oklahoma City with a large Western delegation present.[63] A motion by Philip C. McGahey of New Mexico substituted Glorieta, New Mexico, for Harrison, Arkansas. The Convention accepted the McGahey motion. In the next order, Duke K. McCall moved "that the motion as amended be referred to the Sunday School Board as to what is involved in the development of site at Glorieta, New Mexico, and no other site, and the Sunday School Board report to this Convention next year." The motion was approved. The Sunday School Board completed its investigations; and in 1950 the Executive committee recommended that The Sunday

School Board be authorized to develop the assembly and that the property be deeded by the Executive Committee to the board.[64] Earlier that year the Executive Committee had accepted conveyance from the New Mexico Convention. Over a five-year period, the Executive Committee had been drawn into the struggle to begin the Western assembly, partly because of legal reasons, and partly because of the inability of a large annual Convention to examine carefully all of the details necessary for a right decision. At one point, the Executive Committee appeared to have the right to act on the acceptance of property, but it declined to do so without Convention sanction.

This was in 1950 at the same annual Convention in which the two new seminaries were approved. The Convention met that year for the first time in a city that was not in the traditional South—in Chicago on the banks of Lake Michigan. In touching both ocean shores, and in meeting inside the doors of the North, the Southern Baptist Convention declared itself a truly national body. A few weeks later Northern Baptists, meeting in Boston, became American Baptists.[65]

Broadening the Horizons

About the time Duke K. McCall appeared in Southern Baptist life, the denomination became more news conscious. State papers began to change dramatically. Articles were shorter, and less promotional material was printed. There was more news, especially of national and world significance. Where Crouch lingered in the background, McCall was highly visible. Because of his insights, his personality, and his speaking ability, he was quoted frequently in the newspapers and on the radio. A few months before McCall began his work with the Executive Committee, The Sunday School Board employed Porter Routh, a professional journalist, as director of its Department of Survey and Statistics. At the request of the state Baptist editors, Routh began weekly news releases under the acronym, SBPA, for Southern Baptist Press Association. This continued for about a year until the arrival of C. E. Bryant, another professional journalist, as the new director of publicity for the Executive Committee. Routh suggested to McCall that his weekly press releases were more appropriate for the Executive Committee than for Survey and Statistics.[66] The transfer was made, and, in his first releases, Bryant shortened SBPA in keeping with a practice being considered by some state papers. It became BP for Baptist Press. In 1947 the Baptist Press was reported to the Convention as "a completely new service of the Executive Committee."[67]

Bryant's superb news sensitivity and exceptional personal skill gave the Baptist Press an impressive professional content. It was well accepted, both by Baptist newsmagazines and secular newspapers. The Executive Committee told the Convention that the use of the Baptist Press "in the Convention territory, especially in the state Baptist papers, serves as a unifying and promotional stimulant—uniting the brethren in fellowship through information and promoting through sharing of new ideas."[68] When Bryant left the Executive Committee in 1949, he was praised for "the commendable increase in publicity media during his tenure."[69] To him must go the credit for a solid professional launching of the Baptist Press as part of the Executive Committee's responsibility for "the general work of publicity for the Convention in cooperation with the agencies of the Convention."[70]

Ending the Postwar Transition

After the untimely death of President Ellis A. Fuller in 1950, the trustees of The Southern Baptist Theological Seminary searched for almost a year before asking Duke K. McCall to take the president's chair. He resigned from the Executive Committee in the summer of 1951 to assume his new responsibility at the beginning of the fall term. His experiences on the Executive Committee had proved his mettle and had greatly matured his understanding of the denomination. He had made significant and lasting contributions to the life and work of Southern Baptists. While he was with the Executive Committee, he began to show early signs of his interest in Baptist work throughout the world. Though his tenure had been brief, he could leave, assured that he had done his job well. In the five and one-half years since his election in December of 1945, Duke Kimbrough McCall, one of the youngest of all Southern Baptist executives:

- Gave the Executive Committee a visibility and acceptance it had not previously had, accomplished principally through his writing, his public speaking, and his skill in working with the public press.
- Preserved the Executive Committee as a firm and responsible, yet unobstrusive presence in Southern Baptist affairs.
- Served as a wise and impartial counselor in the establishment of Glorieta Conference Center, the two new seminaries, the Historical Commission, the Southern Baptist Foundation, and the Baptist Joint Committee on Public Affairs.
- Maintained a strong head and a steady hand in the interpretation and administration of the Business and Financial Plan.
- More convincingly identified Southern Baptists with world Baptists through his consistent and personable presence in the Baptist World Alliance.
- Helped increase the respect of other denominations for the Convention, while holding firmly to Southern Baptist independence in ecumenical relationships.
- Instituted the management principle of executive control into the Executive Committee program leadership and staff supervision.
- Made the office of Executive Secretary which was important under Austin Crouch even more important.

McCall did not solve all of the problems. There were still critics of the Executive Committee, especially on the fringes of the denomination. Also, after five years he still was not "Mr. Southern Baptist" to all Baptists, East and West. Born in Mississippi, reared in Memphis, educated at Furman and Southern, he was regarded by some as Eastern in his thought and spirit. Though he regretted leaving the Executive Committee, the call to Southern Seminary was an honor and a challenge he could not resist. So, suddenly, with his resignation in the hot summer of 1951, a very brief but luminous postwar transition came to an end. With new institutions, new leaders, and new challenges, the Executive Committee once more was moving forward into a new and different era.

Notes

1. QR, July 1983, pp. 70-71.
2. Words from a popular folk funeral song of the times.
3. SBC, 1945, p. 23.
4. ECM, June 13, 1945, pp. 145-146.
5. Ibid., p. 146-147.
6. Ibid., p. 147.
7. Mrs. Raymond Rogers to AM.
8. Porter Routh to AM.
9. ECM, September 19, 1945, p. 172.
10. ECM, December 12, 1945, p. 186.
11. Norman W. Cox to AM.
12. SBC, 1957, p. 78.
13. SBC, 1947, pp. 53-54.
14. SBC, 1947, pp. 36-37.
15. SBC, 1944, p. 37.
16. SBC, 1942, pp. 23. 106-107.
17. ECM, March 15, 1944, pp. 93-95.
18. SBC, 1944, pp. 40-42.
19. ECM, June 14, 1944, p. 114.
20. SBC, 1946, p. 55.
21. QR, July 1983, pp. 70-71.
22. SBC, 1946, p. 48.
23. ECM, June 11, 1946. pp. 1-2.
24. SBC, 1947, pp. 61-62.
25. ECM, March 1, 1946, p. 193.
26. SBC, 1952, pp. 70-71.

27. SBC, 1948, p. 86; Cf. E. C. Routh, "Foreign Mission Board," ESB, Vol. I, p. 464.

28. ECM, December 15, 1943, pp. 76-78.

29. ECM, September, 19, 1945, p 165.

30. Ibid., pp. 170-171.

31. SBC, 1950, pp. 39-41.

32. WR, October 31, 1940, p. 8

33. ECM, March 15, 1944, pp. 98-99.

34. ECM, May 15, 1944, pp. 103-104; 107-109.

35. The severely unfunded Old Annuity Plan was the first retirement plan for ministers set up by the Relief and Annuity Board before actuarial needs were well understood.

36. SBC, 1944, pp. 35-37.

37. ECM, March 1, 1946, pp. 189-191.

38. SBC, 1946, p. 47.

39. ECM, March 1, 1946, p. 191.

40. SBC, 1947, p. 34; 1948, p. 36.

41. SBC, 1946, pp. 31, 68.

42. ECM, December 12, 1945, p. 181.

43. Judson Boyce Allen, "Southern Baptist Foundation," ESB, Vol I, p. 1263.

44. ECM, June 22, 1927, p. 7; cf. January 11-12, 1928, p. 20; cf. SBC, 1927, p. 71. SBC, 1928, p. 30.

45. ECM, December 16, 1942, p. 45.

46. ECM, June 16, 1943, p. 66.

46. ECM, May 15, 1944, p. 105.

47. SBC, 1944, pp. 54-55.

49. SBC, 1946, pp. 26-28.

50. Ibid.

51. ECM, September 19, 1945, pp. 167-168.

52. Ibid., p. 169.

53. ECM, December 11, 1946, p. 21; cf. SBC, 1947, p. 34.

54. SBC, 1949, pp. 15, 44.

55. SBC, 1950, pp. 38-39; pp. 407-417.

56. Porter Routh to AM.

57. SBC, 1946, pp. 11, 48.

58. SBC, 1947, pp. 12, 41, 339.

59. Judson Boyce Allen, "Historical Commission of the Southern Baptist Convention," ESB, Vol. I, 623-625.

60. SBC, 1940, p. 39.

61. SBC, 1947, p. 36.

62. ECM, December 15, 1948, p. 110.

63. SBC, 1949, p. 45.

64. SBC, 1950, pp. 41-42.

65. R. Dean Goodwin, "American Baptist Convention," ESB, Vol. I, p. 36.

66. Porter Routh to AM.

67. SBC, 1948, p. 73.

68. Ibid.

69. ECM, June 15-16, 1949, pp. 132.

70. ECM, 1949 Bylaw 20, (5) h., p. 22.

8

The Executive Committee and Convention Growth 1951-1958

Porter Routh did not know in advance of the September meeting of the Executive Committee that he would be nominated to succeed Duke K. McCall.[1] Two members of the nominating committee had mentioned it as a possibility. The session opened, and immediately Routh was routinely reelected recording secretary. Then Austin Crouch was elected interim executive secretary and authorized to sign checks. As far as Routh could see, there was to be no election of an executive secretary at that meeting. Just when Routh had relaxed, J. W. Storer announced that his nominating committee was ready. After a few crisp words, he nominated Porter Routh. The vote was unanimous. Without fanfare, he was called to one of the most responsible offices in the Convention. The simplicity and informality of the election exactly fitted his open spirit and his democratic character.

Friends from across the Convention responded enthusiastically. Henry G. Bennett, president of Oklahoma A and M wrote, "I knew full well that you had served the long, tedious and exacting apprenticeship so necessary for those new duties."[2] J. D. Grey, president of the Convention said, "You are eminently fitted for the post by heritage, background, capacity and experience." Brooks Hays, the Arkansas congressman, called his election, "Universally popular." His aged father, E. C. Routh, wrote Louie D. Newton, "We who know him best believe that he can do the job, all the while maintaining poise and walking humbly before the Lord."

Austin Crouch had one of the shortest interims on record—

twelve days, from his election on September 12 to the day Routh assumed office on September 24. During those days, Southern Baptists learned much about their new leader. Born in Lockhart, Texas (1911), Porter as a child moved with his family to Dallas, where his father was editor of the *Baptist Standard*. There Porter came under the influence of such men as J. B. Gambrell, George W. Truett, and Wallace Bassett. The chief spiritual motivation of his life appears to have come from his mother, who in Porter's early years was stricken with tuberculosis. He was fourteen years old and helping her in El Paso when his mother died. His father had arranged for them to live there temporarily, hoping that the dry climate would restore her health. His mother's faith, courage, and patience endowed her son with a special kind of Christian experience.

About the time Porter graduated from high school, his father became editor of the Oklahoma *Baptist Messenger*. Porter worked for a year after high school for the Southern Pacific Railroad in Houston. He then followed his family to Oklahoma and entered Oklahoma Baptist University. While there he met, and later married, Ruth Purtle of Sulphur, Oklahoma. After graduation, he stayed with the college for three years as a teacher of journalism and political science and as manager of the Bison Press. He also served as a reporter for newspapers in Oklahoma City and Shawnee. He then took a leave of absence to attend the University of Missouri and Southern Seminary. After returning to Oklahoma Baptist University, Porter was asked by Oklahoma Baptists to be their state Brotherhood secretary. When his father was elected by the Foreign Mission Board to the editorship of the *Commission,* Porter succeeded him as editor of the *Messenger,* the first layman to serve the paper. In 1945 he was called to The Sunday School Board as director of the Department of Survey and Statistics and six years later to the Executive Committee.

Porter Routh came to the Executive Committee with three basic convictions about Southern Baptists: (1) The Convention belongs to the churches and not the churches to the Convention. (2) The Convention objective is to assist the churches in bringing persons to God through Jesus Christ. (3) The Convention is workable because of the reality and the power of its fellowship. He also had a few clearly set ideas for conducting his work. As he felt the heavy responsibilities of his new office, he expanded them into nine personal principles for administration:

> I will encourage business practices that will build the confidence of the people who give the funds in the way the Convention uses the funds.
>
> I will operate with openess in the decision-making process.
>
> I will exercise fairness to all parties, taking care in considering any problem before me, not to be prejudiced by personal friendships.
>
> I will seek the best professional assistance on all matters beyond my knowledge.
>
> I will match freedom with responsibility in dealing with staff.
>
> I will keep open to invitations from all types and sizes of churches.
>
> I will speak only when the Convention has spoken, and I will not establish myself as the voice of all Southern Baptists.
>
> I will provide full information on all matters before the Executive Committee to all the members of the Executive Committee and to all others who are party to the deliberations.
>
> I will keep firmly in mind that the organization is no stronger than individuals who comprise the whole; therefore, I must keep my personal integrity, practice good stewardship, perform the work of a faithful churchman, and live a life-style which does not separate me from the masses of church members.

There was no hesitation in Porter Routh's approach to the office. From the day he first sat behind his big desk, those who worked with him sensed his goodwill, his fairness, and his firmness. He did not have to say, "I am in charge here." This was understood from the power of his presence, which was never overbearing or intrusive. Perhaps his firmness came from a memo J. W. Storer handed him when he was first elected: "While you will move with softness and courtesy, you are, when the time comes for asserting it, the boss there in the office."[3] More likely it came from his vast intuitive ability, which from his first day in office was evident in every decision and relationship for the twenty-eight years he served the Executive Committee. He seemed to have been endowed from birth with the poise of easy command.

From where he sat at his office desk on September 24, 1951, Routh could not see the avalanche of challenges that would descend upon it, but he was ready. The one task from which the executive secretary can never escape is the management of the Convention's general business, particularly the management of the funds that flow through his office to all the causes included in the Cooperative Program and for that he was more than ready.

Looking After the Business

The Korean war, which had started in 1950, threw the country into an uncertain mood. Though the economy continued strong, the people, fearful of a war such as they had known in the early 1940s, were hesitating in addressing the future. The Baptists, not much inclined to follow the mood of the country, continued to vigorously support their churches. Total gifts to the churches increased from 1950 to 1951 by 13 percent; and total gifts to missions by 11.6 percent.[4] The difference between total gifts and mission gifts was probably due to more church budget money spent for church extension and church building. The denomination was well into a long period of unprecedented growth in church property and new churches, and these new ventures were demanding sources from which the smaller and newer congregations without established credit could borrow money for use in construction.

Responding to this need, J. B. Lawrence, the determined executive secretary of the Home Mission Board, decided that the board could help the smaller, newer churches by borrowing money and lending it to them for building purposes. To do this, Lawrence needed Executive Committee approval for a line of credit. He apparently felt that some members of the Executive Committee would resist his idea. It was true that some of those faithful guardians of

Southern Baptist financial integrity were so conditioned by the long struggle through depression and war to rid the Convention of its debts that they would be reluctant to create new ones.

Eighty-one years old and still going strong, Lawrence had been a wily fighter all of his life. He understood his problem and went straight to the Convention. In May 1952, he secured the passage of a resolution favoring his cause. Laying a careful foundation that described the need, he asked: "That this Convention authorize its Executive Committee to consider and act upon such requests as the Home Mission Board may make looking to the usefulness of its three loan funds."[5] It was a bold digressive strategy that worked. A month later the Executive Committee approved a request of the Home Mission Board to borrow $500,000 at 3 percent to be lent to the churches at 5 percent.[6] At the next meeting, the Executive Committee commended the Home Mission Board for its loan programs and suggested that it find ways to expand them.[7]

Was the pressure brought by Lawrence necessary? Perhaps not. Many of the old leaders had disappeared, not lasting as long as the ageless J. B. Lawrence. New leaders were appearing on the Executive Committee, among them Casper C. Warren, Carl E. Bates, J. D. Grey, Herschel H. Hobbs, G. Allen West, Jr., and others with forward-looking commitments.[8] This was the beginning of a long, successful relationship between the Executive Committee and the Home Mission Board in support of the church loan programs, support that included further lines of credit and allocations for loan purposes from the Capital Needs Program.

In 1954 the Executive Committee approved a request of the Home Mission Board to borrow $3,000,000 for church loan purposes. In 1955 members of the Executive Committee and the Home Mission Board helped to put down a move to create a separate Church Loan Agency.[9] The members believed that such an agency would duplicate services long offered by the Home Mission Board as a vital part of its mission programs.

In 1956 a group from California presented the Executive Committee with a resolution asking that the Relief and Annuity Board

Funds be released for church loan purposes.[10] Such an arrangement would require a major Convention bylaw change. This was unlikely because: (1) it would create a duality of interest by asking the Relief and Annuity Board to promote two competing programs in the local church, (2) it would endanger the board in time of extreme depression if it could not meet its commitments to pastors because of defaulting church loans, (3) it was strongly opposed by competent financial advisers as an unwise business practice, and (4) it was against the banking laws of the state of Texas in which the Relief and Annuity Board was chartered. The Executive Committee made no recommendation.

The most scrutinized task of the Executive Committee has always been the formation and recommendation of the annual Cooperative Program Allocation Budget. Until about 1950, the budget was a list of percentages used to divide undesignated funds forwarded by the state conventions to the Southern Baptist Convention. This method was first employed in 1919 as a way of dividing funds from the Seventy-Five Million Campaign. Until about 1934, some of the states changed the percentages and remitted directly to the agencies. After 1927 the SBC percentages were fairly constant, and some years there were no changes at all.

In 1927 an effort had been made to substitute dollars amounts for percentages, but it was a proposal out of due season. The Convention messengers, long accustomed to percentages, found it difficult to apply other terms to Cooperative Program distributions. The older, stronger agencies with long histories of fixed percentages could defend them much better than they could deal with the more flexible dollars. The season for change to dollar allocations finally arrived in 1946 with the introduction of the Capital Needs Budget and the addition of new agencies, though it was ten years before the effect was fully felt. It should be kept in mind that from the 1940s the Cooperative Program Allocation budget has been divided into three tiers: (1) The Cooperative Program Operating Budget, (2) The Cooperative Program Capital Needs Budget, and (3) the Cooperative Program Advance Budget (later Challenge Budget). Before

1946 the table of percentages was applied to all undesignated money received. In 1946 a definite budget was adopted: $6,000,000, half for operations and half for capital,[11] meaning that the budget then had two tiers. The existing tables of percentages still applied to the operations budget: however, for the first time there was a ceiling on operations. In 1949 the third tier of the Advance Program was added.[12] The Convention still voted percentages, but it began thinking dollars.

The last year the Executive Committee recommended only a table of percentages for the Cooperative Program Operating Budget was in 1949.[13] The next year it recommended a combination of percentages and dollars. The percentages were dropped in 1955 with the recommendation of the budget for 1956.[14] In 1955 if someone had challenged the new budget with the simple question, "Where is the table of percentages?" the process might have been thrown temporarily into confusion because the bylaws specified that the Executive Committee was to recommend a comprehensive budget that "included the percentage of Convention funds to be allocated to each cause," and the Business and Financial Plan specified, "The agencies sharing in the table of percentages."[15] The change from percentages to dollars was surely necessary for three reasons: (1) Dollars provided a much clearer picture of what the agencies would be receiving for their work, (2) dollars provided more flexibility for the budget-making process, and (3) dollars provided in times of rapidly escalating gifts a way of edging in new causes with a minimum of distress to other causes.

Another forward step in Cooperative Program allocations came in 1954 when the Executive Committee asked the five seminary presidents to devise a formula for dividing the funds for theological education among the five seminaries.[16] The committee believed that the procedure in use at the time had "the possibility of promoting rivalry, ill-feeling, overselling, the dramatization of difficulties, action too late to meet specific needs, and grossly inaccurate evaluations of needs and opportunities."[17] A variety of pressures from many sources had created the problem, such things as changing enrollments, alumni advocacy, trustee concerns, building campaigns, and differences in endowments, enrollments, debt loads, and personalities. The presidents immediately responded. The following December, Duke K. McCall reported that the presidents had approved a satisfactory formula devised by a group of Southern Baptist educators.[18]

In the 1950s, the Executive Committee recommended other significant fiscal policies that would seem now to be of only minor importance; but at the time, they were significant forward steps in the continuing effort to bring order into Convention finances and to improve relationships. In 1954 the agencies were asked to secure permission of the Convention or its Executive Committee for any debt incurred above that which could not be repaid out of operating income within three years.[19] That same year, the gift annuity policy was relaxed to allow the Home Mission Board to write gift annuities at Relief and Annuity Board rates.[20] In 1956 the Executive Committee asked the Convention to reaffirm the 1934 agreement with state conventions on the management and promotion of the Cooperative Program.[21]

In four years, from 1956 to 1959, the Southern Baptist Convention created three new agencies and raised three existing ones to full-time staff status. Fitting their rapidly expanding needs into the Cooperative Program Allocation Budget was like shoehorning a big foot into a tight boot. Only when the boot stretched did the foot feel natural; and, in the case of the Cooperative Program, adding the agencies required a lot of stretching. Though some were added in the late 1940s, most of them were added in the 1950s. Not only did the Executive Committee have to find start-up money, even more money had to be provided the second year, and on indefinitely into the future. The new agencies added after 1951 to the already large family of agencies were:[22]

> 1957 Carver School of Missions and Social Work
> 1957 Midwestern Baptist Theological Seminary
> 1959 Stewardship Commission

Carver School of Missions and Social Work at Louisville, adjacent to the campus of Southern Seminary, came under the control of the Convention in 1957, after it became apparent that the Woman's Missionary Union could no longer carry the heavy educational responsibilities. It became official when the women in their annual meeting voted for the Southern Baptist Convention to elect the school's board of trustees. Midwestern Baptist Theological Seminary was established by the Southern Baptist Convention at Kansas City in 1957. Both the Executive Committee and its executive secretary-treasurer were deeply involved in the negotiations leading to Convention approval.

Not only did money have to be found for these agencies but also it had to be found for the older, established agencies who had huge inventories of unmet needs that had accumulated in twenty-five years of depression, debt, and war. The larger agencies, both new and old, had larger needs, both for annual operations and for capital purposes. Of all the subcommittees of the Executive Committee in the 1950s, the Finance Committee, which then had the task of developing the Cooperative Program Allocation Budget, seemed to meet longer and have the most to do. In some ways, these recurring demands were the supreme challenge to Porter Routh's resourcefulness and diplomacy. Not one time did he falter.

Three things made the task possible. (1) The economic prosperity of the 1950s. Almost anyone could find a job anywhere, anytime. People were employed, and the country was booming. (2) Southern Baptist stewardship; it was the season for growth in tithes and offerings. And (3) vigorous evangelism and church extension in the churches. There was not much question then, and even less now, that it was a period of revival in Southern Baptist life, as the following simple table surely reveals:[23]

	1945	1962	Gain
Church membership	5,865,554	10,193,052	74%
Churches	26,191	32,892	26%
Sunday School enrollment	3,525,310	7,570,455	115%

Total gifts	$98,458,425	$540,811,457	429%
Gifts to missions	$22,490,751	$91,433,845	307%
Ch. bldg. value	$276,089,771	$2,562,836,860	828%
Total Coop. Program	$10,485,571	$53,532,617	411%
SBC Coop. Program	$3,859,231	$18,868,840	389%

By the end of the decade, a few voices were heard advocating even more agencies for such causes as chaplains, pastoral counseling, children's homes, evangelism, and family life. Looking ahead, some thought that they could see the need for agencies to promote alcohol education, care of the aging, and missionary travel. But more and more, the church members were saying, "Let us not start other agencies, but strengthen the ones we now have." The members of the Executive Committee were inclined to agree with them.

Building for the Present and the Future

Southern Baptists were still building, and it appeared they would never stop. The first capital needs program was completed in 1951. Begun in 1946, with a goal of $7,000,000, it underwent several adjustments, including the addition of other causes and the increasing of original goals. Planning for the next phase started in 1950.[24] The second program, projected for 1952-1956, was approved by the Convention for $15,000,000.[25] The chairman of the committee that developed that program was Henry W. Tiffany, a thoughtful pastor committed to the traditions of the Virginia Baptist experience. In 1954 the second program was extended through 1958.[26] When it ended, Southern Baptists had invested since 1946 a total of $32,028,983 in capital needs, mostly in seminary and mission construction. The specific accomplishments of the programs were impressive. For the first time in their history, Southern Baptist institutions were leaving depression-time stinting for postwar prosperity. It could not have been done without dedicated leaders, both in the Executive Committee and in the agencies. The capital needs funds were used as follows:

Foreign Mission Board: $6,066,108 for the building of

schools, hospitals, missionary homes, and meetinghouses on foreign fields.

Home Mission Board: $4,826,870 for building purposes on the home mission fields, and for lending to small churches to help meet their building needs.

Relief and Annuity Board: $3,005,180 to support inadequately supported retirement funds for ministers.

Golden Gate Baptist Theological Seminary: $3,032,166 to buy and begin to build the magnificent Strawberry Point campus in sight of Golden Gate Bridge and across the bay from downtown San Francisco.

New Orleans Baptist Theological Seminary: $3,591,766 for a completely new campus.

Southeastern Baptist Theological Seminary: $3,094,423 for purchasing and refurbishing the old Wake Forest College campus. The president during this time was Sydnor L. Stealey, a peppery, insightful Westerner whose specialities were church history and classical devotional literature.

Southern Baptist Theological Seminary: $3,500,623 for campus construction, including a new library and apartment conversion.

Southwestern Baptist Theological Seminary: $3,242,198. $1,612,467 for new buildings.

American Baptist Seminary Commission: $350,017 for buildings.

Brotherhood Commission: $81,250, for capital expansion.

Radio and Television Commission: $285,122 for equipment needs and film production.

Southern Baptist Hospitals: $953,250, a heroic effort by Southern Baptists but little compared with need. The inability of the Convention to meet the total needs of a local service institution finally led to the hospital's independence.

Looking back, many wise observers have concluded that the 1945 beginning of the Capital Needs Program was one of the most creative and forward-looking steps the Executive Committee ever made.

Improving Communications

For eight years from 1927, the only other professional officer of the Executive Committee, besides the executive secretary, was a specialist in communications: at first, Frank E. Burkhalter, a Texas layman and a trained journalist, and following him in 1929, Walter M. Gilmore, a North Carolina pastor and a skilled general writer and editor. The employment of dedicated writers to help the executive secretary says something about the importance the early Executive Committee placed upon communication, even though, at first, it was not mandated by the Southern Baptist Convention. Mandating came in 1934 with a bylaw that said that the Executive Committee was "to conduct the promotion work of the Convention through the heads" of Southern Baptist Convention agencies.[27] Not only did the bylaw prescribe the area of communication (promotion work of the Convention), it made an important point in polity (through the heads of the agencies).

In 1946 the mandate was broadened when the bylaw was changed to say that the Executive Committee was "to conduct the general work of promotion and the general work of publicity in cooperation with the other agencies."[28] The principle of Executive Committee's cooperation with the agencies has been a vital point in Southern Baptist Convention polity since the organization of the Executive Committee in 1917. It assumes a partnership, not a hierarchy.

In a family of brothers and sisters, misunderstandings are always possible. For many years there were slight tensions between The Sunday School Board and the Executive Committee over various aspects of stewardship promotion. In 1927 the Executive Committee had received the Baptist Bulletin Service from the Cooperative Program Commission. It had been started by the Conservation Commission of the Seventy-Five Million Campaign and was the publishing name for the Sunday worship folders used to present general denominational information to Southern Baptists. As finan-

cial conditions improved in the churches, the circulation greatly
increased, and profits were used for publishing the *Baptist Program.*
As the Bulletin Service grew in importance, The Sunday School
Board, with some justification, began to feel that it was an impinge-
ment upon its publication responsibilities.

To ease the tensions, Duke K. McCall and C. E. Bryant worked
out an agreement in 1948 for the board to publish the bulletins.[29]
The arrangement was mutually advantageous to both the Executive
Committee and the Sunday School Board. Ownership and editorial
control remained with the Executive Committee, and, in return, it
received royalty payments from the board. Immediately, color was
added and a variety of styles offered. Circulation began to climb.
In 1951 weekly circulation was 582,500,[30] and in 1957 it was
1,169,400. Also, in 1957 the bulletins were used in 6,600 churches.
In many of them, the bulletins were the sole source of general
denominational information. For this reason, the Executive Committee regarded the Baptist Bulletin Service as an essential part of
its "general work of publicity."

In the mid 1950s, Sunday School Board officials began once more
to object to Executive Committee ownership of the Bulletin Service,
not only because of its increasing circulation but because the Executive Committee was publishing and selling other materials for use
in the churches. In 1956, for example, it published and sold
8,352,884 tracts and posters (57 titles) to state conventions.[31] Also
in 1956, the Executive Committee initiated The Forward Program
of Church Finance and began selling church budget promotional
material directly to the churches.

At the same time, The Sunday School Board felt strongly that
several of the Convention agencies were selling materials beyond
their basic promotional needs. The multiplication of these publication centers appeared to some Sunday School Board officials to
threaten the board's unique position as the Convention's publication arm. It did not help matters in 1949 when the title of the
director of publicity was changed to the director of publications. He
was then frequently introduced as the director of publications for

The Sunday School Board, and on one occasion an enthusiastic deacon introduced him as "head of all the publications, Sunday School literature and everything," which, of course, was far from the truth. He was embarrassed because there were Sunday School Board employees in the congregation. As the Forward Program grew, The Sunday School Board became even more sensitive. Some were afraid that some leaders of the board were attempting to bring all stewardship promotion under its control. The Forward Program required heavy local church concentration in the fall of the year, and Sunday School Board program leaders felt that this was preempting local church leadership time and energy that should be used in promoting Sunday School work. The Executive Committee was not in violation of any rule, but Sunday School Board officials felt that it was setting a precedent damaging to the board's interests.

These differences were surfaced in a friendly atmosphere; though at times, both sides were frank in their discussions. One bitter winter day, the director of publications of the Executive Committee told the executive secretary of The Sunday School Board that he had been offered a responsible leadership position in another agency. The executive secretary, always marvelously articulate and never uncertain of his positions, without bothering to explain, abruptly said, "You should take it."

The director asked, "Why should I take it?"

The reply, "Everything you do for the Executive Committee is out of bounds."

There was no twinkle in the executive secretary's normally twinkling eyes. What light the director of publications saw was more like ice, but not the ice of animosity or rejection; it was merely the ice of commitment to principle. He still dates his determination to stay with the Executive Committee from the hour of that conversation.

Everything he did was not out of bounds. Least controversial among Executive Committee communications projects was the *Baptist Program*. This magazine, exclusively for professional church leaders, grew in popularity in the 1950s with the addition of church-related advertisements and occasional color. It became

more professional in appearance when Leonard E. Hill, a trained
journalist, was employed in 1957 as managing director. He was
highly skilled in taking full advantage of the advertisers' use of
color. Leonard came to what he had been told might be a temporary
job. The magazine's publication was tied to the profits of the Baptist
Bulletin Service, and at the time there were questions about its
future. Twenty-five years later, still with the *Baptist Program,* Hill was
praised by an Executive Committee official as a graphics genius who
could work miracles in putting together a magazine on the limited
budget required by an almost totally subsidized publication. Circulation in 1957 was 31,000. The size of the monthly editions ranged
from twenty-four to forty-two pages.[32]

More controversial was the Baptist Press. By 1951 it had reached
an annual level of 519 news stories on 372 legal-sized pages and
mailed to about one hundred Baptist and secular newspapers.[33] In
1955 Theo Sommerkamp, with an master of arts degree in journalism, joined the Baptist Press as its first fully trained, full-time
newswriter.[34] A capable, prolific reporter, and tireless in his work,
he helped build the service into a mature news operation. In 1957,
to facilitate quicker dispatch, the Executive Committee authorized
a system of stringers (regional reporters) and a branch office in
Washington, D. C.[35]

The annual recharger for the Baptist Press operation was the
newsroom of the annual Southern Baptist Convention that attracted
an increasing number of secular journalists. In the newsroom,
church and secular editors began in earnest to talk to each other.
More and more the church editors accepted and profited from secular methods. But there was a problem that arose out of SBC polity
in conflict with modern journalism. On the one hand, the newspapers addressed the Baptist Press and said, "We have the right to
know." On the other hand, a Southern Baptist Convention bylaw
said that the Executive Committee was "to conduct the general
work of publicity in cooperation with the other agencies and institutions of the Convention."[36]

When a legitimate news story was in conflict with the perception

of agency officials as to what really happened, they naturally regarded the story as in error; moreover, some of them strongly held to
a traditional Baptist view of journalism—that good relationships
build the fellowship and that false information weakens the relationships, thus destroying the fellowship. A popular view at the time
was: "It is just as important what an editor leaves out of the paper
as what he puts in it." It is a view that has often been challenged.
Still, what does the Executive Committee do, when caught on the
horns of the dilemma, being responsible both for the news and the
fellowship?

The issue came to a head in the late 1950s when Southern Baptist
Seminary underwent its trauma over the firing of thirteen faculty
members. The news had to move, for both church and secular
papers were demanding it. Seminary officials did not want the Baptist Press to circulate harsh, negative stories, even summations of
those being daily printed in the Louisville newspapers, because the
seminary claimed that the stories did not accurately portray what
was really happening. It was an impasse that remained unsolved for
a long, long time. Generally, the theory has been to give Baptist
people the facts and let them make up their own minds. As to the
facts, at the time, the administrative decision was to make state
Baptist editors and the agency people closest to a potential news
story responsible for accurate information and, in general, to report
only the facts, not opinions. It was a decision that was not entirely
pleasing to either journalists or administrators.

Stepping Up the Tempo

Because of its special relationship to the agencies, the Executive
Committee has not intentionally promoted major programs in competition with the agencies. This does not mean that it foregoes
leadership of important forward movements. In 1954 the Convention appointed a special Committee to Promote World Evangelism
and instructed it to confer with the Promotion Committee of the
Executive Committee in order "to step up the tempo of our effort
as Baptists to lay hold on that for which we were laid hold of by Jesus

Christ."[37] This was about the time of the popularity of the phrase,
"Christ Is the Answer." Baptists believed that the world was in crisis
and that its only hope was Jesus Christ. As a result, the Executive
Committee recommended to the 1955 Convention a mammoth forward step for the Advance Program, in essence,[38] as follows:

- Calls for more mission volunteers.
- Enlist the personal support of all Baptists for a great world
  mission advance program.
- A call to Baptists of the United States and Canada to celebrate
  together the one hundred and fiftieth anniversary (1964) of
  Baptists in North America organized for the support of mis-
  sions.
- Increasing the help provided for all missionaries.
- State world mission conferences similar to state evangelistic
  conferences.
- Annual steps by the local churches toward raising Coopera-
  tive Program to one-half of the total church budget.
- Setting of 1957 as the year of World Missions.

Thus, the Baptist Jubilee Advance was born, a program to bring
all Baptists closer together in pursuance of the Convention objective of taking Christ to the world. It pointed up that the premise of
Baptist interdependent relationships is cooperation in missions.
The climax came nine years after the movement was launched, in
1964, when Southern Baptists joined with other Baptists in America
a mammoth celebration at Atlantic City.

Simultaneous with the increased tempo in world evangelism was
an increased tempo in personal stewardship. In September 1955,
Merrill D. Moore secured approval of the Executive Committee for
a workshop of denominational leaders "to work out details for a new
program of church finance."[39] The meeting was held the following
December and attended by state secretaries, state editors, state
stewardship promotion leaders, and SBC agency personnel.

As a result, the new Church Finance Program was tentatively
approved by the Executive Committee for testing in June of 1956.[40]

The plan combined Southern Baptist stewardship methods with modern fund-raising techniques, using a variety of up-to-date materials, and binding them together with strict nomenclature and a comprehensive calendar. The name was later changed to The Forward Program of Church Finance. After a year of careful testing, the plan was officially approved by the Executive Committee and the Southern Baptist Convention.[41]

The Forward Program was an immediate success and became for many churches the standard pattern for promoting annual stewardship programs. The names of Merrill D. Moore and the Forward Program were almost synonymous. Without him it would not have happened. He brought the leaders and the facts together, and he kept them together until the plan emerged out of their knowledge and cooperation. He refused to promote the plan publicly until it had been thoroughly tested in all sizes of churches. And, in a firm and gentle way, he steadfastly discouraged any alteration until the plan had become completely established. Until the Forward Program was replaced by more modern methods, thousands of churches successfully used it to advance their work.

Moving Ahead

Meanwhile, the Executive Committee moved ahead in another important way. In December 1955, Carr P. Collins of Texas moved that a subcommittee of five be appointed to consider recommending to the Convention a study of the total program of Southern Baptists.[42] The next June the Convention approved the formation of the Committee to Study Total Program.[43] What started as a seemingly routine motion by a Texas layman turned into a movement as far-reaching and long-lasting as the work of the Efficiency Commission of 1913-1915. The changes produced were like a driver taking a car to the garage to have the spark plugs cleaned, only to learn that he must have the engine reconditioned.

In a way the Executive Committee and the Convention move on, as the hands of a clock move on—slowly, persistently, inevitably. One hour passes the hand to the hour that follows it. Time disappears and new leaders take the places of old leaders. The hours that are given to the new leaders always seem new, but they are not entirely new. The new leaders work at the old problems in new ways; they work at new problems, sometimes in old ways. Like the hours, the leaders also fall away and merge into the timelessness of remembered leadership that reflects the character and the form of Southern Baptists. Thomas Carlyle once said that "History is the essence of innumerable biographies."[44] People make the difference, and so: the people of the Executive Committee.

In 1951, when Porter Routh assumed office, the Convention president was the energetic, overflowing, and witty, though sophisticated, J. D. Grey. Pastor, evangelist, leader, counselor whose superb pulpit manner and unfailing humor gave him remarkable public acceptance. He was broadly supportive of the entire denominational program, from the local association to the last foreign mission field. Never idle and always prepared, J. D. Grey was a pleasingly dominant personality in any group and in the Southern Baptist Convention.

James Wilson Storer was elected to succeed J. D. Grey in 1953. His insight, uprightness, loyalty, and supportiveness seemed to give him a periscopic view of the denomination. Superb preacher, and an even better presiding officer, like so many of the previous presidents, his sparkling wit carried the Convention through many tense moments. It was known by some that his wit, sometimes laden with satire, could cut like a surgeon's scapel. He rarely pushed it to its limits. In the secular world, J. W. Storer could have been a nationally known pundit; in the Baptist world, he was a sterling leader of matchless character and of unsurpassed value to the Executive Committee. Porter Routh was his special friend. They became acquainted when Porter was selling magazines door-to-door to pay college expenses. He was canvassing Richmond when one of his crew became ill, and all Routh knew to do was to ask a local Baptist pastor for help in finding a doctor. Storer responded; from the meeting, there developed a lifelong friendship and possibly a career for Porter Routh. Storer was a leading member of the Executive Committee when Routh was elected executive secretary.

In 1955 Casper Carl Warren was elected president of the Convention to succeed J. W. Storer. He lived close to the basic instincts of Southern Baptists—local church, missions, and evangelism. More than some other presidents, he was a dreamer whose vision called for mighty works to be undertaken by faith. Warren was chairman of the subcommittee that opened the way for the Home Mission Board to first borrow for church loan purposes. Founder of the 30,000 Movement and a key leader in the Baptist Jubilee Advance, he was always in a hurry "to get to the next village and knock on the last door." There was no doubt about Casper Warren; he had heard the hurry call of Jesus. His term of office ended in 1957.

The chairmen of the Executive Committee also made their contributions to the increasing strength and acceptance of the Executive Committee. The considerate Washington, D. C., attorney, George Broadrup Fraser was chairman when Porter Routh was elected executive secretary in 1951. Big in body and gentle in bearing, Fraser projected a quiet but commanding presence. He was faultless in his courtesy and untiring in his faithfulness. Fraser was succeeded in 1953 briefly by Storer and then by Warren. In 1955 Judge Frank C. Hooper was elected. He presided in a quiet, soft way that seemed inconsistent with his federal court experience, yet he was always firmly in control. Hooper was one of the most thoughtful men ever to serve as chairman, especially for the rank and file. During his term of office, he seldom missed stopping by the desks of the Executive Committee employees to thank them for their services to the Executive Committee. He could make anyone feel important, and he could do it without condescending or patronizing. And so another era ended, but not without its wistful notes.

In 1955 Louie D. Newton rotated from the Executive Committee membership, having served for twenty-five years, which was longer than any other person. He was the last of the pioneers to leave. Some of the staff felt that Louie would someday return, but he didn't; and the Executive Committee has never been the same.

A different kind of a transition was signaled by the death of J. E. Dillard in 1953. He had been ill for more than ten years. Twice before his retirement in 1947 he had taken leaves of absence because of illness. His handsome grandfather clock stands in the parlor of the Immanuel Baptist Church in Nashville. Visitors who read on the tiny brass plate the name of James Edgar Dillard may wonder: Who was this man who lived so long ago, and why did he own a massive eight-foot timepiece? Whatever the reason, today that clock symbolizes the James Edgar Dillard spirit: bigness in all the things that count—compassion of heart, loyalty to Jesus Christ, faithful to the Baptist mission, unfailing humility, unquenchable optimism, boundless world vision, a creative mind, and the willingness to cooperate in a fully democratic setting with all Southern Baptists. He helped pay Baptist debts, but the Baptists can never pay the debt they owe to him.

Three years later Austin Crouch died. In the ordeal of blindness, he had demonstrated a sublime and translucent Christian spirit. He went every day, often alone on the bus, to his tiny room in the offices of the Executive Committee. Here, faithful women read to him and helped him with his diminishing correspondence. He once wistfully said, as many old men say, that his cronies were all dead. In his case, it was not quite true because he had the precious ability, even in his blindness, to make friends with younger men and women. He always knew them. In fact, he knew them so well that some of them believed that his blindness was not as severe as he thought.

Even at his advanced age and with his limited eyesight, Crouch was still alert, though more and more his mind was attracted to the great spiritual issues that troubled Baptists in his youth. He was especially delighted when his young friends shared with him a few moments of their time. Once he took one of them aside for an unforgettable experience. In 1953 the Executive Committee had employed a nationally known artist to paint Crouch's portrait. When it was unveiled, all he could see was the blurry golden frame and a rough mass of color that could have been anything. Crouch asked his young friend to tell him what the portrait was like, and about all the young man could say was that it was exactly like him. The painting completely portrays the character and spirit of the man. His eyes, as seen by the painter, indicate a man of spirit, devotion, and thought. The artist once said that he always painted a portrait from the "inside out" and that Crouch was one of the most transparent characters he had ever painted. By looking at his portrait, young people of later generations can surely see something of the integrity, the fairness, and the future of the Executive Committee.

In September 1957, late in the afternoon, Austin Crouch stepped from a bus, one block from his home, and out of the perpetual dimness that surrounded him, an automobile driven by another old man struck the great leader. The heart that had beat so truly for eighty-seven years ceased beating. In an instant, Austin Crouch was with his Lord and with Little Jap. No one doubted his belief in eternal life, and no one doubted his faith in Jesus Christ. He lived his faith to the end; in the end, he leaned upon it, at peace with himself and with God, an unforgettable symbol of the greatness, the endurance, and the triumph of Southern Baptists. Who was Austin Crouch? He was a man whose own character is written indelibly into the character of the Executive Committee.

Notes

1. The author was present for the election. From this point to the end of the book, he was an observer of most of the events and persons discussed and was involved with many of them.

2. *Porter Routh - 1951,* A bound volume of letters received by Dr. Routh following his election.

3. J. W. Storer, "Ideas about the Executive Secretary of the Executive Committee," an undated note from J. W. Storer to Porter Routh, given to him after his election.

4. *SBC Handbook,* July 1984, pp. 70-71.

5. SBC, 1952, p. 54.

6. ECM, June 11-12, 1952, pp. 6-8.

7. ECM, December 17-18, 1952, pp. 6-9.

8. Ibid. p. 1.

9. ECM, December 15-16, 1954, pp. 11-13; ECM, May 17, 1955, pp. 10-13.

10. ECM, December 12, 1956, pp. 12, 26-27.

11. SBC, 1946, pp. 46-48.

12. SBC, 1949, p. 35.

13. Ibid. p. 35; SBC, 1950, 40.

14. SBC, 1955, p. 37.

15. SBC, 1955, Bylaw 9. (9) (g), p. 26; Ibid., Business and Financial Plan, paragraph 3., p. 28.

16. ECM, June 23, 1954, p. 12.

17. Ibid., p. 11.

18. ECM, December 15-16, 1954, p. 32. The educators included R. Orin Cornett of the Education Commission and Doak Campbell of Florida State University.

19. SBC, 1952, p. 37.

20. ECM, June 11-12, 1952, p. 10.

21. ECM, May 29, 1956, pp. 6-7.

22. Information on each of the new agencies may be found in the *Encyclopedia of Southern Baptists*, Volumes I, II, III and IV.

23. QR, July 1983, pp. 70-71; cf. "State/SBC Cooperative Program Totals," a report of the SBC Executive Committee.

24. ECM, May 8-9, 1950, pp. 3, 15, E.

25. SBC, 1952, pp. 38-39.

26. SBC, 1954, p. 40.

27. SBC, 1934, p. 37.

28. SBC, 1946, pp. 70-72.

29. ECM, June 15-16, 1948, pp. 97, 108-109.

30. SBC, 1952, p. 70; SBC, 1958, p. 96. In 1959, the Executive Committee relinquished control of the Bulletin Service in exchange for an annual contribution to the SBC Operating Budget.

31. SBC, 1957, p. 89.

32. SBC, 1958, p. 96.

33. SBC, 1952, p. 70.

34. ECM, December 14, 1955, p. 2.

35. ECM, December 11, 1957, p. 11.

36. SBC, 1957, p. 31.

37. SBC, 1954, pp. 19, 58.

38. SBC, 1955, p. 53.

39. ECM, September 7, 1955, pp. 7-9.

40. ECM, June 20, 1956, pp. 10-11.

41. ECM, May 28, 1957, pp. 5-6; cf. SBC 1957, p. 67.

42. ECM, December 14, 1955, p. 6.

43. SBC, 1956, p. 44.

44. Thomas Carlyle, *Essays: On History,"* quoted by Burton Stevenson, *Home Book of Quotations (New York: Dodd Mead, 1949,* p. 599.

9

Full Visibility for the Executive Committee
(Part I)
1959-1969

When the Committee to Study Total Southern Baptist Program made its preliminary report concerning the Executive Committee, it requested the consultant, Lawrence Wilsey of Chicago, to make a summary statement.[1] He told the group that another management firm had recently conducted a similar study for the Roman Catholic Church. When the consultants had finished, they told the bishops that the Church needed few, if any, changes because with final authority vested in one person at the top and with an unbroken chain of command all the way to the last priest and congregation, the church had a near perfect organization.

Wilsey said that his conclusions about Southern Baptists had been slightly different. At first he had been astonished at the looseness of the structure. With so many independent churches, associations, and conventions, and with their networks of unrelated agencies, he wondered if it were not a dream of some kind; for according to the rules of sound organization, nothing so loosely organized would work. But, as he had continued his study, he had been even more astonished. Not only did it work, it worked better than most. The work that Wilsey did for the Southern Baptist Convention demonstrated that he understood very well the unifying principles that hold Southern Baptists together.

These principles have been stated in many different ways and are well known to most informed Baptists. Ultimately, there is a very special binding principle that takes precedence over all the others. E. Y. Mullins, in his book, *Baptist Beliefs,* said:

201

Baptists have a very special interest in the doctrine of Holy Spirit and
need to reassert it with vigor. We believe in a regenerated church
membership, in individualism and freedom of conscience, in the right
of private judgement, and in the autonomy of the local church, in an
open Bible and freedom to witness for Christ. Hence, we are peculiar-
ly dependent upon the Holy Spirit for the successful prosecution of
our work.[2]

The ruggedness of Baptist faith stands out in Mullins's use of
strong, liberating words: regenerated church membership, individualism, freedom of conscience, local church autonomy, open
Bible, and freedom to witness for Christ. For many people, it is a
wonder that Southern Baptists have held together through inevitable divisions and disagreements. But it is no wonder at all for those
who understand Baptist dependence upon the Holy Spirit for to-
getherness.

Southern Baptists exist to witness for Christ in all the world, and
they are organized to accomplish this task together. This mission
was in the minds of the members of the Executive Committee in
1956 when they recommended a major study of the work the Convention and its programs, the first such study in the Convention's
111-year history. The recommendation said that the committee was
to find "the most effective way of promoting the Kingdom of God
through the Southern Baptist Convention."[3] The members were
well aware that in recommending the study they were also putting
the Executive Committee under the microscope. To leave the Total
Program Study Committee free to do its work, the members of the
Executive Committee recommended: "No employed personnel of
the Convention shall be appointed to the committee."

Redirecting the Executive Committee

The introduction of the 1958 report of the Total Program Study
Committee to the Southern Baptist Convention contained an important definitive paragraph:[4]

The Executive Committee should assist the Convention in its work without infringing upon the authority and responsibility of the agencies. The Convention meeting once a year does not have ample time or information necessary to carry out detailed operation of its many ministries. The Executive Committee is established to assist the Convention in carrying out its programs without assuming either the Convention's responsibilities or those of the agencies.

The chairman, Douglas M. Branch, North Carolina, asked Kendall Berry, Arkansas, to present six recommendations that both reinforced and redirected the Executive Committee. They were adopted without amendments.[5] The key provisions are summarized as follows: The Executive Committee should

- Provide an appropriate budget-reporting format to provide more information about agency program plans, accomplishments, and costs.
- Review as information, the budgets of all Convention agencies, but should not approve them.
- Study the need for an expanded public relations program, and if found appropriate, recommend an agency to conduct such a program. Meanwhile, the Executive Committee should be assisted by a public relations advisory committee with members from the agencies, the state papers, and the state conventions.
- Be relieved of the responsibility of stewardship promotion with its transfer to a new Stewardship Commission.
- Organize itself into four subcommittees: program, finance, administrative, and public relations.
- Have a small executive staff headed by the Executive Secretary-Treasurer, including a program analyst, a financial analyst, and a director of public relations. The Executive Secretary-Treasurer "should direct the members of the staff in their work."
- Have an office building of its own, large enough for space to be made available to smaller SBC agencies.

In 1959 the Total Program Study Committee made one other

recommendation to the Convention concerning the Executive Committee:[6] "The Executive Committee should be assigned responsibility for maintaining an official organization manual. . . . Each agency will have a single document to refer to when questions concerning responsibilities arise."

The report clearly addressed pressing Executive Committee needs: (1) clearer and more comprehensive reporting of agency programs and finances, (2) public relations on behalf of the Convention and its agencies, (3) office facilities apart from the premises of The Sunday School Board, (4) an enlarged executive staff, (5) a systematic listing and description of all agency programs and services, (6) release from the supervision of stewardship promotion.

For the second time in the Executive Committee's life, its responsibility for stewardship and Cooperative Program promotion had been questioned, this time, not because of any neglect or failure on its part. The study committee gave two reasons for the separation:

[1]"This change will relieve the Executive Committee of operating responsibility and permit it to serve the Convention more effectively and more objectively as an advisory body. [2] Establishment of the new commission will give to this important program status equal to that of other agencies and permit and encourage more rapid expansion of the stewardship promotion program."[7]

Not all members of the Executive Committee were happy about the separation. Also, some state executive secretaries objected. Some of the reasons heard in opposition were: (1) Cooperative Program administration and promotion should not be divided. (2) The Executive Committee had successfully managed the program since 1933. (3) Separation made stewardship promotion more expensive to finance.

The creation of a new agency required a second approval of the Southern Baptist Convention. This was given in 1959 when the Convention met at Louisville.[8] As soon as the recommendation was presented, Findley Edge, a professor in Southern Baptist Seminary,

moved that the responsibility of stewardship promotion be transferred to The Sunday School Board. He was supported in this by
his colleague, Ernest Loessner. After extensive debate, in which
Porter Routh, among others, defended the report of the Total Program Study Committee, the Convention voted second approval and
the Southern Baptist Stewardship Commission was born. The
professors argued that stewardship in the church is fundamentally
an educational matter and that the literature and programs of The
Sunday School Board would provide direct access to the churches
and their members. In rebuttal, others said: (1) stewardship promotion includes the Cooperative Program and both belong together,
(2) assignment to the board could create a duality of interests, (3)
all the agencies have stewardship responsibilities and should appropriately use their facilities to advance stewardship education, (4)
assignment to The Sunday School Board would place too many
programs in one agency, and (5) it would put the board in the
position of promoting competing programs for local church support, the sale of church literature, and the Cooperative Program
support. The recommendation to separate prevailed.

Moving the Executive Committee Offices

Before February 1963, when the Executive Committee moved
into offices of its own, it had been the welcome guest of The Sunday
School Board for thirty-six years. James L. Sullivan who succeeded
T. L. Holcomb as executive secretary of the board in 1953 was just
as open and understanding as his predecessors had been. In every
way, he made the Executive Committee and its employees feel welcome at The Sunday School Board building. In 1941 the Executive
Committee had moved from the Frost Building at 161 Eighth Avenue, North, to the new Sunday School Board administration building at 127 Ninth Avenue, North, where it occupied "seven
attractive, comfortable and commodious rooms."[9] At the time, the
Executive Committee had five or six regular employees. By 1949 the
staff had increased to nine regular employees and occasional part-
time helpers. That year, the Executive Committee requested an

entire floor in the tower planned for The Sunday School Board administration building.[10] In generous response, the board made available the entire third floor, including an office for Austin Crouch, offices for the Southern Baptist Foundation, storage rooms, a small kitchenette, and three committee rooms that could be opened into a large assembly room. The space was ready for occupancy in 1952. On the day the staff moved in, it appeared to be all the space the Executive Committee would ever need.

By 1959 the staff had expanded to fifteen people. In addition, four other agencies were looking to The Sunday School Board for office space. Demand for committee rooms had also increased. The various governing boards tended to hold their meetings in connection with the semiannual meetings of the Executive Committee and The Sunday School Board, so that sometimes the board committees were crowded out of their own facilities. Frequently, Executive Committee subcommittees had to meet in three different locations. The Executive Committee continued to have a hazy, uncertain public profile, especially in Nashville. The work it did was much more important than the people's knowledge of it.

When the 1958 annual Convention mandated a new building, it did not say where the building should be located.[11] About that time, James L. Sullivan conveyed to the Executive Committee an offer of The Sunday School Board to give the completely renovated Frost Building to the Executive Committee, but making clear that if the offer were not acceptable, the Executive Committee was welcome to stay in its present offices.[12] Though the Frost Building was old and somewhat dated, it appeared at first to meet Executive Committee needs. The Executive Committee agreed to accept the offer and and arranged for architects and engineers to develop a plan for its adaptation.[13] After further study, the building was found unsuitable for multiagency occupation. In February 1960, Porter Routh suggested "restudy of the the entire matter of the occupancy of the Frost Building."[14] The committee then agreed to a possible change of plans.

This opened the question of possible removal of the Executive

Committee from Nashville. Surprisingly, among the members of the Executive Committee, there seemed to be considerable support for the idea. At first the special committee to study relocation settled on Tulsa, Oklahoma. Centrally located between the East and the West, and with superior air service, the Western city seemed to be an ideal choice. But before the special committee could make its recommendation, opposition developed to so distant a removal. Finally, on May 17, 1960, it recommended that the Executive Committee relocate in Memphis, Tennessee.[15] Immediately, objections were raised, not so much from members of the Executive Committee as from from visitors who were present in the meeting. Other cities were proposed. Several people spoke in opposition to removal from Nashville, among them Norman W. Cox and J. R. White, whose arguments seemed to have most influence on those present.[16] A motion prevailed to refer the matter to the special committee for further study and report in September.[17]

The following September (1960), the special committee recommended that the Frost Building be returned to The Sunday School Board and that a site committee be appointed to study future location but that construction and removal be postponed until after 1964, the year of the Baptist Jubilee Advance celebration.[18] Some of the lawyers present said that the report was self-contradicting. Others said that the building itself should be part of the celebration. Sentiment developed for moving ahead. A site committee was appointed and the $1,200,000 that had been assigned by The Sunday School Board for renovation of the Frost Building was placed in the care of the Southern Baptist Foundation for use by the Executive Committee in constructing or purchasing a suitable building.

The next May (1961) the Executive Committee unanimously approved a recommendation of the site committee to locate the new headquarters building at 460 James Robertson Parkway in Nashville.[19] A building committee was appointed with Charles E. Curry, a Kansas City realtor, as chairman. Hart, Freeland, and Roberts of Nashville were employed as architects. In order not to be overwhelmed by the imposing architectural forms in the neighborhood, the committee approved an impressive four-floor octagonal building sheathed with attractive Virginia greenstone and a bold aluminum solar screen. Over the front doorway, there was placed a handsome bronze medallion, consisting of an open Bible and the world, superimposed with a cross, clearly announcing to those who pass the building the vision and the mission of Southern Baptists.[20]

The building's eight-sided form was modeled from ancient church buildings in the early Christian world, one example of which is the Charlemagne Chapel still standing in Aachen, Germany (ancient Aix-la-Chapelle).[21] The building provided offices for the Executive Committee, the Stewardship Commission, the Education Commission, the Christian Life Commission, the Southern Baptist Foundation, and later, for the Seminary Extension Department. Formal dedication was on February 20, 1963.[22] The Executive Committee rarely sang in its sessions, but that day it sang the spiritual purpose of the new building:

> The church's one foundation
> Is Jesus Christ her Lord;
> She is his new creation,
> By Spirit and the Word.

In the 1950s, the trauma of the hot Korean war, the terror of the Russian cold war, and the racial distress stirred up by the Supreme Court decision of 1954 veiled an otherwise prosperous decade with a vague sense of unceasing turmoil.[23] It began with the threat of the hydrogen bomb (1950), and it ended with a chagrined Eisenhower and an angry Khrushchev going home from an aborted summit after the U-2 spy plane squabble (1960). In between, the president of the Southern Baptist Convention, Brooks Hays, lost his seat in the United States Congress because he dared stand up for the blacks in the Arkansas school desegregation fight (1957).

The first five decades of the twentieth century had been decades of turmoil, each seeming to bring worse problems than any of the others. So it was for the 1960s, which undoubtedly was a record breaking ten years of social unrest. Those restless times produced racial strife, youth rebellion, urban crises, the Vietnam war, and the death-of-God theology of Thomas J. J. Altizer and William W. Hamilton.[24] For the Baptists, there was also doctrinal unrest. From time to time, the Convention spoke on all of these issues; in at least two of them, the Executive Committee played important parts.

In 1962 shock waves were felt throughout the Convention when Broadman Press published a book by Ralph H. Elliot, entitled, *The Message of Genesis.* Some of Elliot's interpretations did not agree with traditional Southern Baptist views. Protests were heard from all parts of the nation. One of the most effective was an article by a Texas pastor, K. Owen White, entitled "Death in the Pot" and was published in many of the state Baptist papers. Sometime before the meeting of the Southern Baptist Convention, it appeared that something had to be done, else the Convention would suffer broken fellowship. The conflict was very much on the mind of Porter Routh. Late in the spring he went to Oklahoma City with Albert McClellan for the fiftieth anniversary of the *Baptist Messenger,* of which they both had been editors. The morning after the celebration Routh and McClellan called on Herschel H. Hobbs, pastor of the First Baptist Church and president of the Southern Baptist Convention. The conversation turned to the Genesis crisis. As they talked, a plan of action unfolded. Routh brought it into focus. He suggested that a statement could be framed by a responsible and representative committee that would become a norm for general agreement. When the visit ended, the three had agreed that a good approach would be to propose to the Executive Committee the appointment of a committee to secure the rewriting of the Statement of Baptist Faith and Message approved by the Convention in 1925.

As a result, the Executive Committee presented to the San Francisco Convention (1962) a recommendation that reminded the messengers of the 1925 statement and that called for a committee of state convention presidents, chaired by the president of the Southern Baptist Convention, to draft and present to the Convention in 1963 a similar statement "which shall serve as information to the churches, and which may serve as guidelines to the various agencies of the Southern Baptist Convention."[25] In traditional Southern Baptist openess, the recommendation also said, "It is understood that any group or individuals may approach this committee to be of service." The Convention approved, and a committee of twenty-four presidents began their work.

The Baptist Faith and Message Committee, with Herschel H. Hobbs as chairman, met throughout the year and brought its report to the Convention meeting in Kansas City in 1963. After lengthy discussion, the report, including the introduction from the 1925 statement, was approved by the Convention, with the understanding that both statements would be printed side by side in the Convention Annual.[26] As a norm, the statement was heartily approved; as a creed, it was thoroughly rejected. The statement was reaffirmed in 1970, during the Denver Convention, at the height of the debate over Volume I of the *Broadman Bible Commentary*. Again, a Genesis commentary was in question, and the Convention voted 5,394 to 2,170 for The Sunday School Board to withdraw the volume from circulation "and that it be rewritten with due consideration to the conservative viewpoint."[27] That same year a motion was ruled out of order that would have made the Executive Committee a sentry to stand guard against agency violations of the Baptist Faith and Message statement.[28]

Racial strife in the 1960s led to major crises in American cities. In 1962 James H. Meredith was escorted by U. S. marshals to register as the first black student in the University of Mississippi.[29] In 1963 Martin Luther King, Jr. addressed 200,000 blacks and whites in a civil rights rally in the mall at Washington, D. C. Also in 1963 President John F. Kennedy was shot and killed in Dallas, Texas. In 1964 three civil rights workers were murdered in Mississippi. In 1965 Martin Luther King and 2,600 other blacks were arrested while marching in Selma, Alabama. That same year, black riots in the Watts section of Los Angeles resulted in 34 dead, 1,000 injured, 4,000 arrested, and $175 million in fire damage. In 1968 Martin Luther King, Jr. and Robert F. Kennedy were assassinated. The Vietnam war was accelerated in 1964; by 1968 there were 525,000

American troops in the beleagured country. Frustrated, and with his popularity waning, Lyndon Johnson announced in the spring of 1968 that he would not seek another term as president of the United States.

Porter Routh was driving from Charleston, South Carolina, to Savannah, Georgia, in 1968 when he heard on the radio that Martin Luther King, Jr. had been killed in Memphis, Tennessee. Deeply aware of the tensions tearing the country apart, he was fearful that the long, hot summer ahead would accelerate the bitterness. The question on his mind was: *Is there something Southern Baptists can do to help reduce the frustration and the anger?* That night in Savannah, rebellious arsonists burned property not far from the motel where he and Mrs. Routh were staying. The next day Routh had lunch with black civic leaders in Atlanta and found them distressed and afraid.

At home he talked with his pastor, H. Franklin Paschall, who was also president of the Southern Baptist Convention, and with James E. Pleitz, a Florida pastor, who was also chairman of the Executive Committee. While Routh was still pondering the problem, Victor Glass, director of the Home Mission Board's program of work with National Baptists appeared in Routh's office with the word that black Baptist leadership was greatly distressed and looking to Southern Baptists for reassurance. Routh and Paschall then agreed that the next step was to call an informal conference of Baptist leaders. After long, earnest conversation and prayer, most of the members of this group agreed to sign a "Statement Concerning the Crises in Our Nation" prepared by Clifton Judson Allen and to refer it to the Executive Committee for possible recommendation to the Convention.

When the Executive Committee assembled in Houston in 1968 for its pre-Convention meeting, the statement was presented by the chairman, James L. Pleitz.[30] After some revision, it was approved with only three dissenting votes. The next day, on June 5, the Executive Committee presented the lengthy statement to the Convention.[31] The appeal was straight to the Baptist conscience:

We appeal to our fellow Southern Baptists to engage in Christian
ventures of human relationships, and to take courageous actions for
justice and peace. We believe that a vigorous Christian response to
this national crisis is imperative for an effective witness on our part
at home and abroad. Words will not suffice. The time has come for
action. Our hope for healing and renewal is in the redemption of the
whole of life. Let us call men to faith in Christ. Let us dare to accept
the full demands of the love and lordship of Christ in human relationships and urgent ministry. Let us be identified with Christ in the
reproach and suffering of the cross.

The statement was approved, 5,687 for and 2,119 against.

That evening, Robert F. Kennedy was assassinated in a Los Angeles hotel after winning the California presidential primary.

Distraught youth were part of the national travail and among
them were Southern Baptist young people. Mindful of this and of
their own stewardship, Southern Baptist leaders became concerned
about the future of Christian higher education. Administrators and
professors in the Baptist colleges were facing difficulties in maintaining focus on Christian values among youth influenced by the
youth rebellion. Baptists generally believed (1) that denominational
stability depended on trained leaders for both the churches and the
general Baptist bodies and their agencies and (2) that the colleges
needed a helping hand from the Southern Baptist Convention.

The Executive Committee responded by supporting the Education Commission and its executive director, Rabun L. Brantley, in
a three-year study of "the problems and opportunities in the field
of Christian higher education" in Baptist colleges.[32] The Executive
Committee (1) appropriated $25,000 for the Baptist Education
Study Task (BEST) and (2) permitted some of its staff to work
closely with the project. In September 1967, after two national
conferences of Baptist college leaders and eighteen regional seminars involving 8,000 youth and adults, the study was finished and
the report published in a book entitled, *BEST.* Ten years later, it was
republished, "Because of the historical significance of the Baptist
Education Study Task (BEST) . . . and because of the relevance of

this report to the contemporary educational situation in the Baptist colleges."[33] Reflecting on its significance, Ben C. Fisher, who had been a member of the steering committee and later the executive director of the Education Commission, said in 1984 that the Baptist Education Study Task has been "pivotal in the progress of Southern Baptist Education."[34]

The decade of the sixties was the decade of the hippies. They could be seen in every community, and especially in the cities. Youth were being led by scores of pied pipers into the highways and hedges of irresponsibility. Again, taking note of Southern Baptist young people, the Executive Committee in June 1969 voted to invite three to five "outstanding youth to participate in the September meeting of the Executive committee."[35] This was continued into the 1980s.

Strengthening the Budget Process

One of the toughest jobs of the Executive Committee is the development of the annual Cooperative Program Allocations Budget. None of the agencies is ever wholly satisifed; most of the time some are totally dissatisfied. J. Ralph Grant, a tall Texas pastor and a member of the Executive Committee, after listening for hours to the urgent pleas of the agency heads, said, "We would not have them to be any less concerned or any less aggressive. They are not doing their job unless they want more for their causes than the Convention is able to supply." The Total Program Study Committee recommendations led to a better method of determining the allocations by (1) establishing the Program Committee with the responsibility of looking at programs and dollars together and (2) by requiring the agencies to furnish more systematic information on "program plans, accomplishments and costs."[36] For the Program Committee to do its work, three things had to be done: (1) the completion of the Organizational Manual, (2) the perfecting of a reporting format that would relate work planned and accomplished to dollars requested, and (3) the organization of all the steps into a manageable calendar. To help it do this, the Executive Committee employed the consultant used by the Total Program Study Committee, Lawrence I. Wilsey.

Six months later Wilsey submitted his report under the title, *Program Budget Reporting Survey.*[37] It included, in addition to suggestions for a reporting format, the job descriptions of the executive secretary-treasurer, the program planning secretary, and the financial planning secretary, showing the responsibilities that each had for the process. In essence, the suggested format required:

- a highlight statement of the agency's activities and accomplishments for the year;
- listing of all agency financial sources applicable to operating and capital needs, comparing the present budget year with the past budget year and the future budget year;
- identifying specific program areas in which the money from all sources would be spent, also on a comparison basis by budget years;
- reasons for the requested increase of Cooperative Program allocation for the next budget year;
- descriptions of present and planned capital needs projects;
- listing of all debts;
- listing of all assets, including endowments and funds functioning as endowments;
- suggestions and requests; and
- certification that the report had been approved by the agency's trustees or other officially designated committee of the board.

The processing of an annual Cooperative Program Allocation Budget was discovered to take about eighteen months to complete. In order to make the process clear, the Program Committee used a calendar showing steps taken by groups and individuals.[38]

At first complaints were registered from some of the agencies: (1) objection to some of the terms used for reporting agency income, (2) reluctance to report reserves in ways that would compare them with other capital assets, (3) dissatisfaction with the tight calendar that required completion so soon after the close of the audit year, and (4) uneasiness by some because of the discrepancy between estimated program costs and actual program costs. On the other hand, there were some questions by the staff and the members of the Program Committee: (1) some of the agencies appeared not to take program projection and program costing seriously, (2) differences between program goals and actions projected and program results and actions reported, (3) seeming inability of agencies to stay with projected capital needs programs, (4) tendency of some to go into debt for operating expenses—occasionally long-range debt beyond three years duration without Convention permission—and, (5) neglect of some agencies to include in their reports full information on subsidiary corporations. Few, if any, of these irregularities were intentional.

No process is entirely satisfactory when the fate of institutions and the destinies of people are at stake. At times strong men wept. One crisis-ridden night an executive fainted with an apparent heart attack when he learned the proposed allocation to his agency. Happily, he lived to successful retirement, knowing that in spite of its financial problems his agency was alive and doing well. On the other side of the table were the men and women who made the decisions and the staff who sat with them all through the long sessions were often exhausted and sleepless. They could not forget the earnest pleas and the inevitable bottom lines that never seemed to meet the needs. For some, it took days to recover from the budget-making trauma. With experience the format and the calendar were adjusted to correct misunderstanding and timing. Generally, the process became as satisfactory as could be expected of such an emotionally oriented experience.

Notes

1. ECM, December 11, 1957, p. 12; January 23, 1958, pp. 2-3. Lawrence Wilsey, a Presbyterian, was a partner in the management consultant firm of Booz, Allen, and Hamilton, and later president of Texas Christian University.

2. E. Y. Mullins, *Baptist Beliefs* (Louisville: Baptist World, 1912), p. 38.

3. SBC, 1956, p. 44.

4. SBC, 1958, p. 430.

5. Ibid., pp. 55-57; cf. 430-434.

6. SBC, 1959, pp. 74-75.

7. Ibid., pp. 66-67.

8. Ibid.

9. SBC, 1941, p. 30.

10. ECM, June 15-16, 1949, p. 134.

11. SBC, 1958, p. 433.

12. ECM, May 20, 1958, p. 3, Appendix C.

13. ECM, December 17, 1958, pp. 3-5.

14. ECM, February 24, 1960, pp. 18-19.

15. ECM, May 17, 1960, pp. 4-5; Addendum C.

16. Norman W. Cox, who was not a member of the Executive Committee at the time, later admitted to the author of this book that he had prompted some of the opposition expressed in the Executive Committee debate.

17. From 1927 many denominational leaders had attended the Executive Committee meetings. Until about 1963 they participated freely in debate, a participation that was encouraged by the informal seating of the semiannual meetings.

18. ECM, September 21, 1960, pp. 3-5.

19. ECM, May 23, 1961, pp. 2, 5.

20. The author while in Europe in 1962 drove an ancient Fiat, 100 miles over torturous Italian roads to a foundry where he inspected the wet sand model identical in size and form to the bronze medallion placed on the building six months later.

21. The building was designed for two additional floors and for possible extensions on three of the eight sides.

22. ECM, February 20, 1963, pp. 4, A.

23. For information on the current events cited, see *Information Please Almanac-1983*, pp. 119-121.

24. The controversial book, *Radical Theology and the Death of God* by Thomas J. J. Altizer and William W. Hamilton appeared in 1966.

25. SBC, 1962, pp. 27, 64. Only those presidents from state conventions officially recognized as such by the Southern Baptist Convention were included.

26. SBC, 1963, pp. 63-64, 269-281.

27. SBC, 1970, pp. 63, 66, 68, 72, 76-78.

28. Ibid., p. 64.

29. *Information Please Almanac, 1983,* pp. 119-121.

30. ECM, June 4, 1968, pp. 2-3, A.

31. SBC, 1968, pp. 68-69, 73.

32. ECM, February 24-25, 1965, pp. 9, 14.

33. Ben C. Fisher, editor, *BEST,* (Nashville: SBC Education Commission, 1977) p. ii.

34. Ben C. Fisher to AM, September 15, 1984.

35. ECM, June 12, 1969, p. 2.

36. SBC, 1958, p. 56.

37. ECM. December 17, 1958, pp. 5, 10. Cf. *Program Budget Reporting Survey.*

38. See pp. for a schedule of events and decisions required for the development of the Cooperative Program Allocation Budget. Note also that in 1959 the Cooperative Program Allocation Budget included an increased amount from The Sunday School Board for the Southern Baptist Convention Operating Budget. This was by agreement between the Executive Committee and the board in exchange for transfer of the SBC Bulletin and Mat Service to Sunday School Board ownership. The annual amount allocated was based on a formula related to annual contributions made by the Board to the state conventions for promotional support of Sunday School Board programs. The arrangement solved three problems. (1) It assured an annual allocation from the board to Convention operating expenses. (2) It removed the Executive Committee from direct sales to the churches. (3) By specifying that the Executive Committee would continue to control the editorial content of the Baptist Bulletin Service, it provided permanent media through which the Executive Committee could conduct "the general work of promotion and the general work of publicity for the Convention in cooperation with the agencies of the Convention" in keeping with SBC Bylaw 20. 5. (h). For further information see the 1959 SBC Annual (p. 47).

10

Full Visibility for the Executive Committee
(Part II)
1959-1969

The meetings of the Executive Committee in the mid sixties were different from the ones of the mid fifties. In the fifties, seating was informal with members and visitors sitting side by side. A new member could have difficulty in telling them apart. Some of the better-known visitors participated freely in debate, and a few of them sat close to the front of the room. By the mid sixties, with formal seating in the Austin Crouch Room of the Southern Baptist Convention Building, debate was also more formal. Most of the visitors, while willing to make their views known, were less inclined to argue their points. Some of the older ones were as eager as ever. The size of the Executive Committee had increased from thirty members in 1930 to fifty-eight members in 1967. The center of discussion slowly shifted from the plenary sessions to the subcommittee and work group sessions. The agendas had become much too heavy and too involved for everything to be debated fully by the committee of the whole.

The Austin Crouch Room was arranged for members to sit at tables facing the platform. A low banister separated them from the visitors who were seated in opera chairs slightly elevated on three sides of the room. There were about 230 chairs, most of them occupied during the plenary sessions. By the late seventies, the room had become crowded with extra chairs. Frequently attendance in excess of 300 spilled over into the halls.

The subcommittees and work groups were fully open to the visitors. There were no restrictions, except that anything said in the

219

smaller groups was not for quotation in the public press.[1] The reasons for this were that the views expressed in the smaller groups were the tentative views of individuals and that only the final actions of the Executive Committee were "on the record."

Developing the Organizational Manual

Many of the changes in the sixties were initiated either directly or indirectly by the Committee to Study the Total Program. One of them was the new responsibility assigned to the Executive Committee for the development of the Organization Manual. This related to the new Convention requirement for the agencies to "present their reports on a more appropriate and comparable basis and to provide more information about program plans, accomplishments and costs."[2] To do this it was necessary to develop orderly descriptions of agency programs on a comparable basis; for these descriptions, the organization manual was needed.[3] The task of developing this manual was assigned by the Convention to the Executive Committee and then was passed to the new Program Committee. The Program Committee began its work, knowing that it would take considerable time and effort to complete the organization manual. The general program picture was by no means uniform, and the extremes were discouraging. Some of them were:

- Some agencies grew as a house grows when rooms are added to meet family needs. Some of the rooms become obsolete and are maintained for appearance only.
- Some program workers were working outside their assigned tasks, some of them in the program domains of others.
- Hurtful competition existed between some programs, both within agencies and across agency lines.
- Some program areas were subdivided between other programs and even other agencies, without clear lines of separation.
- A few program leaders openly claimed areas of work that were jealously guarded by other departments and agencies.

- The successes of some agency programs were measured exclusively by results in the churches, with indifference toward how well the agency programs were achieving their own specific goal and action plans.
- Sometimes questionable programs staffed with popular program leaders secured excessive financing when other more important programs secured far less financing than needed.
- There was a slight tendency to give all program areas equal status, regardless of the value of their work for achieving Convention or agency objectives.
- Some of the agencies listed only line budget items, such as salaries, travel, and rent, thus obscuring what the money actually accomplished.
- Occasionally, there was little relationship between work planned and results accomplished.

This list does not imply general denominational chaos. There were problems, but the work was done and, in most cases, done well. But the time had come, when, due to the increasing complications of modern organizational life, changes needed to be made for the sake of future efficiency.

Before the programs could be identified and described, several barriers had to be crossed. A program definition had to be written, a format developed, a procedure agreed upon, and a calendar set. Also, accurate background information showing the relationships of the agencies to the Convention had to be developed. Most of all, both the Executive Committee and the agencies had to come to a clear understanding of the Executive Committee's role in the process. Among some agencies, there was mild resistance. For example, in the first full-scale meeting of the Program Committee following the release of the *Program Budget Reporting Survey*, the members met with agency representatives to discuss the project. In the meeting with the Foreign Mission Board, the executive secretary, Baker James Cauthen, quietly listened to the presentation. At the end he had little to say, but it was obvious that he was disturbed and wanted to avoid dialogue. Someone made the point that the Executive Committee had been mandated to get on with the job. His very silence took compelling possession of the room. Then sternly —almost indignantly—he said, "Executive Committee? The Foreign Mission Board is its own Executive Committee."

Cauthen's feelings were not hard to understand. The Foreign Mission Board had existed for eighty-two years before the reorganized Executive Committee and ninety-three years before the Business and Financial Plan. The Constitution and Bylaws of the Southern Baptist Convention give the boards control of their internal affairs, and the Executive Committee cannot interfere. This is on the assumption that the agencies alone are responsible for their own work.

The Executive Committee does have the authority to study and recommend. Traditionally, studies and recommendations have been in cooperation with the agencies and have dealt with general denominational policy, not internal agency operations. The power to study and recommend has been used sparingly, lest the Executive Committee influence become eroded. Special instructions involving the agencies have been followed from a posture of trust and cooperation built upon the Executive Committee's long reputation for honor, integrity, fairness, reasonableness, and caution. With this background clearly in mind, the Executive Committee and its staff were able to establish good working relationships in the development of the Organization Manual. It must be said of Baker James Cauthen—as for all of the agency executives—that when he understood the cooperative spirit of the Executive Committee and its staff in the effort to bring about an orderly description of Convention programs he cooperated fully and happily.

The Program Committee hoped to finish its task by 1963,[4] but the development moved much slower than had been anticipated. Almost the first step was the development of background information on Convention assignment of programs and projects to the agencies. To do this work, the Executive Committee turned to the SBC Historical Commission. A recent Th.D. graduate of New Orleans

Seminary, Lynn E. May, Jr., was assigned to make the compilation. As each of the agencies were studied, May would furnish a lengthy summary of actions drawn from the SBC annuals. It was exhaustive work, meticulously drawn and essential to the process.

The development of the Organization Manual was a slow and intricate process, with everyone having to learn everything about it step by step. The plan was to begin with the smaller and simpler agencies and then move to the larger and more complicated ones. The documents had to be written with great care and circulated to all the other agencies. This was necessary because of the overlapping areas of work. The venture was much like a homeowner blasting a huge rock in his own yard to find after the explosion that the rock extends hidden underground across his property line and is the foundation on which his neighbor's house is built. The fear of these hidden rocks kept all of the agencies minutely aware of each other's programs.

Another helpful person in the process was James L. Sullivan, executive secretary of The Sunday School Board. Because of his leadership in the advanced development of program budgeting at the board, Sullivan was able to supply reliable counsel to the other agencies and to the program planning staff of the Executive Committee. The last program statement was approved in 1967, and the *Organization Manual* was printed.[5] It had been discovered in the course of the study that Southern Baptists had eighty-eight programs,[6] and that these fell into five categories:

Self-supporting programs	12
Channel (church organization) programs	7
Emphasis programs	9
Church Service programs	14
Representative programs	46
TOTAL	88

All of the agencies cooperated fully in the completion of the program statements. The next step was to give the organization manual enough prominence that it would not be forgotten. To do this, it was first printed in the 1967 Convention Annual and then made available in book form to the agencies and state conventions. The final enabling act of the Convention was to approve Bylaw Fourteen:

> *Program Statements.* The program statements of the agencies as approved by the Southern Baptist Convention and published in the 1967 *Annual* and subsequently amended express the policy of the Convention with respect to the programs of the agencies of Convention.

In 1964 the Executive Committee unintentionally raised the issue of program budgeting at the Southern Baptist Convention level.[7] Pressure was great for increased seminary faculty salaries. Some of the teachers were earning less than some of their students. After review of their problem, the Executive Committee recommended that $100,000 of the allocation to the seminaries be designated for improvement of teacher's salaries.[8] The seminary presidents had not requested it as a specific appropriation; but obviously, they could not oppose it. The recommendation was approved without comment by the Convention. Sometime later a strong protest was heard, surprisingly from a Southern Seminary professor, Findley B. Edge of Louisville. As a result, it soon became clear that in keeping with its polity the Southern Baptist Convention should allocate funds to agencies, not to the programs of the agencies. Exceptions have been made at the request of the agencies. This limitation may be the one of four reasons why the Executive Committee could not do detailed program evaluation. The other three are the lack of sufficient staff, the lack of Executive Committee authority to direct the agencies to change the ways they carry out their programs, and the need to hold, as much as possible, the power to study and recommend on the policy level, not on the administrative level.

Increasing the Finances

Foremost among the duties of the Executive Committee is its responsibility, as the Convention's fiscal agent, to look after Convention finances. This was as true in the abundant times of the 1960s as it had been in the sparse times of the 1930s. This required a variety of duties, among them (1) the allocation and distribution of Cooperative Program funds, (2) cooperation with the new Stewardship Commission in the promotion of the Cooperative Program, and (3) careful and responsible administration of the Business and Financial Plan.

In 1959 the Executive Committee received $17,101,216 for distribution to the agencies.[9] In 1969 it received $27,433,440.[10] This was a gain of $10,332,224, or 60 percent. But the gain did not come easy. Twice, due to the recession of the early 1960s, the Executive Committee asked the agencies scheduled to receive capital needs funds not to expect more than 70 percent of what had been promised for the year. The relative financial tightness of some of the years can be seen in the table of Cooperative Program operating budgets approved by the Convention:

Year	SBC CP	Annual Increases	
1959	$10,800,000		
1960	$12,311,900	$1,511,900	(14.00 percent)
1961	13,938,500	1,626,600	(13.00 percent)
1962	13,938,500	none	none
1963	14,217,500	279,000	(2.00 percent)
1964	14,626,500	409,000	(2.88 percent)
1965	17,590,850	2,964,350	(20.27 percent)
1966	19,016,000	1,425,150	(8.10 percent)
1967	21,950,500	2,934,500	(15.43 percent)
1968	24,484,000	2,533,500	(11.54 percent)
1969	26,561,019	2,077,019	(8.48 percent)

The variances in annual percentages of increase reflect: (1) the economic outlook at the time a budget was set, (2) the pressures of the capital needs budgets, (3) the need to catch up from previous year capital needs budget shortfalls, and (4) the spirit prevailing in the denomination at the time the budget year was completed.

The third and largest Capital Needs Program was voted in 1957: $24,000,000 to be funded in four years,[11] which no doubt would have been spread over more years if the Executive Committee and the Convention could have looked ahead. But looking ahead is not always possible. It created some pressure on the Cooperative Program Allocations Budget in 1963 and 1964, but it did accomplish a great deal of good, especially for missions and for the seminaries. The new Capital Needs Program included $5,000,000 for the Foreign Mission Board and $1,300,000 for the Home Mission Board, which since 1949 had been partially used for board operations by permission of the Convention.[12] The 1959 program also included $4,000,000 for the Home Mission Board's Church Extension Loan Fund. A total of $11,700,000 or 49.16 percent was for much needed seminary renovation and expansion of the six seminaries.

In the 1960s, the Executive Committee developed very close ties with the new Stewardship Commission. In September 1960, in a simple ceremony during which the members and the staff of the new Commission were recognized, "Kendall Berry, chairman of the Executive Committee, made the official transfer to Harold G. Sanders, chairman of the Stewardship Commission."[13] The staff and the members of the new commission were recognized. At the same time, the Executive Committee set aside $75,000 "to serve as operating capital" for the commission. There was no sadness in the transfer, though the Executive Committee staff had some wistfulness in the loss of daily contact with dedicated people with whom it had worked for so many years. Merrill D. Moore, the new executive director of the commission would still be close by, as would the friendly and helpful Robert G. Capra, the assistant director of Cooperative Promotion. But the quiet and serious-minded Robert J. Hastings, the associate director of church finance would be farther away. He had recently accepted a position with Kentucky Baptists as state director of promotion.

As the number of agencies increased and as the financial responsibilities of the Convention expanded, the Business and Financial
Plan became even more important in the management of Convention affairs. Changes and additions were inevitable, and the Executive Committee was in the best position to see the ones needed.
From 1952 to 1969, nineteen proposals for changes were made to
the Convention. All except one were originated by the Executive
Committee. That one was referred to the Executive Committee for
study.[14] The other eighteen were passed, one or two with amendments. Occasionally, the changes were initiated at the request of an
agency or a committee. Sometimes they were made in response to
existent or anticipated problems. Usually they were for minor,
though significant, changes in wording. Some of the typical changes
for 1952-1969 were:

> **1952:** Debts for capital purposes, not payable from anticipated
> sources within three years, must have Convention or Executive
> Committee approval.
> **1953:** Agency subsidiary corporations are subject to the Con-
> vention regulations on debts, the same as the agencies.
> **1959:** The Executive Committee must review but not approve
> agency budgets. The Sunday School Board is neither permitted
> nor required to make direct appropriations to the agencies; it
> must make an annual contribution to the convention operating
> budget, and it must report all allocations it makes to state
> conventions.
> **1964:** Agency employees or board members who also have
> interests in businesses may not do business with the agency of
> which they are employees, except under exceptional circum-
> stances. Capital needs are defined as whatever adds value to the
> long-range assets of the agency. Agencies must maintain any
> income-producing property out of the income. The Executive
> Committee is permitted, for study purposes, to employ audi-
> tors to work with agency auditors in the study of agency audits
> in light of Convention action.

1967: The Convention's film, publication and merchandising policy was incorporated into the Business and Financial Plan.

Porter Routh was as fully alert to the importance of the Business and Financial Plan as was Austin Crouch. He realized that it is always possible for the limits of the plan to be be overstepped by eager executives, either unaware of the boundaries or in desperate hurry to achieve agency objectives. In the management of the Business and Financial Plan, Routh brought to his office both a temperament and an ability suited to the times. He was instinctively conservative but in no way fearful of moving ahead; and he was rarely ruffled. He met problems head-on, without fears of failure or feelings of impending crisis. He spoke with firmness, but not in storm or in anger. Like Moses he could walk for a time with those who wanted prematurely to cross Jordan and for a time with those who wanted to go back to Egypt; but he never forgot the masses whom God had appointed him to lead.

Routh could quickly see the crux of a problem; and almost instinctively, he could spot infractions of the Business and Financial Plan. Never given to timidity or procrastination, he frequently took initiative in a frank, short letter or a quick, direct conversation, but never without being sure of his facts. If asked by an executive for clarification of the Business and Financial Plan, he was swift, open, clear, and just in his response. Routh was impartial in his decisions and would rule against himself as quickly as against others.

By the 1960s, Routh had come to see his job in the simplest possible way. Caring little for unnecessary amenities, and less for self-display, he was direct and open in his administrative style. His communication with his staff was almost always in person. Without in the slightest letting go his lines of leadership, he trusted the SBC agency and state convention executives, careful always to listen to any who wanted to talk with him. He would not, under any circumstances, knowingly upstage them. It was his conviction that, due to the unique polity of the Southern Baptist Convention, for the Executive Committee to properly do its work it had to share the stage with the SBC agencies. He believed that each of them should be given its chance to star with Southern Baptists. Perhaps it was awareness of his egalitarian temperament and his deep Christian conviction that enabled the agencies to accept the toughness of some of his decisions.

Acting in "an Advisory Way"

One of the original duties assigned the Executive Committee was "to act in an advisory way on matters of policy and co-operation arising between the agencies of the Convention, or between the agencies of the Convention and the cooperating state agencies."[15] Occasionally, this extended to helping agencies with internal problems. This happened in 1959 at Southern Seminary when trouble developed between the faculty and the administration. The trustees attempted to negotiate the personal differences into a workable partnership, but one group would not negotiate except as a block and would not yield in its demands. This collusion resulted in the dismissal of thirteen of the professors.[16] But the problem would not go away. Finally, in December of that year, the trustees appealed to the Executive Committee for help. A committee of present and past Southern Baptist Convention presidents was appointed: (1) to study the organization and administration of the seminary, (2) to review the problem of the dismissed faculty, and (3) to report "to the people of the Convention." After many months of careful investigation, including an all-night meeting with dismissed faculty members, the seminary administration and the trustees, and the rest of the faculty, the committee of SBC presidents reported that the school had been reorganized with a new dean and that the action against the dismissed professors had been changed from outright dismissals to requests for resignations. In this way, the Executive Committee arranged the easing of a delicate disagreement without itself becoming the arbitrator.

Another example of the Executive Committee "acting in an advisory way" came in the sixties when differences developed between the Radio and Television Commission and the Foreign Mission

Board. In its search for a wider and more substantive program base, at various times the commission had been in conflict with the Home Mission Board over radio and evangelism policies and with The Sunday School Board over music and record merchandising and film production and distribution. Some of the commission's leaders apparently did not regard radio and television as a service available to all the agencies to be used on their behalf and without competition with them.

Even from 1953, when Paul M. Stevens first joined the commission, he talked of expanding the work of the commission into all the world. Committed to missions, Stevens was totally sincere in his belief that his commission had the right to go across international boundaries to wherever the radio waves went, regardless of the assignments that the Convention had made to other agencies. Stevens was an unusually gifted man with many innovative ideas for advancing the use of radio and television in missions. He was also very forceful in persuading people to accept his points of view.

Though heavily in debt, the commission began arranging radio and television programs in countries occupied by Foreign Mission Board missionaries already at work in broadcast ministries. Naturally, Baker James Cauthen, the executive secretary of the Foreign Mission Board, and his staff were much concerned. They were fearful that there soon would be two foreign mission boards at work with two different sets of policies in competition and conflict with each other. The problem was brought to the attention of the Executive Committee, and the task of finding a solution was referred to the Program Committee.[17] Position papers were developed, and conferences were held with both parties, at first separately and then together. In the end, both Stevens and Cauthen agreed that, with some adjustment in the commission's program statement, the two groups would work together in radio and television. The Foreign Mission Board would lead and furnish the finances, and the Radio and Television Commission would contribute its technical skills and materials. Stevens led the commission to employ a person to live in

Richmond and to promote better communications between the two agencies.

A different kind of problem requiring assistance from the Executive Committee arose between state directors of campus ministry and The Sunday School Board. The directors objected to some of the board's policies for Baptist Student Union work. Among other things, they wanted the student program substantially changed, the department transferred out of the Education Division of The Sunday School Board, the financial assistance to state BSU departments increased, and some of the supervisory people removed. The board felt that it could not meet any of these requests in ways that were satisfactory to the directors. When conference after conference netted no results, the board's executive secretary, James L. Sullivan, aware of the needs of Baptist young people in the midst of the youth revolution, led his board to ask the Executive Committee to conduct a major study of campus ministry work.[18] The study involved hundreds of young people, pastors, campus directors, and denominational leaders. It was climaxed with a national conference of students and student leaders held on the campus of Southwestern Seminary. The report was made to the Executive Committee in February 1970. The program was left with the board and in the Education Division, but the board agreed to give it more visibility and to increase its quality. A special interagency advisory committee was created to help campus ministry leaders keep in touch with the agency services available for youth work.

Celebrating the Dream

Southern Baptists debate and celebrate. They plan and talk about their plans. They get some things done and wish they could do more. From decade to decade, the Executive Committee is involved very much in helping with the celebrations. It does this by joining with others in marking the Convention anniversaries and planning the Convention emphases. The more important the anniversaries, the more impressive the celebrations. Sometimes the emphases are tied to the anniversaries. Thus in 1964, on the 150th anniversary of

Baptists in America organized for mission work, the celebration involved nine major Baptist bodies and climaxed with a great rally at Atlantic City in tribute to the Triennial Baptist Convention organized at Philadelphia in 1814. Preparation for the celebration began in 1954 when the Executive Committee approved a world evangelization drive for 1959-1964.[19]

The other Baptist bodies joined in the program under the name Baptist Jubilee Advance. Besides initiating the project, the Executive Committee contributed the services of its staff to the general leadership. In reviewing its accomplishments, Porter Routh cited five important gains in Baptist work resulting from the Baptist Jubilee Advance: (1) rekindling of the mission fires, (2) communication of Baptist leaders across structured denominational lines, (3) practical program assistance, especially for the smaller groups, (4) increased awareness of Baptist history, and (5) the creation of the permanent North American Baptist Fellowship.

Beginning with the Baptist Jubilee Advance, the Executive Committee became intensively active in Convention emphasis planning. This was in keeping with the Convention bylaw that stated that one of the Executive Committee duties was to conduct the general work of promotion for the Convention in cooperation with the other agencies and institutions of the Convention.

The next major emphasis was set for the decade of the seventies. In 1964 the Executive Committee called for the development of a plan for 1969-1979.[20] The general outline was developed by the Inter-Agency Council and the Executive Committee working together and was approved by the Convention in 1967 as the '70 Onward emphasis.[21] It included a massive church organization face-lifting plan led by William L. Howse, Jr., of The Sunday School Board. Much of this planning was done by a special committee of representatives of the major boards and involved more than a score of program leaders. The '70 Onward emphasis brought changes in the grading system, in the names of educational organizations, and in the titles of educational magazines. It also brought an increased variety of educational materials. The four-year emphasis attempted to rekindle Southern Baptist enthusiasm for traditional Baptist values. Annual themes were: *Living the Spirit of Christ* in

Belief and Relevance	1969-1970
Openess and Freedom	1970-1971
Expectancy and Creativity	1971-1972
Faith and Conquest	1972-1973

Honoring the People

In the 1960s, the chairpersons of the Executive Committee were elected by the group. There were no nominating committees. Usually two or three people were informally nominated from the floor in an atmosphere of general goodwill. The fellowship was so even that it was difficult to guess just who would likely win until the votes were counted. There was no lack of talent. For each person nominated, there were a half dozen others who could have served with equal distinction. Those who elected during the period were:

Kendall Berry, Arkansas banker	1959, 1960
John H. Haldeman, Florida pastor	1961, 1962
Harold W. Seever, Alabama pastor	1963, 1964
W. Douglas Hudgins, Mississippi pastor	1965, 1966
James L. Pleitz, Florida pastor	1967, 1968
James L. Monroe, Florida pastor	1969, 1970

Berry was a devout and unassuming Arkansas layman who later became executive director of the Southern Baptist Foundation. He had an interest in art and shared his paintings with his friends. Haldeman was a realtor turned Baptist minister and was generous with his souvenir gold pieces. Seever, though reared in Cincinnati, adapted naturally to the South. A thoughtful, proud man, his distinguished ministry was cut short by diabetes and blindness. Hudgins was an Old South Baptist, an eloquent preacher, and exceedingly conscious of traditional denominational values—a gatekeeper for agency rights. Pleitz, despite his youthful appearance when he joined the Executive Committee, was recognized as a denominational leader when he left. He covered all the bases and played them well. James L. Monroe, a natural leader, could rise to the top of any group he joined; his forte: plain talk on responsibility.

The presidents of the Southern Baptist Convention, as always were influential in Executive Committee affairs. They were:

Brooks Hays, Arkansas congressman	1958, 1959
Ramsey Pollard, Tennessee pastor	1960, 1961
Herschel H. Hobbs, Oklahoma pastor	1962, 1963
K. Owen White, Texas pastor	1964
W. Wayne Dehoney, Tennessee pastor	1965, 1966
H. Franklin Paschall, Tennessee pastor	1967, 1968
W. A. Criswell, Texas pastor	1969, 1970

Brooks Hays, whose humor and humanity were surpassed only by his love for the church and his understanding of the Spirit of Christ, lived for the Baptists and bled for America. Ramsey Pollard, superb preacher and indefatigable evangelist, was a Christian gentleman in the evangelistic tradition of George W. Truett, L. R. Scarborough, and C. E. Matthews. Herschel H. Hobbs, child of God, disciple of A. T. Robertson and Hersey Davis, will long live through his theological legacy to Southern Baptists. K. O. White, a quiet, unassuming man, spoke firmly and Southern Baptists heard him clearly. Wayne Dehoney, a man of ideas and unfailing accomplishments, loved the denomination. Franklin Paschall, preacher, pastor, and prophet; the larger his audience, the brighter his humor and the sharper his message. Wallie Amos Criswell, compelling preacher, had some of the qualities of the prophet whose name he carried.

Executive Committee staff retirements and additions inevitably changed the committee's fabric and brought new perspectives. Wilmer C. Fields, a pastor from Mississippi, became director of Public Relations in 1959 and was assigned responsibility for the Baptist Press, the Baptist Bulletin Service, and the *Baptist Program.* A tall, soft-spoken man, he came to the Executive Committee from a background of wide experience, both in the pastorate and in publications. At the time of his election, he was editor of the Mississippi *Baptist Record.* Though he was a fluent writer and excellent preacher, his most effective work was in public relations and communications planning. He developed the newsroom of the annual Convention into one of the most efficient of any organized group in America. Another notable contribution in leadership was Field's development of the annual public relations seminars for Southern Baptist press and public relations personnel. He succeeded splendidly as a leader, a fact proved in his simultaneous election as president both of the Associated Church Press of America and of the Religious Public Relations Council in the mid sixties.

One of the blessings of the work of the Committee to Study the Total Program was the relief it brought to the office of the executive secretary. That committee's report recommended assistance for Porter Routh in handling the many details related to the business of the Executive Committee and to the planning for the annual Convention. For this new position, the Executive Committee turned to John H. Williams, a layman who had worked for The Sunday School Board since 1935. He began work for the Executive Committee as the financial planning secretary on January 1, 1959. A friendly, even-tempered man, he brought with him an intimate knowledge of the denomination and a host of personal contacts. Skilled in all phases of business, he carried his load with aptness and promptitude. For seventeen years, until his retirement in 1976, he made friends for Southern Baptists, not only in Nashville but in every city where the Southern Baptist Convention met and in every state convention that he attended.

In 1965, when Theo Sommerkamp resigned as associate director of the Baptist Press to become European press representative for the Foreign Mission Board, he was succeeded by James (Jim) Newton, another professional journalist, a young man of deep Christian commitment and intense personal integrity. Also in 1965, Ruth Nelson retired from her position as bookkeeper. It was truly a time of transition, for she had worked for the Executive Committee since 1932 when she had been employed as secretary to Walter M. Gilmore. A modest, retiring woman, whose ability was a hundred times greater than her "size 6," Ruth Nelson blessed the denomination with a happy spirit and an impeccable honesty. The agency treasurers knew her as the faithful cosigner of Cooperative Program checks from the Executive Committee. She was succeeded by the bright and dependable Ada Ruth Cole Kelly, who had faithfully served the Executive Committee as an honored office secretary since 1952. In 1968 Martha Tanner Gaddis joined the staff as administrative secretary for Porter Routh and brought to the Executive Committee a treasure of rich experience and good judgment.

The decade had opened with a somber note from a veteran whose deep Christian concerns were voiced in warning words. In 1960, at the close of the September meeting of the Executive Committee, W. Douglas Hudgins had stood "to express 'a heaviness of heart' concerning certain things happening in our Convention; especially the 'curve of conversions' continuing to go down, fewer ordinations of preachers and fewer commitments for full-time service, fewer students in our seminaries, and a lack of concentration on promoting worship in our churches."[22] Almost from that year the country was in trouble, and Southern Baptists had their full share of burdens.

One quickening night in the Executive Committee meeting of September 1968, W. A. Criswell, then at the height of his preaching power, spoke for more than an hour on "God's Unchanging Hand."[23] The people present were lifted up as he related with intense emotion and tender compassion his personal struggle in overcoming racial prejudice.

America was changing. God's people were changing. Southern Baptists were changing, and the Executive Committee was at the crossroads of everything that was happening. In the materialistic seventies, there would be even more changes and the Executive Committee would find even more to do.

Notes

1. ECM, February 24-25, 1965, p. 17.

2. SBC, 1958, p. 56.

3. The author of this book, who was program planning secretary when the organization manual was developed, believed a clearer title would have been *Program Structure Manual,* or simply, *Program Manual.*

4. ECM, September 23, 1959, p. 8.

5. SBC, 1967, pp. 61, 85-154.

6. SBC, 1967, pp. 184-185. Since 1967, the total has been reduced in number.

7. The Convention did not require the agencies to do program budgeting, but only to submit their annual budget information on a program basis. Some of the agencies did adopt some form of program budgeting.

8. SBC, 1964, pp. 56.

9. SBC, 1960, p. 110.

10. SBC, 1970, p. 261.

11. SBC, 1957, p. 50.

12. SBC, 1949, p. 35.

13. ECM, September, 1960, p. 8.

14. SBC, 1957, p. 53.

15. SBC, 1930, p. 11.

16. ECM, May 19, 1959, pp. 5-7. One of the professors later decided that it was in the best interest of the seminary for him to withdraw from the bloc.

17. ECM, September 16-18, 1968, pp. 7-10. Though other agencies were involved in the study, the focus was on the Radio and Television Commission and the Foreign Mission Board.

18. ECM, February 19-21, 1968, pp. 12, 15-16.

19. Dec. 15-16, 1954, p. 18.

20. ECM, 1964, May 9, 1964, pp. 4, A.

21. SBC, 1967, pp. 62-63.

22. ECM, September 21, 1960, p. 12.

23. ECM, September 16-18, 1968, p. 4.

11

Strengthening Cooperative Relationships
1970-1979

To help prepare the churches for the '70 Onward Emphasis (1969-1979), the director of program planning wrote a book called, *The New Times*.[1] In it he attempted to distill the thought of futurists who claimed special insight into the years ahead. The essence of the book was that America would change and that the Baptists would change with it. America did change. The Baptists changed, too, although much slower than the country.

Racial and social tensions were intensified in 1970, when a riot erupted at Kent State University (Ohio). Four students were killed by National Guardsmen. Then followed disturbances over school busing in 1971 and the shooting of George Wallace in Maryland in 1972. Cooler heads appealed for restraint. But the constant pressure of recurring national crises did not stop. The resignation of Vice President Spiro Agnew in 1973 and later of President Nixon in 1974 shocked Americans. Racial conflict and Watergate scandals had taken their tolls. As if these were not enough, there followed one gasoline crisis after another, raging and seemingly uncontrollable inflation, and finally, a severe financial recession with record unemployment in some industries. America was in a tremendous agitation of change. The war in Vietnam finally ended in 1975, when the South Vietnamese government collapsed and the American troops returned home.

For Baptists the changes were less dramatic. There were a few negative signs. Evangelism seemed less intensive, many members seemed less involved in church programs, and doctrinal disagree-

239

ments seemed more prevalent. There were many more positive signs. Offerings were increasing, especially with the surge of inflation; and larger churches were gearing their programs for reaching youth by building family life centers. The Bible was being seriously taught, churches were experiencing renewal, and Baptist young people were emerging from the influence of the youth rebellion of the sixties. The Convention agencies, reshaped and redirected in the late 1950s, were in seemingly good condition, although there were a few loose ends still left untied from the work of the Committee to Study Total Baptist Program. As the 1970s approached, some leaders felt that the results of that study should be examined. It was needed, they said, as preparation for the new times ahead.

Evaluating the 1958-1959 Changes

In February 1970, the Executive Committee voted to establish a Committee of Ten to review the assignments recommended by the Committee to Study Total Program and approved by the Convention in 1958-1959, "including those to the Executive Committee and report at the soonest possible time considerations which it feels should be given to changing or modifying these assignments."[2] E. W. Price, Jr., a North Carolina pastor, was appointed the chairperson. In June five laymen were added, and the group reidentified as the Committee of Fifteen.[3] In September, it reported: "We have discovered, in light of our present studies, that there is possible need for some re-alignment and modification of these assignments."[4] The Committee of Fifteen requested and received permission of the Executive Committee "to study the entire Southern Baptist Convention structure with the privilege of making recommendations to change or modify these assignments."[5]

The first report resulted in the transfer of the *Baptist Program* and related services from the public relations office to the program planning office.[6] In its second report, the committee recommended that representatives of the four mission agencies, The Sunday School Board, and the seminaries regularly attend meetings of the Brotherhood and Radio and Television Commissions.[7] Their presence was needed, the committee said, to assure proper correlation of the work of the agencies. This measure passed both the Executive Committee and the Southern Baptist Convention.[8] Also in the second report, the committee proposed to merge the Stewardship Commission with the Executive Committee.[9] There was widespread feeling among state convention executive secretaries that the promotion of the Cooperative Program should be related to the same group that supervised the administration of the Cooperative Program. The Executive Committee agreed, but the Convention did not. The recommendation was defeated in spite of efforts to send it back to the Executive Committee for further study.

The final report was made to the Executive Committee in February 1974.[10] There were twenty-two recommendations, most of them either directly or indirectly involving agency interests. Twelve of the recommendations were addressed to the Executive Committee, including several that requested further study of agency problems by other subcommittees of the Executive Committee. Eight other issues were addressed to the agencies. And two were addressed directly to the Convention. Fourteen of the twenty-two were challenged, mostly by representatives of the agencies. The challenges resulted in the withdrawing of one, the tabling of one, and the amending of eleven others. In some cases, the amendments changed the intention of the Committee of Fifteen. Some members of the committee felt that the responses of the Executive Committee took the edge off what the committee was attempting to accomplish. Others thought that Baptist democracy was at work in the process and that as much was accomplished as was needed. In spite of some agency resistance and the changes made by the Executive Committee, the report as finally approved was generally helpful. Some of benefits were:

- Stewardship and Cooperative Program promotion were better understood.
- Trustee-board and trustee-staff relations were brought sharply into focus.

- The Executive Committee organization was strengthened.
- The merchandising and film policies of the Business and Financial Plan were improved.
- Investment guidelines for the agencies were established.
- Retirement plans for the agency employees strengthened.
- The way was opened for the seminaries to consider raising entrance fees.
- Studies were initiated concerning possible overlapping of the interests of the Christian Life Commission and of the Public Affairs Committee.
- Caution was raised against unnecessary staff expansion.
- Attention was focused on the nondegree programs of the seminaries and on the Seminary Extension Department training of ministers without college educations.
- The Executive Committee itself was exhaustively studied by a Convention committee.
- Southern Baptist missions awareness was greatly increased.

In the course of the study, there were two points of tension: (1) Interested Baptists brought their concerns to the attention of the Committee of Fifteen. After carefully checking, the committee developed its own list of concerns. When these were publicly announced, some of the agency executives were offended. One concern focused on office staff expansion, especially at the Home and Foreign Mission Boards. The committee believed that their "concerns" were nothing more than cautions. They were taken, however, as tantamount to instructions, simply because they came from a committee of the Executive Committee. (2) The committee was publicly chastised for the timing of reports and for publicly releasing proposals before discussing them with the agency leaders.

Why did the agencies resist the work of the Committee of Fifteen? Possibly: (1) the mandate to study everything and to recommend changes was open-ended and promoted fear, (2) the committee's study and reporting appeared to the agencies to be taking too long, (3) some agency leaders did not believe that there was need for the

study, (4) some of the executives questioned a listing of concerns
by so important a group, and (5) in the minds of some critics, the
name, "Committee of Fifteen," was ambiguous; it could mean anything.

There was no rancor in the exchange. Strong minds held views
that had to be voiced. Once the right questions were asked and the
answers given, the air was cleared and the Convention moved
ahead. The benefits achieved abundantly offset the negative reac-
tions.

Evaluating the Executive Committee

During its investigations, the Committee of Fifteen decided that
it could not objectively study the Executive Committee. One of its
two recommendations in 1974 was that a Committee of Seven be
appointed to review and evaluate the Executive Committee.[11] C. R.
Daley, the highly regarded, independent-minded editor of the *Western Recorder*, was appointed chairperson. The Committee of Seven
worked steadily for two years and reported in 1976.[12] It listed seven
affirmations:

(1) A strong Executive Committee is indispensable.
(2) The organizational structure of the Executive Committee is essen-
tially sound.
(3) The Executive Committee is blessed with highly capable and
committed professional staff members.
(4) There is evidence that the Executive Committee is endeavoring
to perform faithfully, the functions assigned to it by the Convention.
(5) All meetings of the Executive Committee, its subcommittees, and
work groups are open to concerned constituents although executive
sessions can be called under unusual circumstances.
(6) The *Organization Manual* . . . and *The Southern Baptist Program Budget
and Financial Data* . . . indicate a commendable job in compiling and
updating the documents called for in Bylaw 9.
(7) The Executive Committee keeps comprehensive and accurate
records of its work.

The Committee of Seven also reported "findings and suggestions," most of them directed to the Executive Committee. Some of the more important ones are summarized as follows:

- Improved orientation for new members.
- More involvement of the members in the decision-making process.
- Better communication between the Executive Committee and the agencies, including better relations of the Executive Committee with agency trustees.
- Care lest there be an "unconscious trend toward undue centralization of authority in Southern Baptist organizational life. The usurpation of undue authority by the Executive Committee over the agencies of the Convention would be disastrous."
- Budget requests "should be heard as well as studied by all Executive Committee members."
- Sometimes it appears that the Executive Committee has overstepped its limits in acting "in an advisory capacity on all questions of cooperation among the different agencies." The advisory role "should never become a supervisory or managerial role."
- The right to study and recommend "is by far the most controversial item." There should be periodic evaluation of agencies; however, "far-reaching proposals relating to agencies should be made only after very careful consideration."

One of the suggestions was directed to the Committee on Boards: "While the method of nominating and electing Executive Committee members may be sound in theory, the manner in which it works is not altogether satisfactory. . . . Without information with which to react responsibly, members of the Committee on Boards usually endorse one another's nominations. This makes room for personal favoritism and cronyism in the selection of nominees."

Another was directed generally to all Southern Baptists, including the Executive Committee and its members: "Let there be clear understanding that the Executive Committee is the 'fiduciary, the fiscal, and the executive agency of the Convention in all its affairs not specifically committed to some other board or agency.' " The committee also said that " 'acting for the Convention ad interim' is not the same as 'being the Convention ad interim.' "[13]

Three months later the new president of the Convention, James L. Sullivan, addressed the Executive Committee in its September meeting. He presented three appeals: (1) for communication with understanding, (2) for balance between system and the Spirit and between the pragmatic and the practical, and (3) for a restless patience. It is not clear whether Sullivan had in mind the denomination or the Executive Committee—probably both. If he were thinking of the Executive Committee, there were many sympathetic people in the audience, for his appeals very well described some of the ideals of the Executive Committee in the mid seventies. In the midst of the new times, the Executive Committee was carefully examined, corrected, and given a renewed mandate for the future.

Renewing Mission Commitment

The renewal of Southern Baptist missions awareness was perhaps the most significant outcome of the Committee of Fifteen. Conferences with the leaders of the four missions agencies deepened the interest of the members of the committee in missions education. This resulted in three forward-looking recommendations: (1) that the missions agencies and The Sunday School Board "develop a strategy for mission education using all the channels of all the agencies,"[14] (2) that the mission boards "review thoroughly their present mission plans, and consider the implementation of bold new plans where needed,"[15] and (3) to "involve all appropriate agencies, state conventions, and interested individuals in developing a challenge to Southern Baptists to help meet world needs in the final quarter of this century."[16]

These recommendations led to a Convention committee of twenty-one persons, later identified as the Missions Challenge Committee. Warren C. Hultgren of Oklahoma was named as chairperson. It was this group that led the Convention in 1976 to "set as its primary missions challenge that every person in the world shall have the opportunity to hear the gospel of Christ in the next 25 years."[17] It also led the Convention to reaffirm the Bold Mission emphasis plan previously approved for 1978-1979. The agencies immediately set to work on both of these proposals.

Almost at once mission fires began to burn in unexpected ways. In 1977, when the Convention met in Kansas City, it seemed that almost everyone wanted to advance the cause of missions—and to do it all at once.

(1) For ten years the emphasis planning work groups of the Inter-agency Council had been looking at 1977-1979 as a time for bold missions. The term "bold missions" had been suggested in 1966 to the '70 Onward Steering Committee by Marie Mathis, the director of promotion for Woman's Missionary Union.[18] Specific plans had been approved by the Convention in 1974 for 1977-1979, for engaging in mission action and boldly confronting the secular world in bold mission.[19]

(2) Then, in 1977, after long, careful planning by the Coordinating Committee of the Inter-agency Council and on recommendation of the Executive Committee, the Convention gave second approval to another emphasis plan for 1979-1980.[20] This was part of the carefully integrated Impact '80s plan for 1979-1986 that included an emphasis on the strengthening of local church missions organizations and that had been first approved by the Convention in 1975.[21]

(3) In 1977 the Executive Committee recommended to the Convention a proposal that had been suggested by United States President Jimmy Carter to a group of Southern Baptist leaders calling for 5,000 persons to be funded by churches or groups of churches who would serve for one or two years as volunteer workers on Southern Baptist missions fields.[22] The Convention approved the project which was later known as the Missions Service Corp.

(4) In 1976, prompted by the Missions Challenge Committee report, A. R. Fagan, executive director of the Stewardship Commission, received Convention approval for a Bold Missions Task Force

to develop bold promotional programs in support of missions.[23] The resolution seemed to suggest bold promotional programs for all of the agencies, but Fagan had in mind primarily plans for stewardship support of missions. A year later he presented, on behalf of his Bold Mission Task Force and the Stewardship Commission, a recommendation challenging Southern Baptists to double the Cooperative Program five times by the year 2000.[24]

The resolution from the Bold Mission Task Force and the Stewardship Commission had asked the Executive Committee to assume responsibility for "giving strong administrative leadership in promoting and coordinating all facets of Bold Mission."[25] The Executive Committee had never had an assignment exactly like this. Fully a dozen program leaders whose plans had been approved by the Convention for emphasis felt that their work should have the right-of-way. Because of these commitments, nearly a hundred leaders felt that they should be involved in the decision making. Porter Routh asked Albert McClellan, the director of program planning, to serve as coordinator.

After staff consultations with the Mission Service Corps Committee and representatives of the agencies involved in Bold Missions, the Program Budget Subcommittee approved a coordinating plan that was recommended to the Executive Committee in the September meeting of 1977.[26] The plan, designated as *Bold Mission Thrust,* was approved. Two committees were formed: (1) The Bold Mission Leadership Group, with fifty-five members, included agency heads, their chief associates, representatives of the state conventions, and selected SBC agency board members. This group heard reports from the steering committee and made final decisions. It met once a year or as needed. (2) The Bold Mission Thrust Steering Committee, comprised of representatives of all component emphases. It met quarterly, or as often as needed.

In the months that followed, the Steering Committee identified and the Leadership Group approved guidelines for Bold Mission Thrust planning and promotion. Some of these were:

- Promotion for the component projects and emphasis is the responsibility of the sponsoring agencies.
- No new promotional structures will be established, except as provided by the agencies for the projects for which they have responsibility.
- The Executive Committee will conduct through its various channels, the general work of promotion on behalf of Bold Mission Thrust in keeping with Convention Bylaws.
- A new short-term emphasis plan incorporating the appropriate elements will be developed for Convention approval.
- The Executive Committee, in keeping with the instructions of the Convention, will report annually on the progress of Bold Mission Thrust.
- Bold Mission Thrust is a continuing overall emphasis to be generally followed to the end of the century. It does not preclude emphasis on other aspects of Southern Baptist work.

The Steering Committee worked in cooperation with the Inter-Agency Council Coordinating Committee and the Mission Service Corps. A year later, the Executive Committee presented to the Convention a plan for a 1979-1982 emphases on (1) Bold Going, (2) Bold Growing, and (3) Bold Giving.[27]

Making Changes

Porter Routh strongly believed that most differences of opinion could be reconciled through communication and consensus. With a good sense of timing and the ability to state tersely the heart of a question, he frequently could lead a group to agreement. His ability to negotiate consensus in a positive manner brought two significant changes in agency alignments. In 1962 it became obvious that without accreditation, Carver School of Missions and Social Work could not survive unless it received a great deal more money than the Convention could provide. Sensing that a solution might be realignment, Routh worked carefully, step-by-step, until all parties were in reasonable agreement, and the school was merged with Southern Seminary.

In 1958 the Convention accepted the principle "that sponsorship of hospitals is a function most appropriately performed by the state conventions and local groups.[28] Following World War II, hospitals had become increasingly expensive and more the responsibility of local communities. But ten years passed before Southern Baptists consented to give up the mammoth indebtedness and huge liabilities of the large metropolitan hospitals in New Orleans and Jacksonville. Routh was deeply involved in the discussions and worked closely with the Southern Baptist hospitals and a special committee of the Executive Committee. The negotiations were complex and sometimes tedious; but, finally, consensus prevailed. The separation was accomplished in 1970, when the Convention approved charter changes that set the hospitals on their own.[29]

Early in his administration, Porter Routh sensed a new interest by laity in the work of the denomination, a view that probably came out of his experience as Brotherhood secretary in Oklahoma, and his reading of Hendrik Kraemer's *Theology of the Laity.* Instinctively, Routh believed the day of the laity was dawning and that laypersons, both men and women, should be more involved in the life and work of the Southern Baptist Convention. His interest in the full utilization of the laity was widely known. It surely could not have escaped the attention of the Committee to Study Total Program. This led to a dramatic change in the memberships of the governing boards of the agencies when the Convention by-laws were amended to give the ordained and unordained equal opportunities for membership.[30]

In 1970, Owen Cooper, a Mississippi layman and industrialist, proposed a major lay utilization study. With Routh's encouragement, the Executive Committee voted to sponsor a national conference on the utilization of Baptist laymen. Cooper was appointed chairman, and the meeting was attended by 220 laymen, seventy pastors, and forty denominational leaders.[31] In book form, the report was used by the Brotherhood Commission and other denominational organizations in projects involving laymen for several years afterwards.[32]

In 1978 the Executive Committee welcomed a small delegation of concerned Baptist laymen, headed by C. E. Price, Pittsburgh, Pennsylvania. All of the men were high achievers and most were professionally qualified. For example, Price was an engineer and a vice-president of the Westinghouse Corporation. The men sincerely wanted to be involved in Bold Mission Thrust in keeping with their skills. Porter Routh encouraged them, and this led to a conference of about twenty dedicated men and a similar number of Southern Baptist program leaders. Many channels were suggested for involving highly skilled laymen in Bold Mission Thrust and the general work of the denomination.[33] This was one of Porter Routh's last activities before his retirement. Routh, himself a layman, ended his work for the denomination as he had begun it nearly forty years earlier—encouraging other laymen in their service to the Lord Jesus Christ.

Mending the Rules

Any messenger in any annual Convention can move to amend the Southern Baptist Convention Constitution or Bylaws. It is not often done; but when it is done, the motion is usually referred to the Executive Committee for study. Special care must be taken in the changing of the rules that govern the Convention. An amendment must be properly worded and not in conflict with other Convention regulations. The constitution and bylaws should contain only the foundational principles for operating the Convention and should not be cluttered with trivia. If the proposed amendment has merit, alternative ways of accomplishing its intent should be carefully studied. No amendment should be considered that violates the autonomy of the churches and the general Baptist bodies or that overrides general denominational polity. Also, any proposed amendment must be examined from a legal point of view. Problems like these require more study than the Convention itself can give in its annual session. If the proposal is found to be really needed, and if there seems to be support for it, the Executive Committee sends it back to the Convention for voting. If not, the committee reports to the Convention why it thinks the change is not needed. The Executive Committee itself can propose amendments, and this is the way most of them come to the Convention. The changes it recommends are in keeping with traditional Baptist democracy and have direct bearing on Convention polity.

In the period 1952-1979, the Executive Committee recommended and the Convention approved the following important amendments to the SBC Constitution:

> **1963:** An amendment to Article XIV that required amendments to be "approved by two *successive* Conventions".
>
> **1968:** An amendment to Article VI that extended the length of terms of the elected members of agencies from three to four years. It was thought that the additional time would increase the efficiency of the members.
>
> **1977:** An amendment to Article VI that adjusted the membership requirements of the four major boards.

The Convention bylaws were frequently reviewed by the Executive Committee. When there was need, recommendations were made to the Convention for revisions or additions. Typical of the more important bylaw changes recommended by the Executive Committee from 1952 to 1979 were:

> **1954:** Provision that agency charters must state that all trustees are elected by the Southern Baptist Convention and that the charters may not be changed without Convention consent.
>
> **1959:** Requirement that the Executive Committee provide the agencies with an appropriate format for reporting programs on a comparable basis.
>
> **1961:** The Committee on Boards shall recognize the principle that elected agency trustees represent the constituency, not the staff of the agency.

1965: Messengers to the Convention shall be members of the church that appoints them.

1972: Motions dealing with the internal operations of an agency shall be referred to the elected board of the agency for consideration and action.

1975: Trustees who resign during the year may not be nominated that year to other boards.

1978: The Bylaws and Convention Procedure were combined into one unified document.

Attending the Incidentals

Looking from a distance one is tempted to judge the Executive Committee of the 1970s by its participation in projects that made the headlines, such as the work of the Committee of Fifteen, the report of the Convention's Committee of Seven to Review and Evaluate, the administration of the Cooperative Program, the involvement in Bold Mission Thrust, and perhaps, the visibility the Executive Committee had in the annual Conventions. This view does not include the many lesser problems and projects left out of the headlines. Nor does it include the great amount of work required to support the headline events and to conduct the committee's routine responsibilities. The twenty people who worked for the committee in the seventies were always busy. They frequently worked overtime, and sometimes in the evenings, especially when there were meetings to attend. Their work was the mortar that held the projects in place.

The Seminary Formula. Among the projects that did not make the headlines was the search for a new formula to be used in the distribution of Cooperative Program funds available for theological education. In 1968 the Executive Committee had employed Lawrence Wilsey, a Chicago consultant, to recommend a new formula to be approved by the seminary presidents. After some months, he said that an algebraic formula, such as the one that had been used since 1953, was not a reliable tool and that the allocations and distributions to the seminaries should be based on actual program costs. He also recommended a council composed of presidents and trustees to jointly manage the finances of all the seminaries.

Although the presidents accepted some of the ideas of the Wilsey plan, they did not accept the two principal features. They argued that without adequate funds from the Cooperative Program for all of the needs of the seminaries, financing solely on the basis of program costs was unrealistic. They rejected the council idea outright. Wilsey had proposed an interim formula which the presidents partially installed but which never worked satisfactorily. They did agree with Wilsey that any method or formula should be divided into two sections: an *allocation* section, to be used for determining how much of the Cooperative Program funds would be assigned to theological education; and a *distribution* section, to be used for determining how much of the assigned amount would be given to each of the six seminaries.

In 1972 another consultant was employed, George Kaludis, a financial officer at Vanderbilt University. After a prolonged study and numerous meetings, he responded with methods similar to Wilsey's. Again the presidents would not agree. Some of them were determined to have another algebraic formula, even against the advice of two reputable consultants.

There appeared to be some differences of opinion among the six presidents. But because of their rule that any decision of the group had to be unanimous, movement forward did not seem possible. The problem was still unsolved. Presidents of the smaller schools were having great difficulty in managing their finances, which they said was the fault of the lack of agreement on a new formula. It looked for a time like the unity of the six presidents as a working group would be destroyed. The Institutions Workgroup of the Program and Budget Subcommittee conducted private meetings with each of the presidents to hear from them officially what they had been hearing in the halls and to impress upon them the need of coming to an agreement.

Some of the differences coming to light were: (1) resistance among the presidents to the Executive Committee's insistence that they look seriously at the forming an interseminary council strong enough to deal decisively with the problems of finance, (2) the unwillingness of some seminary presidents to continue the practice of annually changing the interim formula to meet the special needs of others, (3) the determination of some to find and use an algebraic formula, and (4) the differences between schools with large endowments and the schools with no endowments and the bearing that such differences had on the formula.

Finally, the presidents and the Institutions Workgroup of the Executive Committee agreed for the sake of solving the ten-year-old problem: (1) To search for an algebraic formula for both allocation of funds to theological education and the distribution of funds to the six seminaries, (2) to employ as consultant, R. Orin Cornett, a nationally recognized authority on the use of algebraic formulas in allocations and distributions to institutions of higher education, and (3) to include a provision not to alter the formula, except on the advice of the consultant and by permission of the Executive Committee. Cornett was a respected Southern Baptist educator with broad experience. He had been one of the designers of the first formula approved in 1953. Cornett soon developed a computer-based algebraic formula which the Executive Committee approved.[34] Happily, the problem was resolved as well as it could be, given the inadequate amount of money available for the six seminaries.

Capital Needs Programs. Among the many other projects and problems of the Executive Committee in the 1970s were two Capital Needs Programs. The first project, with Preston Callison, South Carolina, as chairperson, was approved by the Convention in 1974 for $4,977,500 to be raised in a five-year period, 1974-1975.[35] There were two small allocations to the Brotherhood Commission and the Radio and Television Commission. Most of the money went to the seminaries and was used either to build new buildings or to rebuild old ones. The schools, in spite of the recent youth rebellion of the sixties, were overflowing with students who appeared more teachable than some of their brothers and sisters of ten years before.

The next program was approved by the Convention in 1978 for $16,705,985 to be raised in seven years, 1978-1984.[36] J. Howard Cobble, Georgia, was the chairperson. This made the seventh program since 1946, to which a grand total of $91,082,468 had been committed.[37]

The Southern Baptist Convention Building. Through the years, the SBC Building was at times very crowded. A major denominational crossroad, its halls were thronged with leaders attending the meetings of the six groups occupying the building. With more and more space needed for offices, the conference rooms were reduced in number. By 1977 there were so many large meetings that parking became a major problem. The members began to talk about more space. Although the building could take two more floors and could be extended on two sides, this was said by architects and engineers to be financially inadvisable. Thought was given to the purchasing of the building next door, but upon investigation, it, too, was found unsuitable. Then, the Executive Committee authorized $250,000 for the purchase of nearby lots for parking; but after further consideration, this was dropped. Meanwhile, it began to appear that the James Robertson Parkway area had failed to develop to the expectation of the city planners; downtown Nashville seemed to be moving in other directions. Office space in the SBC Building continued to be a problem until the 1980s, when a new approach would be taken.

Typical of many other matters appearing on the Executive Committee agenda of the 1970s were:

1972-1973: A study of the problems arising between ministers and churches that resulted in suggestions for relieving the problems.

1973: A change in the procedure for developing the Cooperative Program Allocations Budget. The new feature was a special meeting of the Program Budget Subcommittee in January to provide more time for the agencies to present their needs and for the development of the budget.

1973-1975: A study of the problems of the aging and their implications for Southern Baptists. This resulted in recommendations for The Sunday School Board to assume leadership in providing publications and program assistance to the churches.

1974: Consideration of a request from Bible schools sponsored by state conventions for SBC financial assistance. This resulted: (1) in a reminder that the conventions could assign Cooperative Program funds only to agencies whose trustees it elects, and (2) in a strongly worded suggestion to the seminaries that they strengthen the Seminary Extension Department to help nondegree persons in training for ministry.

1975: A plan for Southern Baptist Disaster Relief.

1975-1976: A committee on capital and endowment giving for the SBC seminaries, an effort to secure coordination of the six special seminary solicitations in progress at the time. It was soon discovered that the larger seminaries had gone too far in their campaigns to change their plans.

Almost every year brought significant changes in the agency program statements, some requiring extensive study and many meetings.

Minding the Shop

The Executive Committee is like a shop that deals in services. There is no way to mind a shop without people, and in the case of the Executive Committee, the members and the staff are the people. Persons elected to the Executive Committee soon realize that being a member is a rare stewardship. It is not uncommon for men and women to grow in ways they had not dreamed possible. Many have come wistfully to the end of their terms, saying that it has been the greatest experience of their lives.

The officers help keep the work moving, and they are usually chosen because of their devotion to the purpose and work of the

Executive Committee and their skills in personal relationships. During the seventies, five people served as chairpersons:

Owen Cooper, Mississippi layman	1971,
Stewart B. Simms, South Carolina pastor	1972, 1973
Charles E. Harvey, Louisiana pastor	1974, 1975
William Ches Smith, III, Georgia pastor	1976, 1977
Brooks H. Wester, Mississippi pastor	1978, 1979

Owen Cooper, a dedicated industrialist, was a man of endless ideas and enthusiasms. Many of these he saw brought to completion; some, however, were beyond the visions of his brethren. His term was cut short when he was elected president of the Southern Baptist Convention. Stewart B. Simms, a cordial friend and a loyal Southern Baptist, also served as chairman of the Cooperative Program Study Committee. Charles E. Harvey, a tireless worker with an unusual sense of propriety, regarded his office as one of the most responsible in the Southern Baptist Convention. William Ches Smith, III, Georgia, conducted the office with rare humor and an unswerving devotion to the cause of Christ. Brooks H. Wester was a sincere, natural leader. He almost invariably was chosen chairman of any group of which he was a member. He did double duty for the Executive Committee as chairman of the search committee for a new executive secretary.

The president of the Convention is an *ex officio* member of the Executive Committee. Not an officer of the committee, he, nevertheless, is an honored member. He usually is asked during the year to make one or two major addresses. Six presidents served from 1969 to 1979:

W. A. Criswell, Texas pastor	1969, 1970
Carl E. Bates, North Carolina pastor	1971, 1972
Owen Cooper, Mississippi industrialist	1973, 1974
Jaroy Weber, Texas pastor	1975, 1976
James L. Sullivan, Tennessee retiree	1977
Jimmy R. Allen, Texas pastor	1978, 1979

W. A. Criswell was a superb preacher and a good presiding officer. On the occasion of his last address to the Executive Committee, he chose the subject: "My Greatest Dilemma—How Far Do You Compromise What You Believe to Stay Together?"[38] Carl E. Bates, a prince of preachers, was unflagging in his loyalty to the denomination. Owen Cooper, a dedicated layman, was a man of rare vision. Jaroy Weber, affable and understanding, was one of the great pastors of his generation. James L. Sullivan, a statesman and a prophet, due to his twenty-three years as executive secretary-treasurer of The Sunday School Board, was one of the best-informed presidents the Convention ever had. He was at times a friendly critic of the Executive Committee. His friends were disappointed when he declined a second term. Jimmy R. Allen, an overflowing, exuberant, and clear preacher, was one of the key persons in the support of the Missions Service Corps. For him, his presidency was a call to minister to key leaders in high places. Bill Moyers, Jimmy Carter, and Menachem Begin were among his friends.

The shop could not be kept without the staff, and one of the most dependable keepers was John H. Williams, who since 1959 had been director of financial planning. In 1975 he came to his inevitable retirement. A happy Welshman, Williams had served so well and so faithfully, that if the rules had allowed, his friends would have kept him around for another sixteen years. He was succeeded by Billy D. Malesolvas, who served faithfully until he felt compelled to return to Texas. He was followed in 1978 by Timothy A. Hedquist, who was well-trained in business at the University of California and in religious education at Southwestern Seminary. Hedquist fitted beautifully into the needs of the Executive Committee in the new times—he understood computers.

The Baptist Press also had personnel changes. In 1973 James Newton, a hardworking newsman of high principle, left his place as assistant director of the Baptist Press to join the staff of the Brotherhood Commission. He was succeeded in 1973 by another mission-minded professional journalist, Robert O'Brien, who was tender in his personal responses and tough in his journalistic ideals. Also in

1973, the Baptist Press added a feature writer, James Young, a friendly outgoing person and a meticulous journalist. He left in 1977 to become editor of the *Rocky Mountain Baptist*. He was followed by Norman Jameson, a young man of unusual spiritual and journalistic insights. These people carried heavy burdens and were well-known in the denomination. One of their chief services to Southern Baptists was the work they did in assisting W. C. Fields in the enormous task of staffing and operating the newsroom of the annual Convention.

A most significant staff change came in 1979. Wistfully, and with some feelings of uncertainty, the staff knew it was coming. Then, with time rushing by, Porter Routh passed his determining birthday in July of 1979 and retired at the end of that month.

Handing on the Seals

Behind the solid steel doors of an old-fashioned safe that stands more than seven feet tall, the official seal of the Executive Committee is safely stored, where it has been since about 1930 when it was purchased that the committee might have "a seal of its own."[39] The Southern Baptist Convention's seal was purchased about that same time. An earlier seal had been approved in 1898. Side by side, waiting for the times when they will be needed for official papers, the seals stand as sentries of the promises made and kept by the Southern Baptist Convention and its Executive Committee. Old, quaint in shape, black, with the gilt almost gone, and heavy to the hand, they suggest the Convention's stability, integrity, and dignity. When they are placed in the hands of the executive secretary-treasurer, the Convention is saying, "We trust you to look after our interests and to care for our needs." From that moment until another takes his place, he is their keeper. As much as anything else, they symbolize his office.

Porter Routh, in his twenty-eight years as executive secretary-treasurer, kept that trust as well as any man could. He made mistakes, as all leaders do; but he did not neglect the trust. His accomplishments were innumerable and have been publicly recorded.[40]

He perhaps would like best to be remembered as a faithful member of a local Baptist church. Others would like also to remember him as (1) a leader who devoutly believed in the world mission of the Lord Jesus Christ, (2) a brother to every Baptist he ever met, (3) a friend of unsurpassing loyalty, (4) an executive mind of unquestioned ability, (5) a workman so faithful that he never claimed all of his vacation time, (6) a layman with the compassion of a true pastor, and (7) a devoted husband. Through the years he had been aided by Ruth Routh, his faithful wife, who provided an immaculate home for him. They had five children, one an invalid. Of Ruth Routh it was often said, "Her children rise up and call her blessed; her husband also, and he praises her" (Prov. 31:28, RSV).

On the last day of July 1979, Porter Routh surrendered his key to the building, said farewell to his fellow workers, and went home. He left office as he had entered it, without pomp and ceremony. One of his friends whom he bade good-bye was the new executive secretary-treasurer, Harold C. Bennett.

In that moment of informal leave-taking, unadorned as it was, the seals exchanged hands—figuratively, of course, for they were locked behind the great steel doors. The future would be different from the past; it always is when administrations change. The new leaders bring new challenges, new dreams, and new problems. The dark times come, and the bright times come. In season and out of season, Southern Baptists remain faithful. They march ahead, and all the great leaders of the past march with them.

Notes

1. Albert McClellan, *The New Times* (Nashville: Broadman, 1968).
2. ECM, February 16-18, 1970, p. 18.
3. ECM, June 1, 1970, p. 8.
4. ECM, September 21-22, 1970, pp. 7, B.
5. Ibid.

6. ECM, September 21-13, 1971, pp. 7-8, 21.

7. ECM, February 21-23, 1972, pp. 5-7, E.

8. Ibid., cf. SBC, 1972, pp. 58-59.

9. Ibid.

10. ECM, February 18, 1974, pp. 28-44.

11. SBC, 1974, p. 60; cf. SBC, 1975, p. 26. Members: C. R. Daley, Kentucky; Daniel Grant, Arkansas; Olin T. Binkley, North Carolina; Herschel H. Hobbs, Oklahoma; W. A. Criswell, Texas; Alma Hunt, Alabama; Harold C. Bennett, Florida.

12. SBC, 1976, pp. 42-49.

13. Ibid., p. 47.

14. ECM, February 18, 1974, p. 39.

15. SBC, 1974, p. 65.

16. Ibid.

17. SBC, 1976, pp. 53-55.

18. Albert McClellan, "Bold Mission Thrust," ESB, Vol. IV, 2,2125.

19. SBC, 1974, p. 67.

20. SBC, 1977, pp. 36-37.

21. SBC, 1975, p 60-61.

22. SBC, 1977, p. 40.

23. SBC, 1976, p. 62.

24. SBC, 1977, p. 37.

25. Ibid., p. 37.

26. ECM, September 19, 1977, pp. 8-12.

27. SBC, 1978, pp. 47-48.

28. SBC, 1958, p. 64.

29. SBC, 1970, pp. 65-70.

30. SBC, 1959, p. 49.

31. ECM, February 22-24, 1971, p. 4.

32. Owen Cooper, *Listen!* (SBC Nashville: Executive Committee, 1971).

33. ECM, February 20, 1979, pp. 7, 34; ECM, September 17-19, 1979, p. 28. Price, who was a member of a small Pittsburg church, worked tirelessly at church planting. In 1983, he was elected vice-president of the Southern Baptist Convention.

34. ECM, February 16, 1976, p. 5.

35. SBC, 1974, pp. 53-54.

36. SBC, 1978, pp. 29-30.

37. "Summary, Southern Baptist Convention Capital Needs Programs," a report prepared for the Capital Needs Committee of the SBC Executive Committee.

38. ECM, September 16-18, 1970, p. 6.

39. ECM, June 12-13, 1929, p. 66; cf. SBC, 1930, p. 88.

40. Albert McClellan, "Porter's Personal Presence," *Baptist Program,* April 1979, pp. 6-8; *"summa cum laude,* Life Distinction," pp. 39, 38.

12

The Executive Committee in Transition
1979-1984

Harold Clark Bennett worked for The Sunday School Board in the early 1960s. One day he appeared in the office of Albert McClellan, the director of program planning for the Executive Committee. After a few friendly words, Bennett came quickly to the point of his visit. He said, "I have an opportunity to go with the Department of Metropolitan Missions at the Home Mission Board. How do you see that position as compared with the one I now hold?" He was at the time superintendent of new work for The Sunday School Board. They talked of the technical aspects of the two positions and then of the challenges of the unfolding future. Bennett then casually asked, "How does one prepare himself for the future?" McClellan's standard answer for this question was, "A decision of this kind turns on two things, basic life commitment and long-range goals. If you truly know who you are and where you belong in God's work, and if you see clearly where you want to serve, you should hold your plans loosely so that the Holy Spirit can freely lead. Also, it is important that you have a variety of experiences."

Whether Bennett heard McClellan or not, he did take the Atlanta position; and doing that job well, he was called to be the director of the Missions Division of the Baptist General Convention of Texas. Then, in 1967 he became executive secretary-treasurer of the Florida Baptist Convention, a position that he held for almost twelve years, until he joined the Executive Committee staff in 1979.

The Search Committee to find a successor to Porter Routh had been appointed in 1977. A year later, in September of 1978, the

263

committee submitted a list of criteria for the approval of the Executive Committee.[1] The list included these items: "unquestioned honesty in financial responsibilities . . . actively involved in the life of a local Baptist congregation . . . possess mediating gifts, which include, openess, fairness, and patience, and . . . dynamic vision of the future of the Lord's work among Southern Baptists."[2] The Search Committee cited the previously approved job description requiring, among other things, that the executive secretary-treasurer "be able to identify quickly basic problems and issues . . . be content to render advice and permit final decision to be made on a group basis . . . be able to integrate the proposals or decisions of a committee and other groups into well-rounded and sound overall plans."[3] The report was approved by the Executive Committee.

The Search Committee then worked through a list of forty-three names submitted to it for consideration and, eventually, in February 1979, nominated Harold Clark Bennett.[4] Then followed a brief interview in the presence of the entire Executive Committee during which some of the members asked Bennett his views on such subjects as: "(1) . . . women as a resource, (2) highest priority of Southern Baptists; (3) leadership style; (4) future of Cooperative Program; (5) . . . how the Convention can involve human resources (men, women, laity, pastors, etc), more effectively in meeting objectives."[5] Bennett was unanimously elected. Then followed a reception when the members of the Executive Committee and the visitors were privileged personally to meet not only the new executive secretary-treasurer but also his wife, Phyllis, whose outgoing presence added warmth and charm to the occasion.

The next day Bennett met with the staff for a few minutes of conversation. He indicated that he knew of no changes he would make in personnel. At the end of the conference, McClellan, speaking unofficially for the group, said: "Dr. Bennett, these people will be as loyal to you as they have been to Dr. Routh. They know things will change, but they are not afraid of change and will work faithfully at whatever you want them to do." Bennett joined the Executive

Committee staff at the beginning of April, to serve as secretary-elect until he officially assumed office on August 1, 1979.

Like most other men, Bennett is a composite of every experience he ever had, from his boyhood in North Carolina to his twelve years in Florida. Pride in excellence is his hallmark, excellence in spirit and excellence in labor. From the time he worked as a paperboy for the Ashville *Times* he never intended to be anything less than the best at any task he was asked to do. He learned discipline as a torpedo bomber pilot in the Navy, and he learned to handle relationships as a pastor for twelve years of both small and large churches. He learned administration in denominational work. Bit by bit, from hundreds of experiences, he acquired a style characterized by careful mastery of detail, punctual attendance to business, easy contact with people, and a steady pursuit of goals. Keener Pharr, one of his associates in Florida said of him, "I doubt not that he could could have succeeded as an editor or executive of the largest of publishing houses or as the chief executive officer of the most complex of businesses."[6] Instead of success as the world knew it, Harold C. Bennett was committed to the Lord Jesus Christ. His devotion to missions was real, as was his commitment to evangelism and stewardship.

Bennett entered his new office determined to continue traditional Executive Committee openness, responsiveness, efficiency, and flexibility in dealing with Southern Baptist business matters. To some observers, the thrust of his approach appeared to be completely open communications.

Taking Hold

Like his predecessors, Bennett showed firmness in leadership from his first day in office. He accepted fully all the responsibilities of his position description.[7] Two of its points seemed especially made for him:

- Be able to plan his work and assign priorities in a fashion that will secure promptness at the time it is required.

- Be able to develop committee agenda and provide advice and assistance without usurping the functions of the committee itself.

To do this, Bennett completely rearranged the way information was presented to the Executive Committee. For his first meeting in September 1979, he was faced with a list of forty-seven agenda items to be considered by the Executive Committee and its three subcommittees. For the sake of order and clarity, he planned a single document organized by subcommittees. The agendas were uniform in structure and keyed to the forty-seven items. Each of the items had four parts: (1) background, (2) request, (3) recommendation, and (4) action. The document was intended as a continuum, used first by the members of the Executive Committee as information, then by each of the subcommittees to be changed as they desired, then again by the Executive Committee for whatever action it wished to take, and finally, included in condensed form in the official minutes of the Executive Committee. At first, the new document seemed to be an excessive amount of paper and an overload of information, but when the members understood the format, it was accepted as an efficient way of handling a massive amount of detail. The new approach with minor changes was continued as a routine procedure for handling Executive Committee information.

The new executive secretary-treasurer's attention to communication was an important part of his staff relationships. He regularly conducted meetings at two levels, with the "executive staff," and with the "professional staff." The executive staff was composed of Bennett, the associate executive secretary and director of program planning, the director of business and financial planning, and the director of public relations. The professional staff was composed of these four and their chief assistants. Bennett also conducted occasional meetings of the entire Executive Committee staff. All of the meetings were devoted to reviews of work underway and work planned. Each worker was encouraged to make suggestions for the improvement of efficiency and relationships. Besides the general enhancement of office productivity, these meetings also were important morale builders.

Bennett's leadership style was open, direct, fraternal, and somewhat formal. Reginald M. McDonough, the associate executive secretary, described it:

> The phrase that best characterizes Harold C. Bennett's leadership style is "directed thoroughness." He gives careful attention to details, yet he is also very goal oriented. While details are important to him, the end result is more important. He uses his ability to investigate, analyze, and organize his ideas as a strategy for achieving goals. . . . He places great emphasis on the staff functioning as a unified team. . . . He is very committed to providing the best resources and training available.[8]

Timothy A. Hedquist described it: "The Executive Committee staff has many diverse responsibilities and this has a tendencey to fragmentation. Bennett's emphasis on communication has gone a long way in producing a spirit of cooperation and teamwork among the staff."[9]

Planned Growth in Giving

In 1977, as part of Bold Mission Thrust, the Southern Baptist Convention set as one of its long-range goals, the doubling of the Cooperative Program giving three times by the year 2000.[10] So great a goal required a restatement of the Cooperative Program in terms of basic principles and promotional methods. To do this the Executive Committee in 1980 established the Southern Baptist Convention Study Committee "to recommend a plan of action to increase the level of giving to the local church and through the local church to Southern Baptist cooperative ministries."[11] James L. Pleitz of Texas was named chairperson. The committee was composed of twenty-one representatives of state conventions, Southern Baptist Convention agencies, and local churches. It reviewed all previous Convention actions on the Cooperative Program and several newly prepared study papers. Twelve listening sessions were held across the nation, and a mail survey was conducted of 1,200 denominational leaders. Using state Baptist papers, the committee appealed to individual Baptists to share their dreams of the Baptist future. Thousands responded, flooding the study of James L. Pleitz. Also, the committee utilized study papers by Lynn E. May, Jr., Albert McClellan, and others. The Committee worked diligently and reported on February 22, 1983.[12]

The Executive Committee approved the report and submitted it to the Southern Baptist Convention the following June.[13] There were four recommendations:

(1) *Principles of Cooperation.* Eight principles pinpointed the assumptions on which the Cooperative Program rests. The first one established the spiritual basis for churches working together:

> Cooperation among Christians finds its purpose and meaning in the nature, plan, and actions of God. God chooses to allow each person to cooperate with him to accomplish his redemptive plan. Through his Spirit Christians are led to initiate cooperative action. The Scriptures reveal God's desire that his people have an interdependent unity of fellowship and service and that they unite in a dependent reliance on him.

(2) *Patterns for Cooperation.* This included the recommendation:

> that the Cooperative Program continue to be the basic process of cooperative funding between churches, state conventions, and the Southern Baptist Convention. This process allows persons making undesignated gifts through their church to support the missionary, education and benevolent works of their state convention and the worldwide ministries of the Southern Baptist Convention.

(3) *Challenges to Cooperation.* The Convention approved the daring annual goal of twenty billion dollars by the year 2000 for total undesignated gifts to the local churches, of which two and one half billion would go to the combined state convention and Southern Baptist Convention Cooperative Program. Also approved, was a goal to secure at the state level, a fifty-fifty division of Cooperative Program funds between state and Southern Baptist Convention

causes. Another goal was to allocate 75 percent of the SBC Cooperative Program funds to foreign and home missions.

(4) *Planned Growth in Giving.* This was a comprehensive plan for promoting the Cooperative Program through the year 2000.

No plan since the Seventy-Five Million Campaign of 1919 had set such lofty goals and demanded so much promotion. The central feature was the enlistment and training of up to seven hundred church and denominational leaders to direct state-sponsored Planned Growth for Giving Conferences and the enlistment of individuals, churches, associations, and state conventions to adopt fifteen-year plans for increasing percentages to Southern Baptist cooperative ministries. A fifteen-member SBC Planned Growth in Giving National Task Force was established with T. T. Crabtree of Missouri as the chairperson. The members included pastors, laymen, and representatives of state conventions and Southern Baptist Convention agencies. Also included were three ex officio members: W. Dewey Presley, chairman, and Harold C. Bennett, executive secretary-treasurer (later, president-treasurer), both of the Executive Committee; and A. R. Fagan, executive director of the Stewardship Commission.

Effective January 1, 1984, Cecil A. Ray of North Carolina was employed as the national director.[14] Ray, with wide experience as general secretary-treasurer of the Baptist State Convention of North Carolina and as secretary of Cooperative Program and church finance for the Baptist General Convention of Texas, was well-known for his innovative and effective approaches to Cooperative Program promotion.

Building for the Next Century

Even before 1980, the need for more space in the SBC Building was apparent, especially to the people who worked in its offices and to the visitors who attended its meetings. Some of the agencies housed in the building were crowded to the point of inefficiency. The Austin Crouch Room was inadequate for large group gatherings. Committee rooms were too small for most meetings. Parking was insufficient for the workers and sometimes impossible for visitors. For several years, the Executive Committee had explored proposals for expansion, but none had been found suitable. Sensing the situation, Harold C. Bennett, early in his administration, suggested an SBC Building Long-Range Study Committee. The appointment of such a committee was approved by the Executive Committee with William E. Fortune of Tennessee as its first chairperson. The committee was instructed to study "the immediate and long-range needs related to the Southern Baptist Convention building."[15] Fortune, an engineer who was involved in the construction trade was later replaced as chairperson when one of his companies was accepted as the prime contractor for the building. He was succeeded by Rodney R. Landes of Arkansas.

The first task of the new committee was carefully to explore the existing building in the light of the needs of the Executive Committee and the smaller Nashville agencies, including the Historical Commission. The Historical Commission, through its executive director, Lynn E. May, Jr., had requested space for its huge collection of Baptist historical materials housed in The Sunday School Board. The committee soon discovered that inflation and zoning problems had made major expansion financially injudicious. It would cost a great deal of money to secure even a little additional office space; and there would be no way in that location to get adequate parking space without an unsightly multistoried garage. The committee continued to work, giving attention to the possibility of another building in another location.

In September 1981, on behalf of The Sunday School Board, President Grady C. Cothen offered a large lot across Commerce street from the board's administration building to the Southern Baptist Convention as a possible site for the new building.[16] Located at the corner of Commerce Street and Ninth Avenue, North, the lot is 178 feet by 239 feet, almost an acre. Cothen, who had succeeded James L. Sullivan as president of The Sunday School Board in 1975, like his predecessor, was a friend of the Executive Committee. A gifted administrator and an eloquent preacher, he stood firm in the faith and wholly loyal to the denomination. In accepting the site, the Executive Committee expressed appreciation to Cothen "for this significant property transfer."[17]

In that same Executive Committee meeting, the SBC Building Long-Range Study Committee was authorized to proceed with planning for the construction of a new building initially suggested for the Executive Committee.[18] Ron Lustig, an architect with Earl Swensson and Associates, Nashville, showed slides of suggested drawings of the building recommended by the committee.[19] The executive secretary-treasurer was requested "to work with the appropriate SBC agencies in formulating a statement of relationships and a suggested policy for the operation of the proposed SBC building."[20] Lynn E. May, Jr., said of the new involvement, "This change of procedure to allow the agencies to be an integral part of the planning process for the design, operation and ownership of the building was a significant development."[21]

A year and a half later, the SBC Building Long-Range Study Committee made a firm recommendation to the Executive Committee: "to proceed with plans for the construction of the proposed new SBC building" at an estimated cost of approximately $8,000,000.[22] The question was raised: Why a new building? Bennett and McDonough were prepared with a closely reasoned paper that showed in great detail all of the needs.[23] Some of its points were:

- The seven smaller SBC organizations in Nashville have all outgrown their present facilities.
- The available rooms for committee meetings whose members come from all parts of the nation are inadequate.
- If Southern Baptists grow only two percent annually, by the year 2000, need for space will be much greater than now.
- As many as 250 or more visitors seek to use the 164 chairs available to them in the present Austin Crouch Room.
- The new building will be energy efficient and will meet Convention needs well into the next century.

The Executive Committee approved the new building.[24] Financing was to be arranged from two sources, from the sale of the existing building and from the Capital Needs Budget for 1984-1988 in which all of the participating agencies would share. The specific allocations were as follows:

Southern Baptist Foundation	$ 320,000
Education Commission	400,000
Six SBC seminaries for the External Education Division	800,000
Stewardship Commission	880,000
Christian Life Commission	1,120,000
Historical Commission	1,250,000
Executive Committee	3,200,000
TOTAL	$ 8,000,000

The $8,000,000 was to be applied to "the cost of construction and interest accrued until the building costs are completely paid."[25] The recommendation for the new Capital Needs Budget was presented to the Southern Baptist Convention in 1983.[26] For the first time in the forty-one year history of the Capital Needs Program, six of the smaller agencies and the Executive Committee had been included. Nevertheless, the proposed new building was challenged. Some messengers felt that it was not needed. The recommendation was adopted with 5,991 favoring the program and 3,449 opposing it. An SBC Building Construction Committee was then appointed with Rodney R. Landes as chairperson.[27] The ground-breaking ceremony was held in September 1983. By the spring of 1984, construction was well underway, with occupancy in early January of 1985.

Ascending Liability

Each passing decade has brought new problems to the Executive Committee. The decade of the seventies was no exception. For twenty years or more, the number of personal lawsuits in the American courts had increased. More and more people appeared to be suing for more and more reasons. Judgments had become larger and larger; and it appeared that neither persons nor organizations were safe from the possibility of either just or unjust lawsuits against them. This meant that Baptist institutions had to increase their liability insurance as a means of coping with the possibility of huge liability judgments. A related problem arose with the question of "ascending liability."

Though not a new problem in the courts, ascending liability was new to most religious organizations. A paper prepared by the Center for Constitutional Studies described it as:

> a shorthand expression coined to describe the legal responsibility which may be attributed to religious bodies as a result of actions taken by institutions related to them such as colleges, schools, retirement homes, hospitals, camps and children's homes as well as various boards and agencies of the religious bodies themselves which have been traditionally viewed as autonomous.[28]

In the case of Southern Baptists, this raised the question, if an agency were sued, would the Convention and its Executive Committee also be liable? The question came to the attention of the Executive Committee early in the decade when a lawsuit was filed against the Brotherhood Commission and certain of its employees and against the Southern Baptist Convention.[29]

On September 21-23, 1981, Harold C. Bennett reported to the Executive Committee that he had contacted the Center for Constitutional Studies School and had found that other denominations were being pressed with the same problem.[30] Bennett also had consulted with the chief executive officers of the SBC agencies and the state conventions and had found that there was concurrence that "ascending liability" was a significant question for Southern Baptists. The SBC executives had agreed to enter into a joint study of the question already in progress by the Center of Constitutional Studies for a number of denominations by the Center for Constitutional Studies. Some of the state conventions had also agreed to participate. As a result of Bennett's report, the Executive Committee voted to participate and authorized a legal affairs committee to monitor the study.[31]

In its first report, the Legal Affairs Committee identified concerns that needed to be faced, some of them by the joint study with other denominations and some of them by Southern Baptists:[32]

> Are the employees of the agencies of the Southern Baptist Convention actually agents of the Southern Baptist Convention? Obviously, an answer for that issue involves matters of polity—How does the Southern Baptist Convention operate? Where are the controls on the agencies of the Southern Baptist Convention, if there are controls on the agencies? How does the Cooperative Program figure in this discussion? To whom do the Cooperative Program funds belong?

The Legal Affairs Committee realized that it would take a long time to find answers to such questions. It continued to meet with the counsel of James P. Guenther, the Executive Committee attorney, who was also a member of the committee. A former employee of The Sunday School Board and a longstanding member of a local Baptist church, Guenther understood Baptist organization and polity quite well. He was also a member of the Advisory Committee for the Center for Constitutional Studies. According to C. Welton Gaddy, chairperson of the Legal Affairs Committee, the study by the center for the denominations would be released late in 1984. Gaddy also said that at that time the Legal Affairs Committee would consider three possible ways of disseminating the information: "(1) a consultation with state convention executive directors, SBC executives, and their attorneys; (2) distribution of appropriate materials to Southern Baptist entities; and (3) a complete report including recommendations to the Executive Committee of the Southern Baptist Convention."[33]

Reporting Bold Mission Thrust

Harold C. Bennett accepted the call to the Executive Committee as a call to Bold Mission Thrust. As he understood the challenge, it was Bold Mission Thrust for the total program—the Southern

Baptist Convention, the state conventions, all the agencies, all the people, all the world. He knew very well that the Executive Committee had pivotal responsibilities for Bold Mission Thrust, some of them by specific assignment from the 1977 Convention and some of them by general assignment from the Convention Bylaws; and Bennett would do his best to implement all of them. Some of the responsibilities were:

- The general work of promotion and publicity for Bold Mission. This was done chiefly through the services of the Executive Committee.
- Correlation of the annual Convention emphases. This was accomplished by working with the Inter-Agency council and its Coordinating Committee.
- Annual reporting to the Convention on the progress of Bold Mission Thrust. The reports were mainly compiled from the reports of the agencies.
- General management of the Cooperative Program. The promotion of the Cooperative Program was principally the responsibility of the Stewardship Commission and the state conventions.

Bennett's commitment to Bold Mission Thrust was both personal and purposeful. One of the initial things that he did in assuming office was to edit and publish a book on Bold Mission Thrust, entitled, *God's Awesome Challenge*.[34] It was a call to return to the biblical basis for missions and to total involvement in missions by all the people in all the churches. The book was also intended to build support for the lifeline of Bold Mission Thrust, the Cooperative Program. For Bennett, both the Cooperative Program and Bold Mission Thrust were Baptist responses to God's awesome challenge. A key point in his vision was local church responsibility. In 1980 the Executive Committee defined Bold Mission Thrust as: (1) churches responding to God's mission in world missions, (2) churches carrying out God's mission purposes, (3) churches strengthened to provide a base for missions, (4) churches involving people in missions, (5) churches cooperating with other churches in meeting world needs, and (6) churches supported (aided) by denominational resources (materials and programs).[35]

In 1981 the Executive Committee reported to the Convention: "The Lord is blessing. Increasing numbers of people are being saved. Baptisms are up. Enrollments in churches are growing. Giving is increasing. People are getting involved in mission projects in increasing numbers."[36] The 1982 report declared: "We believe our vision is from God. It is a bold vision. Southern Baptists must be equally bold in commitment to the task."[37] Then again, in 1983, the Executive Committee reported: "The momentum of Bold Mission Thrust has continued to grow. Many Baptists groups around the world are joining hands with Southern Baptists to give priority to missions and evangelism."[38] Also in 1983, the Executive Committee reported that 1982 had been one of the best years for the Cooperative Program. For four years in a row, it had dramatically increased:

Year	SBC Cooperative Program	Annual Increase
1978	$57,418,384	
1979	64,165,480	$ 6,747,096 (11.75 percent)
1980	71,762,635	7,597,155 (12.00 percent)
1981	81,685,873	9,923,238 (13.83 percent)
1982	93,344,356	11,658,483 (14.30 percent)

Lifted up by the four-year sustained increase, the Executive Committee took courage and in 1983 recommended a substantial 1983-1984 Bold Mission Thrust Cooperative Program Allocation Budget of $125,000,000, an increase of $19,000,000 over 1982-1983.[39]

A year later, in 1984, the Executive Committee reported to the Convention that the SBC Cooperative Program for 1983 was up 9.60 percent, for a total of $102,313,308. Although the increase was less than the previous year, it was a significant gain. A study of the percentages over the years shows many ups and downs in the rate of increase. It is very difficult some years to pinpoint the reasons. The variations are due to such things as levels of employment, rates of inflation, intensity of promotion, general perception of denominational stability, and the intensity of the prevailing denominational spirit. Also in 1984, it had been ten years since the creation of the Missions Challenge Committee which had lighted the fires for Bold Mission Thrust. In 1974 the Convention had instructed the committee to "involve all appropriate agencies, state conventions, and interested individuals in developing a challenge to Southern Baptists to help meet world needs in the final quarter of this century."[40] Even after ten years the goal still was an awesome challenge.

Rising Tensions in the Convention

Periodically, Southern Baptists have experienced seasons of denominational tension. As early as 1814, controversy developed over missions, especially west of the mountains. In some instances ministers were "turned out" of their churches for preaching missions. About the same time, the controversy over the teachings of Thomas and Alexander Campbell swept thousands of Baptists into their "reformation" churches of Christ. Then beginning in 1851, the Graves Landmarkism controversy shook the denomination to its foundation, changing some of its values and semantics and leaving marks that it still bears. Accompanying the Graves controversy was continuing debate over how and who would develop and publish denominational educational literature, a debate not settled until the formation of the second Sunday School Board in 1891. Also in the 1890s, tensions arose over some of the views of W. H. Whitsitt, a Southern Seminary professor, on the origin of Baptists. Then followed the evolution controversy of the 1920s and the Genesis controversies of the 1960s and the early 1970s.

In some ways, these tensions were the result of rugged Baptist individualism and open democratic polity. Controversy developed when persons of strong views disagreed. They accelerated when one group tried to force their views upon another group. The denomination through its many doctrinal controversies worked out a general basis of agreement in statements adopted by the Convention, first in 1925 and again in 1962. *The Baptist Faith and Message* became the generally accepted norm for Southern Baptists, but not a binding creed.

In 1979 the Convention began to show some signs of moving once more into a time of tension and controversy. There were two issues, the nature of initial revelation and the control of the denomination. The word *inerrancy* was one of the focal points of debate. In response to a resolution adopted in 1980 calling for "doctrinal integrity" of the agencies, the Executive Committee assured the Convention that its professional staff over the years had accepted *The Baptist Faith and Message* "as a whole and specifically that portion which addresses the Scriptures."[41]

By 1982 the differences had become intense enough to cause three state conventions (Alabama, Georgia, and Virginia) to pass resolutions asking the SBC Executive Committee to convene itself in a special meeting to deal with the problem.[42] One of the resolutions stated that the meeting should be "for the sole purpose of finding and implementing solutions to this most urgent and serious problem, to devise recommendations to be submitted to the 1983 meeting (of the Convention) in Pittsburgh, and to encourage broad participation of all viewpoints in the deliberations and actions of the Convention." The Executive Committee, after several months of careful consideration, declined the request. Some of the questions raised by observers at the time the proposal was being considered were: Is the timing right for such a meeting? Would the meeting tend to heighten tensions? In a denomination with open polity, would such a meeting be proper for the Executive Committee? Would it be better to arrange discussions of differences in less formal ways? Would such a meeting sponsored by the Executive Committee tend to make the Executive Committee part of the problem? Through the early years of the 1980s, the Executive Committee maintained a neutral stance and was not divided by the controversy.

Changing Personnel

Because of the increased awareness of the importance of women in public life, more women were added by the Convention to the Executive Committee. By 1984, there were six serving as members, including Dorothy Sample, Michigan, who had succeeded Helen Fling, New York, as president of the Woman's Missionary Union and as the WMU ex officio member of the Executive Committee. Though women had been members from 1927, there were usually no more than two or three of them. Through the years, women had become more active as subcommittee members and as officers. Since the mid sixties, five of the women had served as secretaries of the committee:

Gwen Davis, Tennessee	1966
Edith Marie King, Texas	1968, 1969, 1971
	1972, 1973, 1974
Marie Mathis, Texas	1970
Edith Kirkpatrick, Louisiana	1976, 1977
Lois H. Wenger, Florida	1981, 1982, 1984

As was expected, these women, all of them high achievers, served the Executive Committee with great competence.

The chairmen who served from 1980 to 1984 were:

J. Howard Cobble, Jr., Georgia pastor	1980, 1981
John T. Dunaway, Kentucky pastor	1981, 1982
W. Dewey Presley, Texas banker	1983, 1984

J. Howard Cobble, a dynamic young pastor, in a sense was a product of the Executive Committee. He was a graduate of Southeastern Seminary that the Executive Committee had helped to establish in the early 1950s. John T. Dunaway, a wise, loyal, and discerning man, was pleasantly disarming in personal presence. W. Dewey Presley was a towering leader in any situation—open, fair, direct, and immensely practical.

Three Southern Baptist Convention presidents served during the period:

Adrian P. Rogers, Tennessee pastor	1980
Bailey E. Smith, Oklahoma pastor	1981, 1982
James T. Draper, Jr., Texas pastor	1983, 1984

Adrian P. Rogers, a gifted and renowned preacher, served only one year. Bailey E. Smith was a popular evangelist and church builder. James E. Draper, Jr., also an effective church builder, was known as a forthright defender of his convictions.

Following Porter Routh's retirement in 1979, the next staff member to leave the Executive Committee was Robert O'Brien of the Baptist Press who joined the Foreign Mission Board in the spring of 1980 as missionary journalist. He was succeeded by Daniel B. Martin, Jr., a journalist with training also at Southwestern Seminary. A thoroughgoing professional, Martin was the most experienced newsman ever employed by the Executive Committee up to that time. Norman Jameson, feature editor for the Baptist Press, resigned about the same time to enter Southwestern Seminary. To replace him, the Executive Committee turned to Craig Byrd, also a trained journalist and experienced in denominational reporting.

Another new staff member was Reginald M. McDonough, who succeeded Albert McClellan as associate executive secretary and director of program planning. McDonough, trained at New Orleans Seminary for the ministry of education, had been with The Sunday School Board since 1964. He had served as secretary of the Church Administration Department for three years before joining the Executive Committee. An excellent writer and speaker, McDonough was a frequent platform guest at conferences, conventions, and assemblies. He also was the author of numerous articles and eight books. Well-endowed with a Christian spirit, levelheadedness, and easy relationships, McDonough fitted well into the daily demands of his new position.

The Author's Only Personal Words

While I was writing this book, my friends often said, "Write yourself into it." I did, but not in the ways that they had suggested. I am present a few times specifically by name, and most of the time tucked away between the lines. Any book, no matter how objective the author attempts to be, is a point of view. Another author would write another point of view, and the difference in the two would be mainly due to the unique ways the two writers were involved in the material. If a person is present at the time something happens, it is almost impossible for him to describe it as if he were not there.

At the time of my retirement on the last day of December of 1980, I had worked for the Executive Committee thirty-one and a half years, lacking one month. During this long tenure, I had opportunities to take other positions. Tempting as some of them were, I could never escape such questions as: In what other place could I serve more people in more different ways? From what other place could I better see and experience both the micro and macro aspects of all Baptist life? Besides, I found the people that I worked with, both the Executive Committee members and the Executive Committee staff, understanding and affirming. There were little things like Judge Frank Hooper stopping by my desk to tell me how much he appreciated my work and like Carroll Chadwick bringing me a quart of ribbon cane syrup all the way from East Texas. Then there were the big things like the citation by J. W. Storer when I was given an honorary doctor's degree by Oklahoma Baptist University and like the phone call from Louie D. Newton when I was in Dallas considering an invitation to be the editor of *Baptist Standard.* Louie asked me to stay, and I stayed.

In the thirty-one years, I had moments of uncertainty and frustration, but never of anguish and doubt. About the time I was finishing my story of the Executive Committee, my old friend, John H. Williams, the former director of financial planning for the Executive Committee, died from cancer. While he lingered, I often thought of something he had said about the time that he had retired. It went like this: "The Executive Committee gave me pleasant people to work with, pleasant surroundings in which to work, and pleasant work to do, and I am grateful. The Executive Committee and its officers in dealing with great problems are as fairminded and considerate as any group that I have ever known."

Now, in closing this book, I feel the same way. My prayer is: "O Lord, let what John Williams said always be true. Let the Executive Committee be a fair-minded, affirming presence for the weak and the strong, and let its benediction for all Baptists always be: Grace be unto you, and peace, from God our Father, and from the Lord Jesus Christ."

Notes

1. ECM, September 18, 1978, pp. 10, B, 1-2.
2. Ibid., pp. B, 1-2.
3. Ibid.
4. ECM, February 20, 1979, pp. 7-8, A, 10-11.
5. Ibid., pp. 10-11.
6. Keener Pharr to AM.
7. ECM, February 18, 1978, "Job Description," pp. A 1-3.
8. Reginald M. McDonough to AM.
9. Timothy A. Hedquist to AM.
10. SBC, 1977, p. 37.
11. ECM, September 22-24, 1980, p. 30.
12. ECM, February 21-23, 1983, pp. 29-41.
13. SBC, 1983. pp. 41-47.
14. ECM, September 19-21, 1983, pp. 20-25.
15. ECM, February 18-19, 1980, p. 12.
16. ECM, September 21-23, 1981, item 24, p. 113.
17. Ibid.
18. Ibid., p. 103.
19. Ibid., p. 100.
20. Ibid., p. 101.

21. Lynn E. May, Jr. to AM.

22. ECM, February 21-23, 1983, pp. 5-6.

23. ECR, February 21-23, 1983, Harold C. Bennett and Reginald M. McDonough, "Why a New Southern Baptist Convention Building?" pp. 23a-23e.

24. Ibid., pp. 13-13a.

25. Ibid.

26. SBC, 1983, pp. 49-49. See Appendix 3 for a summary of Capital Needs Program, 1946-1988.

27. ECM, September 19-21, 1983, p. 11.

28. ECR, September 21-23, 1981, "The 'Ascending Liability' Question for Religious Bodies and Their Related Institutions (summary)," pp. 45-46, and following."

29. ECR, February 22-24, 1982, pp. 47-49.

30. September 21-23, 1981, pp. 45-46. The Center for Constitutional Studies was located at Notre Dame Law School and later moved to Mercer University Law School.

31. Ibid.

32. ECR, February 22-24, 1982. p. 48.

33. ECR, September 17-19, 1984, p. 15.

34. Harold C. Bennett, *God's Awesome Challenge* (Nashville: Broadman, 1980).

35. SBC, 1980, p. 38.

36. SBC, 1981, p. 38.

37. ECM, 1982, p. 41.

38. SBC, 1983, p. 31.

39. SBC, 1983, pp. 29-29.

40. SBC, 1984, p. 38.

41. ECR, September 22-24, 1980, pp. 46-47.

42. ECR, September 19-21, 1983. pp. 46-48.

Appendix 1
Southern Baptist Convention
Executive Committee Officers, 1917-1984

Austin Crouch was elected the first executive secretary of the Executive Committee in 1927 and served until early in 1946. Duke K. McCall succeeded Crouch in 1946 and served as executive secretary-treasurer until 1951. Porter Routh was elected in 1946 and served until the end of July in 1979. Harold C. Bennett succeeded Routh as executive secretary-treasurer in 1979.

M. H. Wolfe was named the first chairman in 1917 and served until 1919 when the rules were changed to make the president of the Convention also the president (chairman) of the Executive Committee. J. B. Gambrell was president in 1919 and 1920. He was followed by E. Y. Mullins who served in 1921, 1922, and 1923. The next president was George White McDaniel who served in 1924, 1925 and 1926.

Date of Election	Chairman	Vice-chairman	Secretary	Treasurer
5-7-27	George W. Truett		Hight C Moore	
6-21-27	George W. Truett		Hight C Moore	Hight C Moore
6-14-28	George W. Truett		Frank Burkhalter	Hight C Moore
6-12, 13-29	George W. Truett		Frank Burkhalter	Hight C Moore
9-25-30			Hight C Moore	
6-11-30	W.J. McGlothlin	M.P.L. Love	Walter M. Gilmore	Hight C Moore
6-10-31	W.J. McGlothlin		Hight C Moore	Hight C Moore
6-15-32	Fred F. Brown	J.E. Dillard	Hight C Moore	Hight C Moore
5-23-33	M.E. Dodd		Hight C Moore	
6-14-33		C.W. Daniel		Walter M. Gilmore
6-13-34	M.E. Dodd	C.W. Daniel	Hight C Moore	Walter M. Gilmore
6-12-35	J.E. Dillard	H.L. Winburn	Walter M. Gilmore	Walter M. Gilmore
6-17-36	J.E. Dillard	H.L. Winburn	Walter M. Gilmore	Walter M. Gilmore
6-10-36	Frank Tripp			

284

Date of Election	Chairman	Vice-chairman	Secretary	Treasurer
6-16-37	Frank Tripp	J.M. Dawson	Walter M. Gilmore	Walter M. Gilmore
6-15-38	Frank Tripp	J.M. Dawson	Walter M. Gilmore	Walter M. Gilmore
6-14-39	Frank Tripp	J.M. Dawson	Walter M. Gilmore	Walter M. Gilmore
7-17-40	C.W. Daniel	J.M. Dawson	Walter M. Gilmore	Walter M. Gilmore
6-11-41	C.W. Daniel	J.M. Dawson	Walter M. Gilmore	Walter M. Gilmore
6-17-42	C.W. Daniel	J.M. Dawson	Walter M. Gilmore	Walter M. Gilmore
6-16-43	C.W. Daniel	J.M. Dawson	Walter M. Gilmore	Walter M. Gilmore
6-14-44	J. Howard Williams	J.M. Dawson	Walter M. Gilmore	Walter M. Gilmore
6-13-45	J. Howard Williams	J.M. Dawson	Walter M. Gilmore	Walter M. Gilmore
12-12-45				
6-11-46	John H. Buchanan	George B. Fraser	Walter M. Gilmore	Walter M. Gilmore

Date of Election	Chairman	Vice-chairman	Secretary	Executive Secretary Treasurer
1-22-47			Merrill D. Moore	Duke K. McCall
6-10, 11-47	George B. Fraser	George Ragland	Porter W. Routh	Duke K. McCall
6-15, 16-48	George B. Fraser	C.H. Bolton	Porter W. Routh	Duke K. McCall
6-15, 16-49	George B. Fraser	Howard M. Reaves	Porter W. Routh	Duke K. McCall
6-14, 15-50	George B. Fraser	Henry W. Tiffany	Porter W. Routh	Duke K. McCall
9-12, 13-51	George B. Fraser	Henry W. Tiffany	Oliver R. Shields	Austin Crouch[1] Porter W. Routh
6-11, 12-52	J.W. Storer	Casper C. Warren	Oliver R. Shields	Porter W. Routh
6-17, 18-53	Casper C. Warren	W. Douglas Hudgins	Oliver R. Shields	Porter W. Routh
6-23-54	Casper C. Warren	W. Douglas Hudgins	Oliver R. Shields	Porter W. Routh
9-7-55	Frank A. Hooper, Jr.	W. Douglas Hudgins	G. Allen West, Jr.	Porter W. Routh
6-20-56	Frank A. Hooper, Jr.	W. Douglas Hudgins	G. Allen West, Jr.	Porter W. Routh
6-19-57	Homer G. Lindsay	T.K. Rucker	Elwin N. Wilkinson	Porter W. Routh
6-11-58	Ramsey Pollard	Kendall Berry	Elwin N. Wilkinson	Porter W. Routh
5-21-59	Kendall Berry	R. Archie Ellis	A. Barnum Hawkes	Porter W. Routh
5-19-60	Kendall Berry	R. Archie Ellis	A. Barnum Hawkes	Porter W. Routh
5-25-61	John H. Haldeman	J. Ralph Grant	James S. Abernethy	Porter W. Routh
6-7-62	John H. Haldeman	Harold W. Seever	James S. Abernethy	Porter W. Routh
5-9-63	Harold W. Seever		Charles L. McClain	Porter W. Routh

Date of Election	Chairman	Vice-chairman	Secretary	Treasurer
5-21-64	Harold W. Seever	W. Douglas Hudgins	Howard P. Giddens	Porter W. Routh
6-3-65	W. Douglas Hudgins	Rang W. Morgan	Howard P. Giddens	Porter W. Routh
5-26-66	W. Douglas Hudgins	Jay Heflin	Gwen Davis	Porter W. Routh
6-1-67	James L. Pleitz	Joe Coleman	Claude F. Gaddy	Porter W. Routh
6-6-68	James L. Pleitz	R.J. Robinson	Edith Marie King	Porter W. Routh
6-12-69	James L. Monroe	Cooper Walton	Edith Marie King	Porter W. Routh
6-3-70	James L. Monroe	John Parrott	Marie Mathis	Porter W. Routh
6-2-71	Owen Cooper	Stewart B. Simms	Edith Marie King	Porter W. Routh
6-7-72	Stewart B. Simms	R.F. Smith, Jr.	Edith Marie King	Porter W. Routh
6-13-73	Stewart B. Simms	Charles E. Harvey	Edith Marie King	Porter W. Routh
6-12-74	Charles E. Harvey	Walter Gordon Nunn	Edith Marie King	Porter W. Routh
6-11-75	Charles E. Harvey	William Ches Smith, III	Dennis Lyle	Porter W. Routh
6-16-76	William Ches Smith, III	Rufus B. Sprayberry	Edith Kirkpatrick	Porter W. Routh
6-15-77	William Ches Smith, III	Rufus B. Sprayberry	Edith Kirkpatrick	Porter W. Routh
6-14-78	Brooks H. Wester	B. Conrad Johnston	Preston H. Callison	Porter W. Routh
6-13-79	Brooks H. Wester	Rodney R. Landes	Preston H. Callison	Porter W. Routh until July 31. Harold C. Bennett beginning August 1.
6-11-80	J. Howard Cobble	John T. Dunaway	Donald I. Gent	Harold C. Bennett
6-10-81	J. Howard Cobble	John T. Dunaway	Donald I. Gent	Harold C. Bennett
9-21, 22, 23-81	John T. Dunaway	William A. Fortune	Lois H. Wenger	
6-16-82	John T. Dunaway	W. Dewey Presley	Lois H. Wenger	Harold C. Bennett
6-15-83	W. Dewey Presley	G. Nelson Duke	Donald I. Gent	Harold C. Bennett

Note

1. Served twelve days as interim executive secretary-treasurer between Duke K. McCall and Porter Routh.

Appendix 2
Relation of Southern Baptist Convention
to Other Baptist Bodies

According to instructions of the Convention, we submit the following statement of principles:

The relations between this Convention and other Baptist bodies can be understood in the light of a few basic New Testament principles, as follows:

The primary and fundamental principle is the direct relation of the individual soul to Jesus Christ as Saviour and Lord. To his own Master every Christian stands or falls.

All Christian relationships are free and voluntary. To become a Christian is not to be coerced into obedience to Christ, but to choose him voluntarily and freely. Christ's authority is accepted as final for the believer in all things when he is thus chosen freely as Lord and Saviour.

The relations of the believer with other Christians are also free and voluntary and subject only to the authority of Jesus Christ.

A church of Christ is a free and voluntary association of believers, in his name, in obedience to his command, and for the carrying out of his purposes.

It follows that each church is autonomous or self-determining in all matters pertaining to its own life and activities. It is not subject to any other church or organization of any kind whatsoever, but only to Christ and his authority.

All Baptist general bodies are voluntary organizations, established by individuals who wish to co-operate for some common end or ends in the kingdom of God. This Convention is not an ecclesiastical body composed of churches, nor a federal body composed of state conventions. Churches may seek to fulfill their obligation to extend Christ's kingdom by co-operating with these general organizations, but always on a purely voluntary basis, and without surrendering in any way or degree their right of self-determination. These associations, unions, or conventions vary greatly in form, in size, in purpose, in territorial extent and in conditions of membership. But they are all similar to churches in the fundamental principle of their organization and life in that each is independent of all others in its own work, free fraternal, autonomous, or self-determining in its sphere and activities.

The principle of co-operation between individuals and churches and general bodies in pursuit of great common ends is also a basic teaching of the gospel. In all co-operative endeavor the principle of autonomy or self-determination should be carefully conserved.

There is no relation of superiority and inferiority among Baptist general bodies. All are equal. All make their appeal directly to individuals and churches. Each determines its own objectives—financial or otherwise—and allocates its own funds to the interests promoted by it. Each defines and fixes its own sphere of activities. But all is done with due consideration and regard for the functions of other Baptist bodies.

The powers of Baptist general bodies are never legislative, but always advisory in their relations to churches, and to each other.

The co-operation of Baptist general bodies with each other may be desirable from time to time for the sake of greater economy and efficiency. But there are dangers connected with such co-operation due to misunderstanding, confusion of thinking, and sometimes to trespassing upon the rights of co-operating bodies by one or other of the parties to the arrangement.

One of the present danger points is the co-operative relations between the Southern Baptist Convention and the various state conventions. This Convention disclaims all authority over any state convention, but wishes to define its own functions and activities in relation to state bodies. The following points should be stressed:

(1) The co-operative relations between this Convention and state bodies as now established are limited to the one matter of collecting funds for Southwide and state objects in conjunction with a unified appeal for the objects. The state convention boards are at present recognized by this Convention

as collecting agencies for Southwide as well as for state funds. This arrangement, however, is not an essential in Baptist organization, but is made simply as a matter of convenience and economy, and may be changed at any time.

(2) The fact that the state bodies first handle the funds and are more directly related to the churches in the matter of collections does not alter the basic relations involved. For the practical ends in view this Convention co-operates in the unified appeal for funds through state agencies. But in principle it retains as inalienable and inherent the right to direct appeal to the churches. Furthermore, in all matters other than money raising it retains complete control of its own affairs, with the right to fix its own objectives and to determine the amounts of money allocated to its various objects.

(3) The power of appointing the members of all committees and boards of this Convention resides in the Convention itself. When it is desirable that states, as such, or other territorial subdivisions of this Convention's area, be represented on the boards or committees of this Convention, this arrangement can easily be effected by consultation with the respective groups involved. But the power to appoint directly or to nominate the members of its own committees and boards must be retained.

(4) The practice of careful discrimination and mutual respect as between the state bodies and this Convention is called for. The main functions of this Convention and of state bodies remain inviolable. Neither body may impose its will upon the other in any manner or degree at any time. Conference and discussion between committees of the respective groups are always proper in regard to matters involved in joint effort and in so far as necessary to promote good will and mutual understanding. As the work is at present conducted such matters are the division of funds into state and Southwide, ways and means of promoting interest in the various causes, and the burden of cost of collections to be apportioned to state and Southwide funds. These are all matters involved in the one matter of joint effort; viz., the collection of money. In all other matters this Convention pursues its own objects in its own way. It has no authority to allocate funds or to divert funds from any object included in a state budget. In like manner no state body has any authority to allocate funds or to divert them from any object included in the Southwide budget.

(5) The observance of the above principles by this Convention and by state bodies is essential to the integrity and perpetuity of this Convention. Unless the Southern Baptist Convention insists upon its own autonomy in all phases of its own work a process of disintegration, loss of power and initiative, and gradual decline is inevitable.

(6) It is important that the Executive Committee of this Convention receive instructions to conduct all negotiations with representatives of state or other bodies necessary to clarify relations and bring about a satisfactory adjustment, with a view to complete and hearty co-operation in all matters of common interest.

—Taken from the 1956 SBC *Annual,* pp. 56-57

Appendix 3
SUMMARY - SOUTHERN BAPTIST CONVENTION CAPITAL NEEDS
PROGRAM 1946-1984

	46-51	52-58	59-63	65-68	69-73	74-78	78-84	84-88	Total	% of Total
Foreign Mission Board	1866108	4200000	5000000						11066108	9.01
Home Mission Board	1627870	3199000	1300000		1000000			2400000	9526870	7.76
Ext. Loan Fund-HMB			4000000	3225000					7225000	5.88
Annuity Board	1545680	1459500							3005180	2.45
Baptist Hospitals	53250	900000	250000	380000	75000				1658250	1.35
Southern Seminary	1830622	1670001	1700000	735000	950000	1375000	2000000	3858334	14118957	11.50
Southwestern Seminary	1632197	1610001	2000000	910000	525000	1557800	2000000	4233334	14468332	11.78
New Orleans Seminary	1691867	1899909	1300000	1600000	325000	160000	2701295	3341333	13019404	10.60
Golden Gate Seminary	150000	2882166	2400000	500000	182500	593000	4297046	3033333	14038045	11.43
Southeastern Seminary	300000	2709423	1300000	325000	710000	178400	2547444	2703333	10773600	8.77
Midwestern Seminary			3000000	300000	517000	707000	2000000	2945333	9469333	7.71
American Seminary	140017	210000	100000	40000					490017	0.40
Radio & TV Commission	90122	195000	1000000	600000	590500	321300	1000000	2025000	5821922	4.74
Brotherhood Commission	16250	65000	150000	40000	125000	85000	160200		641450	0.52
Public Affairs Committee				300000					300000	0.24
S.B. Foundation								320000	320000	0.26
Christian Life Com.								1120000	1120000	0.91
Education Commission								400000	400000	0.33
Historical Commission								1280000	1280000	1.04
Stewardship Commission								880000	880000	0.72
Executive Committee								3200000	3200000	2.61
	10943983	21000000	23500000	8955000	5000000	4977500	16705985	31740000	122822468	100.

SBC BUDGET CALENDAR

STAFF ACTIONS

GROUP ACTIONS

19BY = BUDGET YEAR
19PY = PAST YEAR
19CY = CURRENT YEAR

Calendar months (center column, top to bottom): JAN., MAY, JULY, SEPT., OCT., DEC., JAN., FEB., MAR., APR., MAY, JUNE, JULY, AUG., SEPT., OCT., NOV., DEC., JAN.

Staff Actions

1 Agency executives begin long-range planning to ascertain 19BY budget needs

2 Request for Budget and Financial Data information sent to agencies by executive secretary of Executive Committee

4 Agency executives present 19BY oral program and budget review to the Executive Committee

6 Budget and Financial Data forwarded to Executive Committee by agency executives

7 Request for agency reports or 19PY for Book of Reports mailed to agency executives by secretary of the Convention

8 Consolidated Budget and Financial Data mailed to members of Executive Committee and other interested leaders

10 Budget program presentations formally made to Program Committee by agency executives. 19BY request from Cooperative Program also presented.

13 Agency executives adjust budget and financial data for 19BY in keeping with recommended allocation

14 Proposed recommended allocation of Cooperative Program funds for 19BY published in denominational press

15 Reports on program basis 19PY due for Book of Reports

17 Stories based on agency reports of 19PY submitted to denominational press

19 Book of Reports delivered to the Convention and made available to messengers

23 Annual published, including essential material from agency audit of 19PY

24 New Convention 19BY begins. The Executive Committee Executive Secretary-Treasurer begins distribution of the Cooperative Program to the agencies

Group Actions

3 The Finance Committee proposes a 19BY total Cooperative Program goal. The Finance and Program Committee jointly recommend to the Executive Committee for adoption.

5 Budget and Data material including special request for Cooperative Program funds for 19BY approved by agency, board, commission, committee, or Administrative Committee

9 Budget and Financial Data studied by Executive Committee including Program Committee

11 Program Committee proposes allocations to Executive Committee for 19BY

12 Executive Committee formulates Cooperative Program allocation recommendation to Convention for FBY

16 The church members study recommended allocations for 19BY as published in denominational press

18 Agency audits of 19PY approved by agency committee and/or full board and submitted to Executive Committee, or within three months after closing of the fiscal year

20 Executive Committee recommends Cooperative Program allocation for 19BY to Convention

21 Convention votes on allocations for 19BY and reviews reports for 19PY and 19CY

22 Members in the churches begin serious evaluation of work accomplished with money spent

Bibliography

Alabama Baptist. Alabama state Baptist paper.

Alley, Reuben Edward. *A History of Baptists in Virginia.* Richmond: Virginia Baptist General Board, 1973.

Annuals, Southern Baptist Convention, 1845-1983. Nashville: The Southern Baptist Convention.

Baker, Robert A. *The Story of the Sunday School Board.* Nashville: Convention Press, 1966.

Baker, Robert A. *The Southern Baptist Convention and its People, 1609-1972.* Nashville: Broadman Press, 1974.

Baker, Robert A. and Craven, Paul J., Jr. *Adventures in Faith.* Nashville: Broadman Press, 1982.

Baptist Courier. South Carolina state Baptist paper.

Baptist and Reflector. Tennessee state Baptist paper.

Barnes, W. W. *The Southern Baptist Convention, 1845-1953.* Nashville: Broadman Press, 1954.

Boyce, James Petigru. *Memoirs.* New York: Armstrong, 1895.

Burton, Joe W. *Road to Nashville.* Nashville: Broadman Press, 1977.

———. *Road to Augusta.* Nashville: Broadman Press, 1976.

Cook, Henry T. *A Biography of Richard Furman.* Greenville; Baptist Courier, 1913.

Cooper, Owen. *Listen!* Nashville: The Southern Baptist Convention Executive Committee, 1971.

Dawson, Joseph Martin. *Baptists and the American Republic.* Nashville: Broadman Press, 1956.

Huggins, M. A. *A History of North Carolina Baptists, 1727-1932.* Raleigh: General Board, North Carolina Baptist State Convention, 1967.

Encyclopedia of Southern Baptists. Nashville: Broadman Press, Volumes I, II.

Norman W. Cox, ed., 1958; Volume II, Davis C. Woolley, ed., 1971;
Volume IV, Lynn E. May, Jr., ed., 1982.

Johnson, Otto J. *Information Please Almanac, 1983.* New York; A and W
Publishers, 1982.

King, Joe M. *A History of South Carolina Baptists.* Columbia: The General
Board of the South Carolina Convention, 1964.

Lumpkin, William L. *Baptist Confessions of Faith.* Philadelphia: Judson Press,
1959.

————. *Baptist Foundations in the South.* Nashville: Broadman Press, 1961.

Masters, Frank M. *A History of Baptists in Kentucky.* Louisville: Kentucky
Baptist Historical Society, 1953.

May, Lynn E., Jr. *The First Baptist Church, Nashville, Tennessee.* Nashville:
Broadman Press, 1970.

Minutes. The Executive Committee of the Southern Baptist Convention,
1917-1984.

Mueller, William A. *A History of Southern Baptist Theological Seminary.* Nashville: Broadman Press, 1959.

Mullins, Isla May. *Edgar Young Mullins.* Nashville: Sunday School Board,
1929.

Owen, Loulie Latimer. *Oliver Hart, 1723-1795.* Greenville: South Carolina
Baptist Historical Society, 1966.

Religious Herald. Virginia state Baptist paper.

Reports. The Executive Committee of the Southern Baptist Convention,
1979-1984.

Robertson, Archibald Thomas. *Life and Letters of John Albert Broadus.* Philadelphia: American baptist Publication Society, 1901.

Rauch, Basil. *Roosevelt Speeches.* New York: Rinehart, 1957.

Routh, E. C. *The Story of Oklahoma Baptists.* Oklahoma City: Baptist General
Convention of Oklahoma, 1932.

Ryland, Garnett. *The Baptists of Virginia.* Richmond: Virginia Baptist Board,
1955.

Shurden, Walter B. *Associationalism Among Baptists in America,* New York:
Arno Press, 1980. First publication in book form.

The Quarterly Review, 1983 and 1984. Nashville: Sunday School Board. A
periodical.

Torbet, Robert G. *A History of the Baptists.* Valley Forge: Judson Press, 1965.
Revised.

Underwood, A. C. *A History of the English Baptists.* London: Carey Kingsgate, 1947, 1956.

Western Recorder. Kentucky Baptist state paper.

Whitley, W. T. *A History of British Baptists.* London: Charles Griffin and Company, 1923.

Van Ness, Issac Jacobus. *Training in the Baptist Spirit.* Nashville; Sunday School Board, 1914.

Key to Symbols Used in Notes

AM   Albert McClellan, associate executive secretary and director of program planning for the Executive Committee of the Southern Baptist Convention, retired.

BC   *Baptist Courier,* South Carolina state Baptist paper.

BR   *Baptist and Reflector,* Tennessee state Baptist paper.

ECM   *Executive Committee Minutes,* 1927-1984. Southern Baptist Convention Executive Committee.

ECR   *Executive Committee Reports,* 1979-1984. Southern Baptist Convention Executive Committee.

ESB   *Encyclopedia of Southern Baptists,* Volumes I (1958), II (1958), III (1971), and IV (1982).

SBCA   Southern Baptist Convention Archive

SBC   *Annuals,* Southern Baptist Convention, 1845-1983.

SSBA   Sunday School Board Archives

QR   *The Quarterly Review.* Nashville: Sunday School Board. A quarterly periodical.

RH   *Religious Herald,* Virginia state Baptist paper.

WR   *Western Recorder,* Kentucky state Baptist paper.

Index

297